Organizational Stress Management

ORGANIZATIONAL STRESS MANAGEMENT

A Strategic Approach

Ashley Weinberg

Senior Lecturer in Psychology, University of Salford, UK

Valerie J. Sutherland

Independent Consultant and Researcher, Alberta, Canada

and

Cary Cooper

Pro Vice Chancellor (External Relations) and Professor of Organizational Psychology and Health, Lancaster University, UK

palgrave
macmillan

First published 2010 by
PALGRAVE MACMILLAN

Palgrave Macmillan in the UK is an imprint of Macmillan Publishers Limited,
registered in England, company number 785998, of Houndmills, Basingstoke,
Hampshire RG21 6XS.

Palgrave Macmillan in the US is a division of St Martin's Press LLC,
175 Fifth Avenue, New York, NY 10010.

Palgrave Macmillan is the global academic imprint of the above companies
and has companies and representatives throughout the world.

Palgrave® and Macmillan® are registered trademarks in the United States,
the United Kingdom, Europe and other countries.

ISBN 978–0–230–20392–1

This book is printed on paper suitable for recycling and made from fully
managed and sustained forest sources. Logging, pulping and manufacturing
processes are expected to conform to the environmental regulations of the
country of origin.

A catalogue record for this book is available from the British Library.

A catalog record for this book is available from the Library of Congress.

10 9 8 7 6 5 4 3 2 1
19 18 17 16 15 14 13 12 11 10

Printed and bound in Great Britain by
CPI Antony Rowe, Chippenham and Eastbourne

To Anne, James and Lottie, Mum and Dad –
thank you for all your love and encouragement.

This book is for all who can improve well-being
through the way we work.

Ashley

CONTENTS

LIST OF FIGURES, TABLES AND BOX

Figures

Tables

Box

ACKNOWLEDGEMENTS

The authors would like to acknowledge the most valuable contribution of Chapter 2 entitled 'Stress and the Law' by Peter Jenkins, the hard work provided by Keith Povey Editorial Services Ltd, and the excellent proof-reading carried out by Risha Weinberg.

LIST OF ABBREVIATIONS

ACAS	Arbitration, Conciliation and Advisory Service
AMT	advanced manufacturing technology
ASSET	A Shortened Stress Evaluation Tool
AWA	alternative work arrangements
CAD	computer aided design
CALM	counselling and life management
CAM	computer aided manufacturing
CBI	Confederation of British Industry
CEO	chief executive officer
CHD	coronary heart disease
CIM	computer integrated manufacturing
CIPD	Chartered Institute of Personnel Development
CNC	computer numerically controlled machining
DDA	Disability Discrimination Act
EAP	employee assistance program
EFP	employee fitness program
EPM	electronic performance monitoring
EU	European Union
Eurofound	European Foundation for the Improvement of Working and Living Conditions
EWCS	European Working Conditions Survey
FMS	flexible machining systems
GHQ	General Health Questionnaire
HSAW	Health and Safety at Work
HSE	Health and Safety Executive
IoE	Institute of Employment
IT	information technology
JIT	just-in-time
NICE	National Institute for Clinical Excellence

NIOSH	National Institute for Occupational Safety and Health
PC	personal computer
PTSD	post-traumatic stress disorder
PWC	Psychosocial Working Conditions
QWL	quality of working life
RSI	repetitive strain injury
SBS	sick building syndrome
SPSS	Statistical Package for the Social Sciences
SWOT	strengths, weaknesses, opportunities and threats
TAB	Type A Coronary Prone Style of Behavior
TQM	total quality management
WHO	World Health Organization

CHAPTER 1

CHANGE AND THE NEED FOR CHANGE

NEED FOR AN ORGANIZATIONAL APPROACH TO STRESS MANAGEMENT

Many of us would subscribe to the adage, "If it's not broken, don't fix it", but we are also aware that if "it" is our workplace, then things are constantly changing. Where jobs depend on success in our area of work – and most tend to – there are nagging doubts and fears that "it" might not be good enough to help us maximize our potential and to ensure that the future is bright for all concerned. These concerns could provide the impetus for the "fix" needed to guarantee performance and effectiveness. In particular, these reflect the health and performance of the organization, which in turn are underpinned by the well-being and job satisfaction of its employees. Therefore, this book addresses the ways in which we can maximize performance and health in the workplace by using an integrated, organizational strategy to optimize well-being and, in turn, manage stress. It differs from other traditional stress management books in three main ways:

1 First, the approach recommended is a proactive model rather than using a reactive stance. This is in contrast to the typical scenario, in which organizations tend to wait for something to happen before they adopt some form of stress management activity. It becomes wrongly acknowledged as a strategy needed to solve the ills of the organization, and implies that the employees have already become casualties or victims of exposure to workplace stress. By leaving the issue in this way, organizations reach a point of needing treatment that tends to be both costly to administer and, all too often, ineffective in the long term.

1

2 Second, we would also suggest that any effective approach to the management of stress should be integrated into organizational processes. It means that the process will become part of the way in which the business is managed on a day-to-day basis. Ultimately, it should be regarded as "the way in which we do things around here", instead of being seen as some stand-alone activity that is introduced in response to a problem. We firmly believe that stress management activities can be a cost benefit to the business.

3 Third, stress management activities tend to focus on the individual in the workplace – inadvertently placing a level of blame on the employee, who is seen as having some sort of problem, or is perceived as unable to cope. This suggests that the individual must change in some way so that the "problem" no longer exists. Empirical studies and evaluation of stress management programs now clearly show the flaws in this simplistic line of thinking, as it is acknowledged that "the sick individual may be the symptom of a sick organisation" (Carroll, 1996). Therefore, for both humanistic and economical reasons, a different approach is necessary. This book offers a holistic organizational approach to the management of stress. It is one that addresses the quality of life for the individual at work, the dynamics and interpersonal relationships of the work group or team, and the organizational structure and climate that shape the working environment. This approach offers many potential benefits to individual employees and business strategists if, in return, they take joint responsibility for the management of stress at work. It must be acknowledged that, by optimizing the health of the workforce, we can ensure the good health of the organization. Most obviously, this becomes manifest in terms of maximum performance and productivity.

ENDORSEMENT FOR CHANGE

National government level

The rationale for our approach to the management of stress in the workplace is endorsed at the highest levels. A joint initiative by the UK government, the Confederation of British Industry and the Trades Union Congress, as well as the Health and Safety Executive, among others, resulted in 2004 in the launch of work stress guidance in the belief that "it is important to manage stress well to avoid its negative impacts on an individual, on employers and on the British economy as a whole". Between 2006 and 2009, three major reports were commissioned by the UK government focusing on the psychological health of workers: the Black Report (2008), the Foresight Project (2008) and the National Institute for Clinical Excellence guidelines for improving the well-being of the UK workforce (NICE, 2009). In addition, and in response to European Union legislation, the UK has continued to roll out directives aimed at capping the weekly working hours of employees.

Health and Safety Executive standards for the management of stress

Towards the end of the millennium, the government's Health Strategy Unit (1998) noted that "people with a job spend a lot of their time at their workplace, so a healthy workplace is vital to their health". The principal targets of this strategic approach have yielded positive outcomes for smoke-free workplaces with disabled access; however, the prospect of psychologically healthier working environments has been shaped but not yet realized. The Health and Safety Executive (HSE) management standards represent a strategic attempt to ensure that organizations comply with guidance on psychosocial working factors, including workload and management practices to "reflect a high level of health well-being and organizational performance" (HSE, 2009a). The six areas covered by the guidance are:

- **Demands:** The focus should be on workload, patterns of work and the working environment, with an emphasis on employees feeling they are able to cope with the demands placed upon them. With this in mind, the HSE standards require that a system exist in the organization to address concerns about workloads. It is recommended that employees are provided with "adequate and achievable demands in relation to the agreed hours of work", and that their skills and abilities are matched to the demands of the job.
- **Control:** Employees should "have a say about the way they do their work" and "where possible have control over their pace of work". Consultation over working patterns and the timing of breaks is recommended, and opportunities to develop new skills should be supported.
- **Support:** Encouragement, information and sponsorship should be provided by the organization to its workers, enshrined in

policies that make support by managers and colleagues – including constructive feedback and access to the necessary resources – the foundation for employee development and success.

- **Relationships:** Positive behaviors in the workplace should be reinforced by policies and procedures for reporting and dealing with unacceptable behaviors such as bullying.
- **Role:** Employees should be clearly informed about their function(s) and carrying out a role should not cause conflict for individuals charged with those responsibilities; where this does arise, systems should be in place to address role conflict.
- **Change:** This should be carried out by engaging with and informing employees, providing opportunities for them to influence proposals for change. Furthermore, employees should be made aware of the potential outcomes of the change process, and training and support should be available to help them adjust.

In order to facilitate the fulfillment of the HSE management standards, organizations are encouraged to conduct surveys and assessments to help identify potential risks for work-related stress, to enable root causes to be tackled and to engage employees in a partnership designed to improve the working experience.

Annual surveys on psychosocial working conditions in the UK, conducted between 2004 and 2008, showed little overall progress across this time period and suggested a time lag between organizations initiating interventions and realizing the benefits – or, indeed, the influence of other factors affecting employee perceptions. However, two reports by the Institute of Employment (IoE, 2009) into the progress made following the introduction of the HSE management standards show that there is widespread recognition of the HSE definition of stress and a degree of progress in taking preventative measures. The key obstacles identified by the IoE were money, levels of training and information, and top-level management support for initiatives.

The Black Report

In the report "Working for a Healthier Tomorrow" (Black Report, 2008), Dame Carol Black acknowledged the positive impacts of working (such as its role as "a key determinant of self-worth, family esteem, identity and standing within the community"), as well as the negative side of the employment equation (for example, 175 million working days lost to illness in 2006). The review detailed the costs of ill-health in the working population, but admitted that the human costs "are often hidden and privately borne". Over 260 contributions were made in response to calls for evidence, and recommendations included an expanded role for occupational health beyond helping employees with ill health to remain in work, facilitating the entry into the workforce of those seeking work or experiencing unemployment. Relevant to the focus of this book, the Black Report highlights the key objectives of preventing ill health, promoting positive health and well-being, and "early intervention for those who develop a health condition". Furthermore, there is recognition that "business is more likely to listen to business than take advice from Government" (p. 56) and, as such, the need to take account of the financial costs of not implementing healthy working strategies is seen as a necessary tool in building the platform for positive interventions to improve well-being at work.

The Black Report pinpointed the key factors likely to promote the success of health-related interventions in the workplace:

- visible commitment of senior level management
- alignment of interventions with business strategy
- two-way communication that facilitates employee influence and participation in the scheme
- evaluation of the outcomes.

The Report highlighted a lack of information and advice for organizations and, to this end, a two-year pilot initiative was operated by the HSE to offer free and confidential support to small and medium-sized businesses on workplace health and safety issues. Initially, this was by phone and was supplemented by follow-up visits as appropriate. Interestingly, 85.2 percent of the initial 3850 calls were related to risk assessment and hazard identification rather than absence management or return to work issues. There was a very high level of satisfaction with the service on offer – not unrelated to it being free – and 87 percent found the advice of use to the organization (Tyers *et al.*, 2007). Of those visited by an adviser, 60 percent felt that their views on health and safety had changed as a result. However, only 1.9 percent of phone calls and 3.4 percent of visits were categorized as relating to psychological issues such as stress (Tyers and Lucy, 2008).

In line with the guidance already offered by the HSE, the Black Report recognized that employee health is likelier to be worse where there is job insecurity, monotony of work tasks, little worker-control over the job, an imbalance between efforts and rewards, a lack of supportive social networks and low expectations of receiving fair treatment from the employer (Coats and Max, 2005). There was recognition that line managers play a key role in determining employee health, well-being and performance, as they are well positioned to identify risks and to foster positive working conditions: "Good health equals good business, and the line manager is the key agent of change" (p. 59). Powerful examples cited by the Report included the *Sunday Times'* survey of the "Best Companies to work for in the UK" – which incorporates aspects of employee engagement including well-being, line management and team working – showing these companies have 13 percent lower staff turnover (less than half of the UK average) and "on the stock market they have consistently outperformed the FTSE 100"! A similar analysis of "The Best Companies to work for in America" highlighted the positive relationship between employee satisfaction and share value, including a doubling of the market return between 1998 and 2005 for such organizations compared with industry- and characteristics-matched benchmarks (Edmans, 2008).

In light of the evidence presented, the Black Report emphasized the important relationship between work and health, and called upon the UK government to collaborate with employers and representative bodies to:

- derive methods for measuring and disseminating "the benefits of employer investment in health and well-being" (p. 60)
- improve employers' understanding of the financial case for prioritizing health and well-being
- examine practical steps to facilitate health and well-being initiatives in smaller organizations.

The Foresight Commission and the National Institute for Clinical Excellence guidelines

The Foresight Project on Mental Health and Capital (2008) was established to identify the opportunities and challenges facing the UK over the next 20 years, focusing on the potential consequences for

6

the psychological development and well-being of the population. In relation to the workplace, suggestions recommended to the Government Office for Science at a Strategy Seminar in 2009 were based on a need to assess work environments for their impact on mental capital and well-being. This could be achieved via stress audits (see Chapter 6) and the development of key performance indicators. In turn, these could lead to:

- improved recognition and interventions to tackle work-related stress
- more flexible working methods
- improvement of managerial competence
- raising the profile of mental well-being at work.

Following on from the Foresight Commission, NICE (2009) coordinated public health guidance, which aimed to build on the groundswell for promoting mental well-being through the fostering of productive and healthy working conditions. Adopting the starting point that work has positive benefits for health and well-being (Waddell and Burton, 2006) and based on the concept of "fair employment" (Commission of Social Determinants of Health, 2008), the workplace is recognized as "an effective site for interventions to improve health and reduce health inequalities" (Head *et al.*, 2002). Furthermore, the cost–benefit analysis undertaken by the Foresight Project revealed the potential economic gains to be made by taking an organizational approach, identifying financial gains from conducting audits of employee well-being of the order of £100 million per annum (NICE, 2009). Additional resourcing of steps aimed at preventing mental ill health at work was predicted to save £275 million, and the economic gains linked to granting employee requests for flexible working were estimated to be approximately £165 million per annum (NICE, 2009).

In November 2009, acknowledging the costs of employee mental health-related problems to individuals, organizations and businesses (discussed later in this section), NICE issued five recommendations for improving psychological health in the workplace:

1 Promotion of employee mental well-being via its incorporation into policies and working practices for all categories of workers, including job design, recruitment, selection, training and appraisal. Taking into account the type of work and the profile of the workforce and

organization, this recommendation addresses the need to promote "a culture of participation, equality and fairness based on open communication and inclusion" (p. 8) which, in turn, relates to the need to raise awareness of mental well-being and decrease the stigma attached to mental health problems. The importance of matching employees' skills to their job demands, and supporting them in their work and during times of change and uncertainty is emphasized.

2 A structured approach to assessing and monitoring employees' mental well-being to highlight both the risks and the potential for positive change. Whilst taking care to safeguard individual confidentiality, the conduct of staff surveys and compilation of absence and turnover statistics, as well as training and development costs, are beneficial to this process of assessment. Employers should make workers aware of their legal entitlements at work, as well as of their own responsibilities for their mental health, whilst responding to the needs of those at particular risk of work-related stress. Where such needs are identified, policies should ensure that support is available at the earliest opportunity – for example, counseling and occupational healthcare.

3 Flexible working conditions where reasonably practical. Whether part-time, home-based, flexi-time or job-sharing, these arrangements are recognized as likely to improve employees' perceptions of control and "promote engagement and job satisfaction" (p. 11). This would necessitate promoting a flexible working culture in which requests should be considered consistently and fairly, whilst managers' ability to manage teams working flexibly might need to be enhanced.

4 Supportive leadership style and management practices. These should demonstrate "participation, delegation, constructive feedback, mentoring and coaching" (p. 12), and feature in the assessment of managers on taking on and progressing within the job. Managers' ability to motivate, train and support employees is seen as playing a crucial role in the mental health of workers, which would also require them to "respond with sensitivity to individual emotional concerns and symptoms of mental health problems" (p. 12) and/or refer them to appropriate sources of help, such as occupational health services.

5 Support and advice is needed for micro, small and medium-sized businesses in taking an organizational approach to improve employee well-being, which might also include enabling access to occupational health services.

Confederation of British Industry and the Chartered Institute for Personnel Development

Based on the credit crunch and recession of the late noughties (2000–10), the Confederation of British Industry (CBI) predicted new approaches in four areas of business development:

- increasing the range of finance options to avoid the pre-crunch risks levels
- development of more collaborative relationships with a range of suppliers
- the integration of sustainability and ethics into business models to engender "corporate citizenship" and help retain staff
- evolution of a flexible workforce, utilizing the opportunities afforded by new technology and training, to produce a smaller core of staff accompanied by a larger "flexi-force".

The implications for organizations and their employees are manifold. Richard Lambert, CBI Director-General, highlighted: "We may be at the start of a new era for businesses. What we need now is a more balanced, less risky pathway to growth – one in which the short-term returns may be lower, but the long-term rewards for management success will be a lot more sustainable and secure. And in a more collaborative, less transactional world, closer relationships with customers, suppliers, employees and shareholders look like becoming the norm". The impetus for strategic management of employee well-being could not be greater.

The practical implications of this refreshed approach to working with employees are echoed in a report commissioned by the Chartered Institute of Personnel Development (CIPD; 2006) and conducted by Ipsos-MORI and the Kingston Business School, which highlighted that where employees are engaged in their work, there is lower absenteeism, better performance and a decreased likelihood of quitting. According to the findings, the key determinants of employee engagement are: having the chance to feed their views upwards, keeping staff well informed, commitment by managers to the organization, and flexible working opportunities. However, the CIPD also reported limited evidence that organizations are matching the benchmark of the "high quality workplace", with only three in ten employees engaged with their work. For the CBI's wishes for closer relationships with employees to be realized, the CIPD's recommendations are clear:

- recognizing the causes of employee stress
- increased autonomy for staff and teams of workers
- more flexible working opportunities
- provision of meaningful work
- encouragement of supportive line management relationships
- promotion of employee engagement.

European Foundation for the Improvement of Working and Living Conditions

The 2005 European Working Conditions Survey (EWCS) of 31 EU member and candidate countries found that, on average, 35 percent of workers felt work impacted on their health; however, these rates varied considerably between nations. Almost 70 percent of respondents in Greece, Poland and Latvia noted this, compared with 20 percent of UK participants and 25 percent of German, Dutch, Irish and French employees. Stress was reported by 22.3 percent of respondents as a leading symptom of ill health at work. The highest prevalence of poor psychological health was recorded in the education, health and public administration sectors, and by professionals and senior managers across the whole survey. Interestingly, the surveys carried out by the European Foundation for the Improvement of Working and Living Conditions (Eurofound) since 1990 have shown that the proportion of employees working long hours has steadily decreased, with an increase in those working shorter hours. Comparisons between nations in terms of working conditions show that the UK, Ireland and Scandinavian countries report the most favorable working conditions, with relatively less exposure to physical risks, a better balance between home and work life, and high levels of social support. However, this picture is more complex when viewed by occupational group, as employees in transport and communication, health, hospitality, education and social work report unfavorable working conditions, including within the UK and Ireland (EWCS, 2009).

We continue by reviewing the reasons why organizational health and performance must be a topic for serious consideration. We suggest that this is not simply a journey of whimsy and indulgence because there are sound, practical business reasons why we need to have a firm understanding about our rationale for adopting an organizational approach to the management of stress at work. This scene-setting is a quite deliberate and vital part of the diagnostic process needed before we are ready to put into place the various strategies and interventions that will ensure good organizational health. We will see that there is not just one problem: neither is there just one solution. Nevertheless, we believe that all organizations, from large multinational institutions right down to small-sized companies and one-person businesses, are able to benefit from adopting this new approach. In the final part of this chapter, we will consider the changing face of the workplace and society itself, and the implications this has for a healthy workforce and healthy organization. At the end of this chapter, evidence for the unacceptable costs of mismanaged stress is presented.

A BRIEF HISTORY OF THE CHANGING WORK ENVIRONMENT

It has been suggested that we have traded a working scenario characterized as "fifty years of work; fifty weeks each year, for fifty hours a week" for a style of living and working that would now be unrecognizable to our grandparents' generation. Indeed, the reality of the workplace in contemporary organizational life differs much from the work environment of a mere two or three decades ago. Advances in new technology and globalization have ushered in seemingly endless possibilities for changes in the work environment, alongside which we continue to face enormous changes to the nature of society itself. The restrictive post-war era gave way to the eagerly embraced 1960s, and the era of the baby boomers soon became the fast pace world of the consumer society "teenager" and, of course, the sexual revolution. This liberated group really believed that they invented the word "sex" and pushed many of society's boundaries beyond the point of no return! Meanwhile, the pace of new technology moved at a dizzy speed. Harold Wilson, the Labour Prime Minister of the 1970s, proclaimed that we were living within the "white heat of technology" that would transform our lives, and produce a leisure age of twenty-hour working weeks. We faced a golden future!

However, this bubble finally burst and the reality of the 1970s, in which energy crises played a crucial role, emerged as one typified by industrial conflict, unrest and strife. Bitter battles were fought

11

between the workers and management, and a strike-ridden society slowly was brought to its knees. A no-win situation developed. Normality in our working lives was gone forever as we moved into the 1980s and the emergence of the "enterprise culture". A decade of privatization, statutory constraints on industrial relations, mergers and acquisitions, strategic alliances and joint ventures followed. Yet, in this free market, hothouse culture of the 1980s and early 1990s, competition, the supremacy of the individual and "youth" were idolized. Fortunes beyond avarice were won and lost by those who dared to reach out into this "have-it-all" society. Whilst this entrepreneurial period improved our economic competitiveness at home and in certain international markets, it was not without tolls, such as strain and burnout. At this time, the word "stress" became familiar in the vocabulary of working people. However, it also meant that "stress" was thus seen only as a negative experience. In reality, it was the mismanagement of the stressful situation – which was an inevitable part of modern-day living and working – that became deleterious in its consequences. Bad press and media coverage served to exacerbate the problem because individuals and organizations began to deny "stress", their physical and psychological condition, and their symptoms of stress, until a crisis or breakdown situation had occurred. Before the 1980s ended, a recession began that continued well into the 1990s. One of the key changes observed during this time was the privatization of the public sector industries, and this laid the groundwork for potentially the most profound changes in the workplace since the Industrial Revolution.

The 1990s were dominated by the impact of the recession and efforts to get out of it. Governments were striving to reduce budget deficits, and thereby were squeezing more and more out of business. As the Western World fought to respond, to halt further losses in market share to their Pacific Rim competitors, gain access to new markets, and respond to market vacillations, we witnessed sweeping changes. One of the ways to respond to global competition was for the organization to become "leaner and meaner". Becoming leaner and meaner was achieved by processes variously described as "downsizing", "right-sizing", "delaying", "becoming flatter" or "process re-engineering". This race to be more customer responsive and to reduce "time to market" brought wave upon wave of change in the workplace, including the emergence of initiatives such as total quality management (TQM) and just-in-time (JIT) technology.

In addition to these constraints were the problems associated with fluctuations in the demographic situation, rising expectations in the labor force, and an increasing reluctance for workers to accept certain jobs.

The "Noughties", as they have been termed, have seen the economic cycles replicated, but on a grander scale, one not witnessed since the Wall Street Crash of 1929. Twenty years after the fall of Communism in Eastern Europe, Capitalism has had its turn to face an uncertain future. The "have-it-all" mentality that had pervaded the western economies back in the 1980s outgrew its own brand of usefulness and nearly sank the banking sector. The ideology that suggested that the markets should prevail had failed to take into account the behavior of those who contribute to those markets. Originating in the "sub-prime" property sector of the United States, fuelled by unsustainable speculation and the institutionalized greed of some money market practitioners, a black hole began to suck in the investment – or so-called "casino banks" – and, with it, the surrounding economy. Survival became the watchword, as many industries ranging from construction to cars and crockery saw long-established companies swallowed up. The efforts of international governments to shore up the failing banks have been cited as the bases for a new era of business survival characterized by austerity but, whatever shape the recession of the late Noughties turns out to be, it is likely to mean even more pressure for those fortunate enough to remain in work as the heat is turned up. Economists are taking stock of the reality check to market-focused theories, and are recognizing the key role of human social and motivational needs in "nudge economics" – in other words, the markets are awakening to the power of psychology in the workplace. While employee well-being might not, on the surface, appear fashionable in such an austere economic climate, it is proving to be the competitive edge that makes it a necessity for all organizations keen to see a profitable future.

THE FUTURE OF CHANGE

The political and economic drivers of change are well known. However, the impact of population, technological and organizational changes tends to be more subtle, as they form part of our everyday living experience. These are considered in turn.

People at work

The lengthening of age expectancy in more economically developed countries (such as the UK), the increase in the number of European Union (EU) member states, and the greater fluidity of employee movement across EU national boundaries have produced changes in the demographic profile of the UK working population. It is predicted that, by 2071, the number of individuals aged over 65 will be approximately 21 million (with almost half of this number aged over 80) (Foresight, 2009), and projected estimates of the increased total size of the UK population by 2031 are in the region of 71 million (ONS, 2007).

As more and more private sector companies have become publicly owned, this has increased our appetite for the privatization of the public sector; this has become manifest as "outsourcing" and "market testing", resulting in more people working in a freelance capacity or employed as part of a contract labor force. The variety of contracts can include very short-term contracts or "zero-hours" arrangements. Employers refer to this as "the flexible workforce" but, in reality, it means part-time working for more and more people.

Higher numbers of migrant workers coming to the UK – which peaked in 2007 (GLA, 2009) – have repercussions at many levels, including legislation that threatens to punish employers who are unsure of their employees' entitlement to work in the UK. These include concerns over lowered expectations of working conditions – and, indeed, maltreatment among those entering the country to work – and attitudes of existing UK-based workers to competition for jobs. The Gangmaster Licensing Act (2005) was passed following the deaths in 2004 of 23 cockle-pickers in Morecombe Bay. This legislation aimed to ensure the establishment of legitimate labor providers in the UK, and provide them with minimum employment standards. However, in doing so it acknowledged the likely existence of 200–300 rogue organizations in addition to the 1000 gangmasters already recognized. Reviews of the Gangmaster Legislative Authority's activity in 2007 and 2008 "found that agency worker exploitation remains a significant feature of the UK economy – which according to DEMOS, the OECD and Eurofound houses one of the least regulated labor markets in the developed world – and that it is particularly an issue for new migrants" (GLA, 2009: 9). It is interesting to note that 25 percent of such agency employees are from the UK.

The proportion of women in the workforce has grown significantly over the last thirty years, with gender parity in some countries and sectors, but not others. For example, less than 50 percent of all women in Italy are in paid work, but women make up 51 percent of professionals in the US (*The Economist*, 2009). The projected increases in women working have continued in a number of more economically developed countries, although in the UK the overall figure of 65 percent has changed little since 1997 (Eurostat, 2008, cited in *The Economist*). Again, within subgroups there are differences and, for UK women aged 25, there was a notable rise in the proportions at work between 1992 and 2005, up from 67 percent to 76 percent (ONS, 2007). The role of family-friendly policies and government-sponsored childcare incentives might well play a part in this increase.

However, the changes to the overall presence of women at work belies enduring differences in the gender-based treatment of employees. The pay differential is perhaps the most glaring symptom of gender inequality, whereby women are systematically paid lower wages than their male counterparts. This gap is equivalent to a 19 percent difference in the UK (Arulampalam *et al.*, 2005/06) and is wider in the private sector, where women are paid on average 45 percent less than their colleagues (*The Guardian*, 2005b). Denmark – which has a higher proportion of women at work than most other European countries, and spends a higher percentage of its gross domestic product on public support for childcare than France and the US (*The Economist*, 2009) – maintains a lower pay differential of 12 percent, while in Austria the gender gap is widest at the lowest end of the wages spectrum: an example of the "sticky floor" phenomenon (Arulampalam *et al.*, 2005/06). However, across the EU27 the average gender pay gap has narrowed from 24.5 percent in 2000 to 15.8 percent in 2007 (Eurofound, 2008).

This contrasts with the "glass ceiling" effect (Davidson and Cooper, 1992), which describes the invisible organizational layer barring access or promotion to the higher echelons of management. This is reflected in the very low proportions of women at board level in the FTSE top 100 companies. Again, there are national contrasts, with 1.5 percent of senior management roles in Sweden held by women, but neighboring Norway has introduced a quota system that ensures there is gender equality at the top of organizations. Failure to address the unequal treatment of employees certainly has its costs. First, the financial costs of failing to facilitate equal participation in the labor markets of men and women means that the UK could be missing out on an 8 percent increase in GDP, and as much as 21 percent in Italy (Goldman Sachs cited in *The Economist*, 2009). Second, there is a reluctance to change long-standing difficulties, which can breed arrogance and even abuse on the part of the perpetrators. Evidence given to the UK parliamentary committee investigating working practices in the banking industry uncovered the use of female prostitutes in one firm as part of business negotiations!

With two out of three families two-earner or dual career, the problem of who plays what role in the family and the conflicts surrounding work and domestic space presents a challenge to the already delicate work–home balance. This is, in part, reflected in UK legislation granting men paternity leave rights (7–14 days to be taken in one block, at the time of writing) and further allowances for parental leave following the birth or adoption of a child (up to 13 weeks, at the time of writing). Such centralized efforts to recognize shared roles in family life are further supported by the right for individuals to request flexible working arrangements, echoed in the NICE recommendations. Indeed, where such flexibility exists and the employee perceptions of their organization recognize this, there is less conflict between home and work-life, and also better psychological health for workers (O'Driscoll *et al.*, 2003).

Technology

The impact of technological changes is clearly tangible, in that we can see how mobile phones and their "offspring" have become ubiquitous in a relatively short span of 15 years, with email and the Internet remolding the shape and pace of work in many sectors. These present challenges and benefits, which range from the shift in expectations of a "waking" to a working week (Parker *et al.*, 2001), as well as the evolution of electronic performance monitoring of employees' computer-time and communications (Carayon, 1994; see Chapter 5). What is less easy for employees to envisage is the level of control they will have over the use of new technology in their work. The blurring of the boundaries between home and work is a common experience, as employees increasingly consider working on the computer at times of the day and week that clash with home life – and might, indeed, be encouraged to do so. The portability of the mobile phone and other electronic organizers contributes to the notion of workers potentially being available to the organization at any time, or in any place. It might not be the issue of the convenience of new technology for the organization to which employees object but, rather, the reasons underlying it, and whether they as individuals have been consulted or have participated in the design of its use (Weinberg, 2005).

Organizational behavior and changes

The colossal damage inflicted by aspects of the banking sector, on itself and the national economies depending on it, has highlighted both public interest and organizational sensitivity to the ethics underpinning corporate governance. Perhaps this was foreshadowed early in the new millennium by the high-profile cases involving the US energy giant Enron and the change in ethos that saw praise for the well-intentioned whistleblowers horrified by an organization's failure to recognize and address moral issues. In the UK, the accountability and conduct of public sector services have been features of their development in the last twenty years – at best creating a mechanism for monitoring and improving aspects of the performance of schools and hospitals, and at worst constricting the creativity and public-centered thinking that led to their existence. This made the expenses scandal involving large numbers of UK Members of Parliament an even more salient indicator of the difficulties in relying on organizations' internal monitoring procedures. Aside from Parliament, the governance of large parts of the UK public sector has been transparent to a far greater degree than has been the case for business and commercial enterprises. This is, in part, due to the global nature of ownership of formerly UK-owned firms, but more so to a reluctance to make organizational processes transparent and to regulate the mechanisms and behavior that drive commerce, particularly in the financial sector. The regularly and well-publicized cases of bullying, harassment and gender discrimination involving macho-styled bosses have contributed to a worrying portrait of working conduct in a number of areas. However, the issues of procedural justice at work are common to all, and are seen as a major influence on employee well-being (Rousseau *et al.*, 2009; Warr, 2007).

Bullying at work has increasingly received attention from researchers and lobbyists contributing to the development of a range of policies aimed at promoting dignity and respect for individuals in the workplace. In the UK, these include the Disability Discrimination Act and initiatives aimed at promoting dignity at work. However, the prevalence of bullying has been detected at worryingly high levels, with 49.4 percent of a sample of over 5000 UK employees either experiencing or witnessing bullying at work in a five-year period (Hoel *et al.*, 2004). Some working environments appear to have higher rates of bullying – for example, prisons (Vartia and Hyyti, 2002) – with some occupations, such as teaching, featuring increased levels of negative behavior from managers. Other organizations where large-scale change is also frequent – for instance, the National Health Service and universities – experience higher rates of bullying by peers.

The roles of leadership style and of organizational culture are crucial in setting examples and "rules" for everyday working life. From the employee's viewpoint, perceptions of organizational support are closely linked with fairness and, in turn, their commitment to their employer. This stems from the tendency to attribute human-like qualities to organizations (Eisenberger *et al.*, 1986), which leads to interpretations of supervisors' and managers' behavior as being representative of the organization, rather than simply those individuals' intent (Levinson, 1965). Fairness, support from supervisors, appropriate rewards and favorable job conditions are frequently noted predictors of perceived organizational support, which translate into employees' levels of job satisfaction and positive mood, as well as improved commitment and performance (Rhoades and Eisenberger, 2002).

One of the ways large organizations have attempted to cope with global competition has been to become a multinational company. The organization is no longer based in one particular country, but has plants or business arrangements in those countries that offer the most favorable conditions. The 1980s saw the biggest and most sustained wave of merger activity, which began a trend that continued into the new millennium. However, the seizure experienced by the money markets, and consequently the rest of the world economy, in late 2008 produced a sudden reversal. From the first to the second quarter of 2009, the value of merger and acquisition activity by firms interested in UK businesses dropped from £12.3 billion to £0.4 billion – the lowest level since 1987, while the value of such deals by UK companies in the UK also dropped, from £8.2 billion to £0.7 billion. Widespread cuts are set to become the new order of things as governments who have bailed out their banking sectors seek to balance their finances and manage their vastly increased budget deficits.

Against the backdrop of twenty years of globalization, the use of the Internet and other methods of electronic communication have permitted the disappearance of the factual, though not nominal, headquarters of multinational corporations (Handy, 1994). It means that different functions could now be performed anywhere in the world and where they were handled best (and/or cheapest)! This situation does not guarantee a natural focal point for monitoring employee well-being. Indeed, assumptions could exist at local management level that corporate responsibility for this lies at organizational headquarters, while head office might assume that this is the business of its local management structures. The employees working in these organizations are simply left to complain about the constant reorganization that seems to take place for the sake of reorganization! As one manager working within a construction company told us:

> Just as we begin to see the light at the end of the tunnel (following yet another restructuring process) we realize that the light is only another train coming towards us, headlong and on our track!

The effects of job cuts are far-reaching and the consequences undesirable, ranging from extreme worry to job insecurity and uncertainty. In 88 percent of studies on downsizing these factors, in turn, have been found to lead to increased risk of injury and/ or violence at work, cardiovascular disease and psychological ill health (Quinlan, 2007). A longitudinal study of job-related insecurity has confirmed the potentially inescapable negative impact of job insecurity on psychological health, as it prevailed regardless of employees' gender, age, tenure, family circumstances and educational level (Hellgren and Sverke, 2003). The repercussions faced by the "walking wounded" are discussed in greater detail in Chapter 3. However, at this point it is relevant to observe that it is often the older employees who are first out of the door in times of economic recession. Organizations tend to get rid of their older workers, who are mistakenly regarded as expensive, inflexible, harder to train, unhealthy and unproductive. The Chief Economist of the Chartered Institute of Personnel and Development, John Philpott, has claimed that, "despite the introduction of age discrimination legislation, older people might still be those more likely to accept voluntary redundancy or be hit by compulsory job cuts" (*Personnel Today*, 2008.) This seems to have been substantiated by findings that benefit claims by unemployed workers over 60 increased by 65 percent in the year up to April 2009 (*Daily Telegraph*, 2010). In terms of psychological well-being, the effects of unemployment have been found to be negative for older as well as younger individuals, with the role of personal choice playing a key role in the positive well-being of older people of working age (Robertson *et al.*, 2003; Warr, 1995) – a choice removed by the job-cutting responses of many organizations to the recession of the late Noughties.

For the prejudices already mentioned, older workers find it difficult to regain employment, leading to higher social security costs and market loss in terms of the reduction in purchasing power of this group. The organization immediately loses a wealth of experience and "knowledge", and the employees left in the jobs feel a mixture of guilt, relief and the impact of the loss of stability. They are also wary of what the future might hold for them if they stay with the company. Many will respond by moving on to another company perceived as safer in terms of job security. This means that the organization can be faced with the unexpected high costs of re-hiring and training new staff, and disruption to operations caused by labor turnover and instability.

Conversely, job insecurity can present a quite different problem for the organization, in the form of "presenteeism". It would appear that employees vie to demonstrate organizational commitment by presenting themselves for work whether or not they are fit enough to do so. The ability to maintain a good record of employment and not be absent for any reason is seen as a necessary credential for avoiding becoming a redundancy victim in the next tranche of lay-offs. This clearly has implications for health and safety in the workplace. There are also potential costs for the organization, such as poor performance from an employee who really should not be at work because he or she is unwell. Some cynics also suggest that older employees are laid off for more devious financial reasons. Organizations that adopt the practice of offering voluntary redundancy to employees aged 50 years or more will be rid of a group of workers who might begin to suffer from symptoms of exposure to stress. This, of course, is the group most liable to sue the organization for cumulative stress trauma!

Grasping the future of change

Towards the end of the last millennium, many authors (for example, Cascio 1998; Cooper, 1998) suggested that change is here to stay because of the business trends that drive it and, indeed, the growth of global markets: the ever-spiraling Internet and continually developing new technology have resulted in "commerce without borders". This, in turn, fuels the demand for a technology that can provide links with customers and access to information any time, anywhere and at speed. These are vital if the organization is to be responsive to market changes, and to gain and maintain competitiveness. Cascio also noted that change drives the need for continuous learning, and that thinking and inventing will be the most valuable assets in today's organizations. This involves the redefinition of careers and opportunities for new products and services, which in turn can raise uncertainty and anxiety for the workers affected. On the negative side of this equation is the increased stress produced. However, it is our argument that stress need not be damaging in its consequences, since only mismanaged stress leads to a state of distress. The concept and underlying theory of stress, the stress response, distress and reasons why "change" is a source of stress are explained in detail in Chapter 3. Perceptions of control can help to mediate the negative impact of an uncertain economic climate and it therefore makes sense to enhance employee engagement, rather than move away from it (Bordia *et al.*, 2004). By ensuring that the agents of change are those that can handle the complexities of the situation and recognize the impact of uncertainty, change can bring more successful outcomes (Hasle and Jensen, 2006). In other words, the concept of "survivor syndrome" in organizations, whereby those that remain in work are subject to a form of trauma, need not be inevitable (Travaglione and Cross, 2006). This is not to ignore the age-old political advice given by Machiavelli, that "There is nothing more difficult to take in hand, more perilous to conduct, or more uncertain in its success, than to take the lead in the introduction of a new order of things", but it helps to recognize that employees under strain will feel less committed to the organization and therefore more reluctant to accept change (Vakola and Nikolaou, 2005).

So, survival of the fittest becomes the name of the game, and the pace and speed at which the players can adapt to the continually changing environment is the factor that will determine this survival. An ability to be flexible is the key characteristic for both the individual employee and the organization. So, the chances of survival might be enhanced by the manner of our adaptation and, if change is implemented positively and sensitively, harmful outcomes might be minimized or avoided, and previously underlying negative factors removed (Schabracq and Cooper, 2000).

The changes we have experienced have produced a revision of the psychological contract that binds workers to the organization and to each other. In the mid-1990s, Herriot and Pemberton famously asserted that "the captains of industry had set in motion a revolution in the nature of the employment relationship the like of which they have never imagined. For they have shattered the old psychological contract and failed to negotiate a new one" (Herriot and Pemberton, 1995: 58). Naturally, a climate of change and uncertainty stimulates renewed interest in the psychological contract, which is the set of mutual expectations existing between employees and their employers. Examples of these are presented in Table 1.1. Fulfillment of the psychological contract can have positive ramifications for employees' commitment to the organization, career development and job performance, while the frustration of expectations is linked to negative behaviors such as absenteeism and turnover (Sturges *et al.*, 2005). However, the impact of an unfulfilled or violated psychological contract can also be harmful for employees' well-being, ranging from a lack of job satisfaction to emotional exhaustion (Gakovic and Tetrick, 2003).

We must acknowledge the demographic changes that are taking place, which include issues related to migrating workers as well as the

TABLE 1.1 **A psychological contract for the new millennium**

What employees expect	What employers expect
Pleasant and safe working conditions	Hard work
Fair pay and rewards	Honesty
Information about changes and participation in solutions where possible	Uphold the positive image and reputation of the organization
Feedback on performance, including recognition for a job well done	Added value – innovation and new ideas
Opportunities for training and progression	Working extra hours when required
Reasonable job security	Flexibility in a globally changing economy

Source: Adapted from the CIPD (2009a).

ageing of the population. The latter will result in a decrease in the number of economically active people in relation to the number of those who have retired. The age structure of our working population is changing as life expectancy increases while the birth rate declines. Projections indicate that the number of workers in proportion to the number of retirees will continue to decrease. This has obvious implications and burdens for our welfare, health and pension systems, and the organization of work. It is widely acknowledged that the current trend to retire at an early age will need to be reversed in order to cope with the problems of an ageing society. Thus, organizations will need to find ways to keep their workforce healthy, active and productive for a longer period of their lives. Early retirement for the "stressed-out" or "burnt out" individuals, aged 50 to 55 years will no longer be acceptable as a standard practice as a or way of avoiding stress litigation procedures. Thus, there is need to combat age barriers, building on the anti-age discrimination legislation introduced in the UK in 2006, to maintain older workers at work and to support their continued health and productivity (Griffiths, 1997). Stress management activities will be necessary in ensuring that work is designed to minimize adverse impact on these and other employees. Worksite health promotion activities and training programs will also help to optimize the full health and productivity potential of this occupational group. However, the barriers to job opportunities that an economic downturn presents to older employees need to be addressed in practice. These include organizational policies and structures, and the attitudes of management, not only in relation to the grounds of age, but also gender, ethnicity, disability and sexuality. It is suggested that a stress audit can be adapted to address the issue of equality of opportunity in the workplace by identifying the barriers that prevent the individual developing their full career potential (Sutherland and Davidson, 1996). More details of this approach and method are described in the case study example provided in Chapter 6.

Whilst the potential for great improvement in communication between us exists, electronic communications media (in the form of voice-mail, email, video conferencing, Internet links, interactive pagers and handheld organizers) can also be potential sources of strain. This is known as "technostress". Rapidly changing dimensions in modern technology will continue to bring dramatic changes to our work environment. For example, it is suggested that more and more of us will no longer be tied to a workplace. For many people, in certain jobs the virtual workplace (in which employees operate remotely from each other) is a reality. Technological developments have encouraged these changes, and there is an urgent need to understand how we can optimize the performance, effectiveness and health of those individuals no longer under direct supervision in the work environment, who might also feel isolated from the social aspects of the workplace.

Nevertheless, it also means that employees engaged in on-site and off-site working are now exposed to the pressures of electronic monitoring or computer-based monitoring. Issues surrounding this method of controlling employees and the impact of electronic monitoring are considered in Chapter 5.

Issues relating to organizational governance have assumed a high profile in recent years and, given its relationship with employee commitment and well-being, not to mention job performance, it is vital that procedural justice and organizational support are maintained and appropriately monitored. Leaders and managers have a responsibility to uphold and promote ethical behaviors at work, providing not only role models but also strategic influence to ensure that problems such as bullying and discrimination are recognized and effectively addressed. In a fluctuating economic climate with its inevitable uncertainties, those leading organizations are well-positioned to inform and engage employees as much as possible, and to implement change whilst demonstrating appropriate concern for its impact. Shifts in the psychological contract should also be made explicit to ensure optimum communication and reciprocal relationships between employers and employees in challenging and changing times.

Meanwhile, we continue by examining the costs and consequences associated with the changing nature of the workplace.

THE CHANGING NATURE OF THE WORKPLACE: CONSEQUENCES AND COSTS

We firmly believe that organizations neither understand nor make enough effort to calculate the damaging costs of stress in the workplace. This part of the stress management process is vital for two main reasons. First, it is a key element of a "diagnostic" phase in the process. It is essential that problem areas are *accurately* identified and that the potential impact of this is described in terms of business costs to the organization. Second, it is likely that the organization will require a budget for the implementation of an effective stress management program that adopts an organizational approach. If the costs to the organization are well documented, the potential savings can be judged against the costs of the stress management activities. However, they also require "up front" expenditure before this investment benefit is realized. Thus, data on costs and cost savings are needed by those making a bid for funds, since, in our experience, this type of activity tends not to be regarded as a priority in many organizations. This is because the organization has failed to understand and acknowledge the true costs to the business.

The costs of mental ill health

The reports described earlier in this chapter drew evidence from a range of sources, and in turn developed estimates of the cost of psychological ill health to businesses, which as Dame Carol Black emphasized, do not begin to take into account the costs to the individuals concerned and their families. Based on the assumptions outlined in the NICE report (2009), the annual cost of mental ill health to UK employers in 2009 was £28.3 billion, with workplaces losing £835,355 for every 1000 staff members. However, this level of lost economic activity represents only two thirds of the costs, a further third being due to health and social care costs (Black Report, 2008). These findings suggest that the NICE recommendations for improving the ways in which mental health is managed at work (see pp. 7–8), not only stand to reduce costs to organizations with 1000 employees by £250,607 annually, but also to lessen the impact on wider public services.

Prevalence of mental health problems at work

The Royal College of Psychiatrists (1995) has highlighted that one in three members of the adult population will experience an episode of psychological ill health at some point in their lives, with 18 percent of women and 11 percent of men experiencing significant psychiatric symptoms at any given time. The Black Report distinguishes between the one sixth of the UK working age population that has symptoms such as fatigue, sleep difficulties, irritability and worry (which are associated with mental ill health) and a further one sixth that has symptoms of the severity and duration that would merit diagnosis of psychological disorder. The most common of these illnesses would be depression, anxiety or a combination of both.

The *Labour Force Survey* provides data on work-related stress that incorporates both groupings identified by the Black Report. Their 2008–09 findings produced estimates that, during that period, 415,000 UK employees "were experiencing work-related stress at a level that was making them ill" (HSE, 2009), while the HSE's own Psychosocial Working Conditions (PWC) survey found that 16.7 percent of the working population felt their job was "very" or "extremely" stressful. These estimates rely on self-reported data, which in themselves show no annual increase in problems over the period 2004–09. However, the insight provided by occupational health physician assessments is alarming, as this shows a 100 percent increase in psychological ill health at work during the longer and overlapping period 1999–2006 (McNamee *et al.*, 2007). The HSE believes that the data collected from occupational health departments actually underestimates the extent of the problem, as the largest proportion of their clients are those with mild to moderate mental ill health who are less likely to be referred on for specialist help (McNamee *et al.*, 2007).

It is important to emphasize that gathering data on the costs associated with psychological ill health is not a purely academic exercise, as it can provide organizations with a baseline from which to progress. Furthermore, the Foresight Commission pinpointed economic benefits following on from the conduct of annual audits of employee well-being "of the order of £100m per annum", which could be augmented by a factor of at least 2.5 through appropriate investment to tackle the issues raised.

Individual symptoms of psychological strain in the workplace

The mechanisms involved are explored in greater detail in Chapter 3, but it is worth noting here that the individual symptoms of strain are manifold and can be found in cognitive, physiological and behavioral outcomes, whether the individual is a member of the working population or not. However, the range of expression of such symptoms within organizations can take on a different significance as these become linked to individual and team performance issues, organizational failures, and possibly financial and legal consequences.

The example of hospital doctors performing clinical tasks with significantly less confidence while reporting higher levels of distress (Williams *et al.*, 1997) is a useful one to help focus the mind. Similarly, one might imagine how difficulty in making decisions or general worries about future performance might impact on job-holders with responsibility for air traffic control or a nuclear power plant. Psychosomatic symptoms of strain – which are physical manifestations of psychological strain – can include headaches, muscle trembling (such as a twitching eye), excessive perspiration, lack of appetite, indigestion, sickness, shortness of breath, and even a decrease in sexual interest (Cooper, Sloan and Williams, 1988). All of these are consistent with over-activation of the body's "stress response" and, while these are often short-lived, it is the chronic presence of physical symptoms that can lead to long-term health difficulties. Most strikingly, a Europewide study of 6467 pregnant women found that it is not only the number of hours, but also the quality of one's working life that can have an impact, as working more than 42 hours per week or having low job satisfaction carry "a moderate excess risk" of premature birth (Saurel-Cubizolles *et al.*, 2004).

The most serious health outcome as a symptom of anything is death! Death from overwork (*karoshi*, as it is known in Japan) is evidence of a cultural emphasis on the significance of work organizations in the lives of employees, placing considerable pressure on workers to adhere to expectations that could, in turn, result in serious health consequences. The death of a junior doctor in the UK after working over 120 hours without sleep demonstrates that overwork is a potential danger wherever it occurs. Netterstrom and Juel (1988) studied 2465 Danish bus drivers over a seven-year period and found that workload – as assessed by measuring the intensity of traffic on certain routes – was the factor most strongly associated with heart disease.

An increased rate of errors in employees' work is consistent with poorer levels of concentration, while symptoms of tiredness and cognitive overload have been blamed by some investigations into fatal mistakes on the UK railways. Additionally, feeling the pressure of a set of demands has been linked to mistakes whilst carrying out everyday tasks (Reason, 1988) and so it is not unreasonable to assume that errors are made in most jobs, but some are more likely to stand out than others. It is how the organization deals with these mistakes that can either compound or exacerbate the problems for the staff concerned – an appropriate organizational culture that promotes safety is not only a clear example of good practice, but also a portent of organizational well-being (for example, Zohar, 1980).

In addition to the availability and quality of work of an employee under strain, their emotional affect might also be transformed, along with a reduced tolerance of challenging situations. This can impair an individual's ability to manage interactions and that person might fail to communicate clearly with others or rise quickly to irritation. Such behavioral symptoms are particularly noticeable in organizations reliant upon the trading of feelings for success. Given the increasing switch from manufacturing to service industries, emotional labor is used by a host of organizations, ranging from call centers to public sector health and social care, which might already be drawing upon strained employee resources. The negative consequences of this can range from low morale among staff to greater dissatisfaction among customers as employees feel unable to put on the face the organization would have them wear. A link between psychological strain and incongruent emotions experienced while doing a job has already been established (Brotheridge and Lee, 2003). Burnout – comprising the negative mix of emotional exhaustion, depersonalization of clients and a lack of personal accomplishment (Maslach and Jackson, 1986) – has become a familiar problem among occupational groups working with the public. The impact on organizational functioning is likely to be evident in many ways, as will be seen in Chapter 2.

Organizational symptoms of strain

As has been discussed, burnout and its symptoms are evident not only in the individual, but also in barometers of organizational well-being. This is because the symptoms, if they are not addressed, can develop into a climate of sub-optimal functioning, in which it is accepted by co-workers that "this is how the job makes us feel". Low morale is often evident in the lack of discretionary activities in which employees engage – that is, those behaviors carried out by workers but not enforced by employers. These include voluntary overtime, attendance on training courses and pro-social activity, which can range from simply being friendly to colleagues to making suggestions as to how to improve the workplace (Warr, 1999). For the receivers of the product or service, low morale can manifest itself in poorer quality, miscommunication and ultimately customer dissatisfaction. Along with complaints, poorer productivity, greater staff turnover, elevated absenteeism rates and industrial unrest, these are also potential symptoms of organizational strain. Furthermore, there is evidence to suggest that the incidence of unacceptable behaviors (such as bullying) is higher in sectors under pressure – for instance, higher education (Kinman and Jones, 2004). Not unrelated to the management of change and the battles that can ensue, there is evidence that revenge by employees is predicted by perceptions of a breach of the psychological contract (Bordia *et al.*, 2008).

Absenteeism

It is instructive to look back and reflect on the strain and burnout caused by the "hot house" culture of the 1980s that proved so immensely costly to industry and society. It was estimated that mental illness was responsible for 80 million lost working days annually in Great Britain, costing in excess of £3.7 billion (DSS, 1993). In the UK, over ten per cent of gross national product was spent each year in coping with the manifestations of job-generated stress (Cooper, Cooper and Eaker, 1988). Annually, the US industry lost 550 million working days due to absenteeism and it was estimated that 54 per cent of these absences were, in some way, stress-related (Elkin and Rosch, 1990). So how have things changed?

Since then, the problem in the US has continued to mount, wiping billions from the "bottom line" (CCH Unscheduled Absence Survey, 2007). The costs in the UK amount to £8.4 billion, with 40 percent of all sickness absence attributed to mental health problems, which is equivalent to £335 per employee (Sainsbury Centre for Mental Health, 2007). These figures stem from 175 million lost working days, with 70 million days lost due to psychological ill health. The latter exceeds the total of 66 million working days lost due to both physical and mental health problems in the UK public sector alone (CBI/AXA, 2006). This is consistent with the finding that work-related stress and mental health disorders have been the single largest cause of absenteeism in each year from 2004–08 (Cooper and Dewe, 2008), with sickness absence high in certain occupations, including teaching, nursing, social work, police and the armed services (Seymour and Grove, 2005).

Psychological health problems constitute 47 percent of long-term sickness absence (Spurgeon *et al.*, 2007), with episodes lasting on average 26.8 days (HSE, 2009). However, the nature of the illness might cause a delay in the individual seeking treatment, which serves to lengthen any period of absence. Furthermore, people with mental health problems are more likely to suffer from musculoskeletal problems at work (Glozier, 2002). Returning to work following an episode of psychological ill health presents a number of challenges too, as colleagues can respond less favorably to the individual than if they had had a physical health problem (Glozier *et al.*, 2006). An added challenge is the perception of the employer, as their criteria for judging an individual's ability to do their job effectively will not be the same as those used by a clinician in deciding an employee is "well" – that is, one's mood and symptoms could improve, but productivity levels might lag behind and not be seen as a legitimate aftermath of illness (Black Report, 2008). However, the continuing evolution of working hours permitted by new technology might necessitate a re-evaluation of how absenteeism is calculated in some jobs. A study of the lost working hours, rather than days, of 54,264 full-time US employees has shown that those experiencing psychological distress make up for lost time, "possibly to stay up to speed with task driven occupation and avoid performance review" (Hilton *et al.*, 2009). Whilst this might lead to welcome flexibility, the pressure that motivates such "catching up" could be less beneficial for recovery from psychological ill health.

Presenteeism and work loss

Presenteeism refers to "impaired work efficiency" (Black Report, 2008), whereby the employee is unwell but continues to work. It is estimated that the associated costs are almost double those of absenteeism, totaling £15.1 billion annually, equivalent to £605 per employee per year (Sainsbury Centre for Mental Health, 2007). Presenteeism is projected to be responsible for 60 percent of the costs of mental ill health in UK workplaces, although the influential studies to date have been conducted in the US and Australia.

The issue of decreased work performance has been scrutinized in a major US study of 4115 employed people: the study projected that, on over 130 million working days per year, employees' performance was impaired by psychological and emotional strain (Kessler and Frank, 1997). More than one fifth of respondents reported the loss or cutback of activities on one work day in the previous month due to physical or psychological health reasons (the average loss is 6.7 days per month), with depression being the largest single category of ill health detected (Kessler *et al.*, 2001). This form of presenteeism, which means the individual that is struggling with psychological symptoms at work and whose performance is impaired, is likely to cost organizations more than absenteeism, with an estimated lost productive time at work equivalent to $44 billion annually in the US (Steward *et al.*, 2003). In fact, some US studies claim that the impact is four or five times greater than that of absenteeism (Goetzel *et al.*, 2004).

Turnover

The cost of replacing employees who have left their jobs due to a mental health problem is estimated at £2.4 billion each year (Sainsbury Centre for Mental Health, 2007), with the CIPD estimating the overall figure, including training and induction of replacements, to amount to £7750 per employee lost (CIPD, 2007). The CIPD (2007) and the CBI/AXA (2007) estimate turnover rates at between 14.1 percent and 18.1 percent respectively, with the "stress of job/role" cited as the reason for turnover by 8 percent of employees, with a further 15 percent citing "ill health – other than stress" (CIPD, 2009c). Analysis of the survey data available led NICE (2009) to assert it is reasonable to assume that, for every 1000 employees, 13 will leave each year due to mental ill health, at an average cost of £6125, which takes into account the range from £3150 for manual employees to £9000 for those at senior managerial level. These figures are utilized in the costing exercise at the end of this chapter.

Job satisfaction

The term "job satisfaction" is an umbrella term for our feelings towards many factors at work, including pay and conditions of work, management style, relationships with colleagues, job security, and even the functioning of tools and software. Job satisfaction can be defined as a "pleasurable or positive emotional state resulting from the appraisal of one's job or job experiences" (Locke, 1976). There is evidence suggesting that those employees who are generally happier are better at their jobs (Wright and Staw, 1999), and can even boost companies' performance (Edmans, 2008). According to the NICE study (2009), in the UK, 27 percent of employees stated they were "very satisfied" with their job and 47 percent were "satisfied". However, the impact of work factors on job satisfaction can be complex and might be mediated by other factors. For example, despite higher levels of psychological strain among UK academics, 58 percent claimed they were at least "moderately satisfied" with their jobs (Kinman and Jones, 2004). It is possible to attribute this to the importance of intrinsic job rewards, such as conducting research and supervision of students in lecturing jobs. However, dissatisfaction with stagnating pay and poor promotion prospects has taken its toll on university employees: "No one seems to enjoy their work any more. I used to love teaching – now it is just what I do" (Kinman and Jones, 2004: 25). In turn, this negative experience can also impact on performance, as research into schoolteachers has previously shown significant associations between teachers' job satisfaction and pupils' academic performance (Ostroff, 1992).

One indication of higher job satisfaction is employees' commitment, demonstrated through a range of voluntary behaviors at work – for example, voluntary overtime and adaptive behaviors such as participating in training (Birdi et al., 1998). Similarly, pro-social behaviors incorporate being friendly and helpful in the workplace, and these are also significantly related to overall job satisfaction (McNeely and Meglino, 1994). Interestingly, from an organizational perspective, where employee trust of managers is increased, so too is the relationship between the pro-social motivation and job performance (Grant and Sumanth, 2009).

The cost of mismanaging stress at work

Before we address the issues surrounding stress and the litigation process in Chapter 2, it is worth listing the deleterious and costly behaviors that can be manifest in response to the mismanagement of stress in the workplace. These could be the result of organizations failing to take notice of or showing no interest in changing an unsatisfactory status quo. Dissatisfied employees that are under stress are more likely to:

- arrive late to work and/or take an early departure
- take extended lunch, coffee and tea breaks
- make more errors, resulting in the need to redo work – due to slow and poor decision making, poor concentration or impaired judgment

- have more rejects in quality inspection
- have increased equipment breakdowns that are sometimes the result of sabotage
- miss deadlines
- have accidents at work; more work-related travel accidents (that is, road traffic incidents that cause damage to vehicles and injuries to employees)
- engage in petty theft
- interpersonal conflict with other people at work – this includes petty bickering and the creation of a climate of unsubstantiated, time-wasting rumors and mistrust at all levels
- be moved around as a result of departmental transfers – for example, a manager might try to get rid of the "stressed" employee, before they become a serious and potentially costly problem, by transferring them to another "unsuspecting" manager or colleague
- be less innovative and creative.

It is clear, that the overall cost of mismanaged stress to organizations, individuals and society itself is immense. Therefore, the potential rewards for effective stress management in the workplace are also very high in both humanistic and business terms.

Calculating the costs: How much is stress costing your organization?

NICE (2009) estimates that £250,607 can be saved by taking steps to address the issue of poor psychological health at work, which is equivalent to savings worth 30 percent for every 1000 employees in an organization. This calculation is derived from average costings attributable to mental ill health under the headings of absenteeism, presenteeism and turnover. Using the figures and the algorithm provided by NICE, it is possible to estimate the costs to your own organization and derive the value of potential savings to be made (see Box 1.1).

For the steps that need to be taken to improve working practices in order to achieve these levels of savings, the following chapters highlight the relevant individual and organizational mechanisms, legal requirements and practical interventions that need to be considered.

BOX 1.1 How much is stress costing your organization?

Calculating costs related to absenteeism per 1000 employees

Average annual sick days per employee (all causes)	8
Estimated total sick days	8 x 1000 = 8000
Estimated proportion and number due to mental ill health	40.5% x 8000 = 3240
Based on CIPD data, NICE assumes the average cost of a day taken as sick leave as	£83.25

Therefore, for an organization with 1000 employees, the annual cost of sickness absence attributable to mental ill health is estimated as:

$$3240 \times £83.25 = £269{,}730$$

By estimating the number of employees and the financial cost of a working day in your own organization, the cost of absenteeism due to mental ill health can be calculated.

Calculating costs related to presenteeism per 1000 employees

It is acknowledged that there is a wide margin for error in estimating these costs, as the studies on this topic have been conducted outside the UK and on a range of occupational groups. However, NICE has assumed the costs to be equivalent to 1.5 times those due to absenteeism. Therefore, for an organization with 1000 employees, the cost of presenteeism is estimated to be the ratio of presenteeism to absenteeism multiplied by the number of sick days taken:

$$1.5 \times 3240 = 4860$$

NICE assumes the costs of a work-impaired day to be 20 percent higher than a day taken as sick leave, based on an average figure of £100 per day. Thus, the cost of presenteeism to your own organization could be calculated by adjusting for the number of employees. In this example, where there are 1000 people in the workplace, the costs of presenteeism would be:

$$4860 \times £100 = £486{,}000$$

Calculating costs related to turnover per 1000 employees

Based on CIPD figures, which show annual turnover running at 15.7 percent for all causes, NICE estimates that 8 percent of turnover is due to staff stress.

Thus, for an organization with 1000 employees, annual turnover would be 157, of whom 8 percent would be leaving due to stress-related illness (13 employees). Taking into account the wide range of costs for replacing employees at all levels of an organization, NICE have calculated an average cost of £6125 per individual. Therefore, for the organization with 1000 staff, turnover due to psychological strain would be:

$$13 \times £6125 = £79,625$$

To calculate the costs of stress-related turnover in your organization, the number of employees and the proportions should be altered.

Total costs of stress to the organization and the value of potential savings

Combining the costs of absenteeism, presenteeism and turnover in this example of an organization with 1000 employees, the overall figure would be:

$$£835,355$$

NICE estimates that adopting appropriate interventions of the nature of those described in Chapter 7 can lead to savings equivalent to 30 percent of this amount:

$$£250,607$$

By adding the costs of all three consequences of psychological ill health in your own workplace, proportional savings of 30 percent can be calculated.

Source: NICE (2009).

STRUCTURE OF THE BOOK

In Chapter 2, we consider issues surrounding the stress litigation process in the workplace, including the implications for employer's liability insurance, and the requirements for health and well-being standards at work. In addition to the health and safety consequences for public and private sector organizations, the potentially high and damaging costs of stress litigation are, and should be, a serious cause for concern for human resource professionals in their role of preventing and treating stress at work.

In Chapter 3, the nature of stress is examined and, in Chapter 4, "hot spot" stressors highlighted by the UK's HSE are considered. In Chapter 5, the issues of rapid technological development and the physical environment are assessed as potential sources of stress at work. Chapter 6 provides guidance on how to conduct a stress audit, and includes examples of three case studies of psychological risk assessments. Finally, in Chapter 7, options for the management of stress are described, with examples of each type of intervention, its effectiveness and potential weaknesses.

CHAPTER 2

STRESS AND THE LAW

Peter Jenkins

Stress at work affects a significant proportion of the workforce in the UK. In 2008/09, an estimated 415,000 individuals in Britain believed they were experiencing work-related stress at a level sufficient to make them ill, according to the Health and Safety Executive (2009c). Almost one in five of those at work thought their job was either "very stressful" or "extremely stressful". Self-reported work-related stress, depression and anxiety accounted for an estimated 11.4 million lost working days in Britain. Certain occupational groups are reported to experience high prevalence rates of self-reported work-related stress. These groups include teachers, nurses, housing and welfare officers, customer service workers, certain professional and managerial groups, and those working in public administration and defense. There are high incidence rates of work-related mental ill health among these occupational groups, together with medical practitioners and those in public sector security based occupations, such as police officers, prison officers and UK armed forces personnel (HSE, 2009c).

One avenue for redress for work-related injuries, whether physical or psychological in nature, is via legal action, either to minimize the perceived causes of stress in the workplace, or to gain compensation for the damage and loss allegedly incurred. However, this is not a straightforward route to take, given that leading legal commentators have concluded that "workplace stress can be a legal and managerial minefield" (Jamdar and Byford, 2003: viii). Furthermore, as the authors point out, "stress can give rise to a variety of different legal liabilities, crossing a number of legal disciplines".

LEGAL PERSPECTIVES ON WORKPLACE STRESS

Re-examining the opening paragraph perhaps offers some clues as to why this should be so. First, there is no such single, actionable entity recognizable as "workplace stress", according to the law. The apparently high levels of stress indicated above are self-reported and thus might well lack credible, objective evidence that would carry sufficient weight within a court of law. Stress is not a widely recognized medical category, such as depression or anxiety; rather, it constitutes a *situation* or *context* affecting the individual employee. Stress, or, rather more accurately, its *adverse effects*, could well be attributed by the plaintiff primarily to the ill-effects of the workplace. In practice, however, it might actually have its main causes *outside* the workplace, in terms of failing relationships, financial problems, or in pre-existing emotional problems or vulnerabilities. Finally, despite the evidence suggested – namely, higher incidence rates of workplace stress amongst certain occupational groups – key legal rulings have strongly *resisted* the argument that some occupations are *inherently* more stressful than others.

Having said this, the relationship of the law to the field of workplace stress is a complex and rapidly developing one. The last two decades have marked a clear recognition by the legal system in the UK that psychological ill-health caused by work is a feature of major social importance, requiring effective recourse to redress in the courts. This chapter will outline the major aspects of the law relating to workplace stress, including both statute and case law.

There are multiple, overlapping elements of the law that relate to the monitoring and minimization of workplace stress, and to providing routes to redress and potential compensation for alleged victims. These elements of the law include:

- health and safety law
- laws prohibiting discrimination and harassment
- employment contract law
- personal injury litigation.

HEALTH AND SAFETY LAW

Employers are under a threefold duty: namely, to provide competent fellow employees, adequate plant and equipment, and a safe system of work (Pitt: 2009: 430). The statutory duties of employers with regard to maintaining the welfare of employees are primarily set out in the Health and Safety at Work (HSAW) Act 1974. This requires employers, "so far as is reasonably practicable":

Section 2	to ensure the health, safety and welfare at work of employees;
Section 2(2)(e)	to provide a working environment that is safe, without risks to health, and adequate for the welfare of employees.

Under the Management of Health and Safety at Work Regulations 1999 (SI 1999/3242), employers are further required:

3(1)	to make assessment of risks to the health and safety of employees and others at work;
6	to ensure employees are provided with appropriate health surveillance.

Risk assessments can relate variously to people, premises, plant and procedures, and are intended to identify potential hazards and the appropriate steps required to minimize them. Other specific regulations (for example, on the use of display screen equipment) spell out the particular risks to health associated with their use, such as musculoskeletal disorders, visual fatigue, and, in addition, stress (HSE, 2004a). Risk assessments can provide clear evidence that an employer has sought to anticipate and reduce occupational hazards that are likely to affect the health and safety of staff. In 2006, for instance, a coroner called for clarification of the risk assessments carried out prior to the death of the journalist Kate Peyton, who had been killed while on assignment in Mogadishu, the capital of Somalia.

Whereas the initial emphasis of the legislation was very much focused on the physical health and safety of employees, over the past two decades the HSE has taken an increasing interest in the *psychological* health of employees, and, in particular, in the issue of workplace stress. The HSE has issued management standards for work-related stress that identify key areas for monitoring and intervention by managers, in relation to work and its demands, the level of individual control, the nature of support systems, work-related roles, the degree of change and the quality of relationships (HSE, 2007). For example, the management standards with regard to relationships at work include the following criteria:

- employees indicate that they are not subjected to unacceptable behaviors – for example, bullying at work
- systems are in place locally to respond to any individual concerns (HSE, 2004a: 14).

The HSE has maintained a record of active intervention, in pursuit of its statutory remit with regard to health and safety at work. In 2005, for example, it brought a successful prosecution, under section 2 of the HSAW Act 1974, against St George's Mental Health NHS Trust, for neglect of its duties, whereby a psychiatric nurse had been killed on duty by a psychiatric patient, leading to the Trust being fined £28,000, plus £14,000 legal costs. The HSE has also exercised its powers in order to issue warning notices to employers, where reported levels of stress amongst staff are held to be unacceptably high, as in 2003, in the case of West Dorset General Hospital NHS Trust, and again in 2004, in relation to De Montfort University. The HSE has a variety of enforcement measures it can apply against employers, including improvement notices, prohibition notices, investigation and, ultimately, as mentioned, prosecution, under section 2 of the Act. However, it has largely opted for an educative and enabling role, taking the stance that workplace stress is primarily an issue to be addressed, in a positive and proactive manner, by informed and effective managers (Davies, 2009).

LAWS PROHIBITING DISCRIMINATION AND HARASSMENT

The employer's responsibility in relation to workplace stress is also covered by legislation relating to the prohibition of *both* discrimination *and* harassment. There is a wide raft of primary and secondary legislation that prohibits unlawful discrimination by an employer against individuals, on the protected grounds of race, gender, sexual orientation, gender reassignment, age, religious beliefs, or disability. "Parliament has recognised that individuals who are subjected to unlawful discrimination generally find the experience hurtful, distressing and humiliating and often suffer stress and stress-related illness as a result" (Gillow *et al.*, 2003: 103). Individuals who are subject to unlawful discrimination might, therefore, often experience stress, or, rather more accurately, emotional *distress*, as a direct result of their experiences. The employee may then seek to bring a case against the employer in an Employment Tribunal, within a three month period of the original incident, or termination of employment, if related to the incident.

The claim for damages can include compensation for the loss suffered and also for injury to feelings. The former cap, limiting awards for damages for injury to feelings in sex and race discrimination cases, no longer applies, and, in consequence, these awards can be substantial in nature. For example, Ms LSM, a 17-year-old recruit to the Royal Navy, was subjected to four years of sexual harassment, resulting in her being diagnosed as suffering clinical depression, leading to her attempted suicide. She was awarded £65,000 damages by an Employment Tribunal, including £25,000 for "for injury to feelings arising directly from the harassment and stress suffered" (*LSM* v. *Royal Navy*, Case No. 55542/95).

Disability discrimination legislation has a particular relevance to the issue of workplace stress. Under section 1 (1) of the Disability Discrimination Act (DDA) 2005, a disability is defined as: "a physical or mental impairment which has a substantial and long-term adverse effect on [the person's] ability to carry out normal day-to-day activities". "Long-term" is defined in this context as meaning over 12 months. Impairment could relate to "memory or ability to learn, concentrate or understand; or perception of the risk of physical danger", according to Schedule 1 of the DDA. Discrimination against a person with disability is unlawful if it takes the form of less favorable treatment than a person without a disability, or a failure on the part of the employer to make reasonable adjustments, or, finally, victimization against a person bringing a complaint on the grounds of disability.

Mental health conditions, such as depression, are considered as a disability within the meaning of the Act. Unlawful discrimination against an employee with mental health problems could result in additional stress (or distress), leading to grounds for action under the terms of the Act. However, an employee subject to workplace stress might also be diagnosed as suffering from a mental health condition, such as depression, or generalized anxiety disorder. The employee would then qualify for protection, in the form of requiring "reasonable adjustments" to their working situation, again, under the terms of the Act.

"If an employee is suffering from stress, an employer should consider making reasonable adjustments to the employee's working conditions, such as allowing the employee to work part-time or allocating less stressful duties" (Gillow *et al.*, 2003, pp. 106). Reasonable adjustment would also extend to offering employees a phased return to work, after absence caused by stress, and sensitive follow-up and monitoring of their situation after their return to work.

HARASSMENT

There is no specific legal definition of "bullying" as such, and the relevant law here is complex and not necessarily consistent. Jamdar and Byford suggest that "the law on bullying and harassment at work is, in fact, a bit of a mess" (2003: 74).The concept of harassment did not appear in the original versions of anti-discrimination law, and its later insertion into regulations has clearly been influenced by practice and policy deriving from the US in this respect (Pitt, 2009: 55). There is currently a range of definitions of harassment that could be applied in the context of workplace stress.

> Unwanted conduct which has the purpose or effect of violating the other person's dignity, or creating an intimidating, hostile, degrading, humiliating or offensive environment for him. (Race Relations Act 1976 (Amendment) Regulations 2003 (SI 2003/1626))

Sexual harassment is also further defined, under the EU Equal Treatment Directive (2002/73/EC), in terms of "unwanted verbal, non-verbal or physical conduct of a sexual nature" that has the equivalent purpose or effects indicated above. In legal terms, the test of harassment applied here is a *subjective* one, dependent on the perceived experience of the person, who *feels* offended by another's behavior. The thrust of anti-discriminatory legislation is, furthermore, to place a *proactive* duty on management, by imposing "a positive duty on employers to take action to prevent discriminatory harassment in the workplace" (IDS, 2007: 99). Management needs to take clear and consistent action to reduce the incidence of workplace stress caused by allegations of harassment, by implementing guidance, monitoring and policies that minimize the risk of unlawful discrimination of employees.

Employees might also be protected from harassment at work by another piece of legislation, originally designed to deal with the issue of "stalking", in the community, rather than in the workplace as such. Under section 1 of the Protection from Harassment Act 1997:

(1) A person must not pursue a course of conduct –
   (a) which amounts to harassment of another and
   (b) which s/he knows or ought to know amounts to harassment of the other.

A "course of conduct" is elsewhere defined as meaning behavior, including speech, that occurs on at least two occasions. It has been the view in the past that there are some difficulties in applying the Act to a workplace context, particularly in establishing that workplace activities, such as an annual review, informal canteen interactions, or communication between staff, amounting to a "course of conduct" analogous to a systematic pattern of unwanted attention that would be consistent with "stalking". However, the Act has been used successfully in major cases to establish a case of harassment at work. The advantage of using the Act is that it makes provision for both criminal and criminal proceedings, and the latter can offer scope for substantial damages.

Helen Green worked for Deutsche Bank Group Services Ltd, where she was subjected to "a relentless campaign of mean and spiteful behavior designed to cause her distress" by four female work colleagues. The court established that she had been subject to harassment and that management bore vicarious liability for the harassment carried out by other employees, even if management was not aware of this situation (*Green* v. *Deutsche Bank Group Services Ltd.* [2008]). Harassment was here defined by the judge, Mr Justice Owen, in an *objective* sense, as constituting conduct:

(a) occurring on at least two occasions;
(b) targeted at the claimant;
(c) calculated in an objective sense to cause distress; and
(d) that is objectively judged to be oppressive and unreasonable.

Helen Green had suffered two nervous breakdowns and a major depressive disorder as a direct result of the campaign of harassment experienced at the hands of her work colleagues, and was awarded damages of £800,000. The potential use of the Protection from Harassment

Act 1997 thus substantially raises the bar for employees seeking redress for workplace stress caused by harassment, offering a powerful option to consider.

For employees, use of the Act holds a number of positive features, in that it is neither necessary to establish a reason for the harassment, as under legislation prohibiting discrimination, nor to require evidence of a foreseeable psychiatric injury. Also, the Act provides a time limit of six years within which to bring an action, as opposed to the period of three months required for cases brought to Employment Tribunals. Given these factors, and the additional element that employees can bring a case under this Act as well as pursuing a personal injury claim as a "second bite at the cherry", it is possible that the use of this action could increase in the future (IDS, 2007). Management therefore needs to ensure that their liability to this kind of legal challenge is minimized by actively monitoring the quality of working relationships, and by implementing the HSE Management Standards for Work-Related Stress (2007) in a systematic and proactive manner.

EMPLOYMENT CONTRACT LAW

Employees suffering from workplace stress may also seek redress by taking action via an Employment Tribunal. This could, for example, be related to psychological stress, or ill-health, induced by working excessively long hours, in contravention of the Working Time Regulations 1998. Originating from an EU Directive (93/104/EC), the regulations stipulate maximum working hours of an average of 48 hours in any seven-day period, together with minimum rest periods.

Employees are also protected under their contract of employment, by the application of an implied term of "mutual trust and confidence". If an employee is subjected to such extreme conditions at work that he or she is forced to resign, then it is possible to bring a case for constructive dismissal against the employer. In the case of *Gogay* v. *Hertfordshire County Council* [2000], the employee worked as a care worker in a children's home, looking after challenging and emotionally disturbed young people. She became distressed by the attention focused on her by one young resident in particular, who had a history of sexual abuse and attachment problems. Following statements by the young person about a therapy session that had taken place, the care worker was suspended by the authority, pending investigation. This investigation found there was no case to answer and the care worker was reinstated. However, she was unable to return to work, because she was now suffering from clinical depression. "The judge held that her employers were in breach of the implied term of trust and confidence because they had no reasonable grounds for suspending her and had failed to carry out a proper investigation of the circumstances before doing so" (Gillow *et al.*, 2003: 118).

Employers need to be aware of this as a potential outcome (that is, action for constructive dismissal) in the case of conflicted relationships with staff that might well be experiencing substantial and damaging levels of stress, due to the nature of their working situation. The existence of this duty of implied trust and confidence carries weight in determining the appropriate standard applied to employers in responding to situations likely to induce significant levels of stress or distress amongst staff. This duty "can require employers to investigate complaints of bullying thoroughly, take steps to resolve workplace conflict, and ensure that strong management and the handling of disciplinary issues do not cross the line into humiliating or offensive treatment" (IDS, 2007: 4).

PERSONAL INJURY LITIGATION

The final area of law relating to stress in the workplace is that of personal injury litigation, where employees seek to bring a civil action for damages for breach of employer duty of care. Under the law of negligence, an employee needs to establish that he or she was owed a duty by their employer to take reasonable care, that there was breach of that duty by the employer and that the employee suffered harm as a result. The harm may be physical or psychological in nature. If alleging *psychological* harm, then the employee needs to establish that this harm amounted to a psychiatric injury, capable of being diagnosed by current diagnostic manuals, such as the DSM IV or ICD 10. Examples of a psychiatric injury could include post-traumatic stress disorder (PTSD), clinical depression, or generalized anxiety disorder, amongst others. Worry, arising from the work setting, is not sufficient to qualify as a psychiatric condition, hence the inadequacy of "workplace stress" as a qualifying factor for compensation in this regard. The nature of the evidence is a key factor here, as a note from a general practitioner indicating distress or anxiety is unlikely, on its own, to be effective as evidence – that is, without a confirmed psychiatric diagnosis (Jamdar and Byford, 2003).

The key case that opened the door to successful legal action for "workplace stress" was the well-known case brought by John Walker against his former employer, Northumberland Social Services Department. John Walker worked as an Area Social Services Officer from 1970 to 1987. There was a high volume of work, often concerning problematic and stressful child protection cases. With no previous history of psychiatric problems, Mr Walker suffered a "nervous breakdown" in 1986, and again after his return to work in 1987. His employer had been alerted to the problems he was experiencing at work after his first absence due to ill-health, but their promised support and supervision was not forthcoming. In 1988, he was dismissed by his employers on the grounds of permanent ill-health.

John Walker then brought a successful legal civil case against his employers. The judge noted the expert evidence, which attested to the intrinsically stressful nature of much social work but also noted an additional factor, which was the structure and resourcing of the relevant social services department. In 1996, two years after winning the court case, Walker reached an out-of-court settlement with his former employer for a compensation payment of £175,000 (*Walker* v. *Northumberland C.C.* [1995]). On the plaintiff's return to work, it was held to be clearly foreseeable that a continuation of the evident pressures of work would undoubtedly cause his psychiatric problems to recur. Judge Colman held that the council "provided no effective help. In so doing, it was, in my judgement, acting unreasonably and therefore in breach of its duty of care".

The *Walker* case was quickly followed by other successful cases in which employer liability for psychiatric injury caused by breach of duty of care was established. Within the legal profession and the media, there was growing concern that the effect of the case would be to "open the floodgates", contributing to the rapid growth of a "compensation culture". This stance overlooked the apparent key message of the *Walker* case, that the claimant, in effect, had to suffer not simply *one* instance of psychiatric harm but, more probably, had to experience a *second* instance as well. An employer could reasonably assume that an employee would be sufficiently robust to cope with the normal day-to-day pressures of work and, therefore, a stress-induced psychiatric illness would not normally be expected to occur as a result of work. However, when there was evidence that an employee had previously developed a psychiatric condition, as a result of work-based pressures, it would then be entirely foreseeable that the condition would return, if subjected to similar pressures of work, without steps being taken to minimize this risk (Jenkins, 2007).

The *Walker* case illustrated the weakness of a naturalistic, or causal, model of workplace stress, as seen from a legal perspective (see Figure 2.1).

This somewhat simplistic model fails to recognize, first, that the crucial intervening factor required for successful litigation is *breach of employer duty of care*, and, second, that the breach must be seen to *cause* the psychiatric injury, via what is referred to as proving "the test of causation". It is entirely possible to establish breach of duty of care, as, for example, in the major class action brought by former servicemen and women against the Ministry of Defence, *without* establishing that the breach actually *caused* the alleged psychiatric injuries incurred by the claimants (*Multiple Claimants* v. *MOD* [2003]).

A more accurate representation would need to include these essential factors, as in Figure 2.2.

Employer liability as set out in *Hatton*

In 2002, the Court of Appeal heard four conjoined cases relating to awards made for "workplace stress", more properly defined, in legal terms, as claims for psychiatric injury, caused by breach of employer duty of care. Only one of the cases was upheld; the other three were dismissed in what was initially taken to be a radical restatement of the law on employer

FIGURE 2.1   **Causal model of litigation for "workplace stress"**

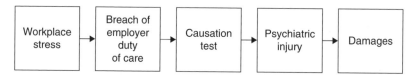

FIGURE 2.2   **Duty of care model of litigation for "workplace stress"**

duty of care. However, read more carefully, the findings and rationale by the then Lady Justice Hale can be seen as a careful, point-by-point restatement of the law as applied in the original *Walker* case, with some additional refinements. The Court of Appeal judgment is now the essential reference for considering cases seeking to establish employer liability for workplace stress. The case set out a number of key points to be considered in future cases, abbreviated and summarized in Figure 2.3.

In the only case to succeed in this appeal, the plaintiff, Mrs Jones, had worked as an administrative assistant at a local authority Training Centre. She was working "grossly excessive hours", which were acknowledged by the personnel officer to be equivalent to the workload of two, if not three, people. The work itself was seen to be very stressful, with tight financial deadlines. Management refused to take any effective action in response to her two formal, written complaints. She had then left work through ill-health, suffering from anxiety and depression, later receiving £150,000 in damages.

Mrs Jones' case can be seen to have satisfied the criteria contained in the checklist below. Her workload was unreasonable in comparison with that of others, had caused a foreseeable psychiatric injury, and was attributable to management failing to take remedial action in order to reduce the evident risk to her psychological health. Other cases failed, however, where the workload, however high, was still comparable to that of others – for example, in schools undergoing an Ofsted inspection, or a major reorganization. Where an employee had failed to alert management to their difficulty in coping with stress in the workplace, or where the employee was vulnerable, because of other *unknown* stress factors in their life outside of work, then the employer

---

- Is the individual subject to undue pressure of work that is:
  - unreasonable by any standard
  - unreasonable judged in comparison with the workload of others in a similar job
  - due to individual vulnerability, which is known to the employer?
- Has the individual received an injury to health, either physical or psychological, that is directly attributable to stress at work?
- Was this injury reasonably foreseeable by the employer?
- Is this injury directly and mainly attributable to the employer's breach of duty of care, in failing to reduce workplace stress (by providing confidential counselling, redistribution of duties, training and so on)?

FIGURE 2.3 **Checklist for employer liability**

Source: Adapted from *Hatton* v. *Sutherland* [2002].

would not be held liable for their subsequent psychological ill-health. Foreseeability is a crucial factor here, in that it must be "reasonably foreseeable" that the employee is vulnerable to psychiatric injury: the employee needs to be proactive in this respect and clearly communicate to their employer if they are experiencing significant levels of stress. However, as in the *Walker* case, where an employee has already had time off for ill-health, or is seen to be vulnerable due to pre-existing mental health problems (that are known to the employer), then the employer needs to anticipate future adverse stress levels – by providing, for instance, a phased return to work, or additional training, support, supervision or mentoring. Providing access to a confidential counseling service for employees will also demonstrate the fulfillment of the duty of care by a reasonable employer and reduce their potential liability (Jenkins, 2008).

The court, in a sense, drew a line that carefully demarcated employer liability with regard to the burgeoning "compensation culture". Not all workplace stress is available for compensation; "some things are no one's fault", according to the Judge. Furthermore, the claim, advanced by HSE and others, that some occupations are inherently stressful – or, at least, more stressful than others – was decisively rejected. The key factor remains that of establishing breach of employer duty of care and, more difficult still, that the breach caused the alleged psychiatric injury.

Case law after *Hatton*

Subsequent case law has provided essential qualifying detail to the key elements of the *Hatton* judgment. Merely providing access or referral to an employee counseling service is not sufficient to protect employers where management has clearly failed to carry out reasonable steps to protect staff from undue workplace stress (*Intel* v. *Daw* [2007]; *Dickins* v. *O2 plc* [2008]). Significantly, a claim may now succeed *without* a "first absence" occurring due to ill-health; the earlier *Walker* case, as with many others, required a "second absence" in order to demonstrate breach of employer duty of care.

Erica Connor was the head teacher of a primary school, where she subsequently experienced a great deal of conflict with two school governors who campaigned publicly against her alleged "Islamophobia". The Local Education Authority sought to introduce mediation and an independent enquiry, rather than respond promptly to her developing risk of emotional ill-health due to the levels of stress caused by this situation. In 2005, Ms Connor was signed off work by her general practitioner for stress and depression, later diagnosed by a psychiatrist as severe depression, with symptoms of post-traumatic stress disorder. She then brought a successful case against her employer, alleging breach of duty of trust and confidence as an employer, breach of statutory duty, breach of the Protection from Harassment Act 1997, and negligence. The case for negligence alone was proven, and she was awarded £388,000 in damages (*Connor* v. *Surrey CC* [2009]). The outcome suggests that employees can continue to succeed with personal injury cases against employers, if these meet the very precise conditions laid down by *Hatton*.

Certain existing company documentation (such as personal files, appraisal records or sickness absence data) might be helpful to indicate evidence of risk that should put an employer on alert. However, as we have stated, to win a stress case the issues of foreseeability and causation must be proved in each case presented. Questions and requests that will be posed are likely to include:

1 Was the employer aware of key documents on stress – for example, HSE reports?
2 Was a risk assessment conducted?
3 What internal procedures and monitoring processes are in place to deal with stress?
4 Is there an adequate health record system?
5 Details about human resourcing and training records, job descriptions, and the physical resourcing of jobs.
6 Details on cost and practicability, in order to measure the "reasonable response" in terms of the magnitude of the risk of injury, the seriousness of the consequences, and the cost and practicality of preventing that risk.

Employers will need to know how safe is the system of work, and to provide documentation to show that they know. It is equally important that complaints and warnings from staff about potential injury due to the work environment are treated seriously, and that they are monitored and dealt with in a systematic and timely manner. The prevention of problems and the avoidance of the stress litigation process are preferable and less costly in the long term. When an employee wins a stress case, in addition to the financial burden of compensation claims, the court costs and unwanted publicity for the organization, there is also the prospect of increased employer's liability insurance premiums.

A POLICY FOR STRESS MANAGEMENT

The objective of a policy for stress is to protect the health, safety and welfare of employees.

An effective policy on stress should recognize that stress is a health and safety issue. It should be developed jointly and agreed with trade union assistance and cooperation. The policy must apply to everyone in the organization and be endorsed from the most senior level within the company. Overt commitment to a policy on stress must be in evidence and it should guarantee a non-judgmental approach. It must include:

- a statement of intent
- an outline of the responsibilities of the employer and the employee
- a description of how the policy is organized and operationalized – specifically it should identify the chain of command and state who is responsible and for what and when; and should show how the policy and the responsibilities described therein are managed, monitored and evaluated
- a description of the specific systems and procedures in place to eliminate, minimize, control or treat stress in the workplace. This might include audit and risk assessment procedures; recruitment and training options; medical services; lifestyle management practices; management systems; organizational development plans; access to referral services such as counseling or employee assistance providers.

Thus, the objectives of a policy on stress should be:

- to prevent stress by identifying causes of workplace stress and eliminating (or minimizing) them – that is, to deal with the source of stress
- to control stress by ensuring that the stress response does not cause negative impact on the individual – that is to deal with the response to stress
- to rehabilitate employees who are suffering from exposure to stress through the provision of a confidential counseling service – that is, to deal with the symptoms of stress.

It is important that a policy on stress is reviewed on a regular basis, since there are likely to be changes both within the organization and to the legislative requirements relating to stress in the workplace.

SUMMARY

The law perceives "workplace stress" in terms of a number of different categories, with various overlapping routes for employees to bring legal action for any alleged harm suffered at work. The law covers the field of stress at work via health and safety legislation, which places statutory duties on employers to provide, so far as is reasonably practicable, a safe place of work, demonstrated by effective risk assessments and the implementation of relevant HSE management standards, designed to minimize the risk of psychological damage to employees.

■ Discrimination law places a proactive duty on employers to implement policies and practices that protect employees from unlawful discrimination on the protected grounds of race, gender, sexual orientation, gender reassignment, age, religious beliefs, or disability.
■ Harassment provides additional grounds for legal action by affected staff, and is subject to statutory definition, unlike bullying. Case law has confirmed the vicarious liability of employers for acts of harassment carried out by its staff in the course of their employment, even if not known to the employer. The contract of employment carries an implied duty of trust of confidence, and breach of this duty could give rise to successful action by an employee for stress-related injuries.
■ Finally, employer liability for psychiatric injury, caused by breach of duty of care, has been tested and comprehensively restated in the *Hatton* appeal.

While the standard remains that of the "reasonable employer", in order to minimize the risk posed by the presence of stress in the workplace, management needs to be alert for signs, or communication, of risk of harm, or of prior vulnerability, on the part of employees, and to discharge their duty by responsible monitoring, appropriate and timely remedial action and the provision of confidential counseling services.

CHAPTER 3

WHAT IS STRESS?

To successfully manage a stress situation, we must first define what we mean by "stress" and identify what causes it in order to recognize the effects of exposure to stress. We have already examined the deleterious costs of mismanaged stress in Chapter 1, and acknowledged the implications of the stress litigation process and the consequences of increased employers' liability insurance in Chapter 2. Now, we need to understand how and why stress is damaging in its consequences.

In order to do this, we will refer to a theoretical framework and describe certain models of stress. Thereby, we can explain how and why exposure to certain conditions and situations can have an adverse impact on performance, health, well-being and quality of life. It is important that we understand how and why exposure to a constantly changing work environment might be manifest in terms of poor performance, productivity and ill-health. Until we can identify the source of stress, it is unlikely that stress management activities will be successful. Therefore, it is necessary:

- to define and clarify what we mean by the word, "stress"
- to recognize our response to stress in behavioral, emotional and physical terms; and to understand how models of stress evolved to influence our thinking about the stress response and stress management strategies
- to understand the differences between adaptive and maladaptive stress coping strategies.

These steps are all vital to the effective management of stress and so will be discussed in the first part of this chapter. However, it is also important that we:

- identify potential sources of stress in our environment.

In Chapter 4, we will use a model of stress to discuss the prevalent sources of stress for a range of occupational groups, including managers and other employees working in contemporary society.

DEFINING "STRESS"

First, pause for a moment or two; then write down the words or phrases that immediately come into your mind when you think about what the word "stress" means to you. If we ask a group of people to take part in this exercise, the list of words produced invariably has three key characteristics.

1 Most of the words or phrases are expressed in "negative" terms – that is, "stress" is perceived as something bad or unwanted. For example, words or phrases such as "depression", "feeling out of control", "overworked", "migraine or headaches", "time pressures", "panic attacks", "anxiety", and "cannot sleep" are commonly used to express what stress means to us personally. Mostly, stress is regarded as a negative experience for the individual.
2 The list usually contains expressions or words that describe symptoms of exposure to a stressful situation – that is, people describe stress as "feeling anxious", "feeling depressed", or having headaches or panic attacks. The stress is being explained in terms of the feelings and reactions that the individual is experiencing. Therefore, stress is being described in terms of a "response-based" model and approach to managing stress.
3 The lists rarely contain words that can be described as "the source of the stress" or the "stressor". In our example in point 1, "being overworked" and "time pressures" are workplace stressors. However, these work conditions and situations need to be explained in greater detail before we are able to use this information to manage the potentially stressful situation effectively. By referring to the source of stress or stressor, we are describing stress in terms of a "stimulus-based" model as an approach to managing stress.

From our discussions so far, we seem to have assumed that "stress is what happens to people". This is misleading, and likely to be the cause of errors in our understanding about the nature of stress. The review of various models of stress later in this chapter will help us to conceive of stress as an interactive process. It is also a dynamic process in which time plays a vital role. It is apparent from the examination of simple dictionary definitions of stress that they also can be traced back to the various schools of thought about the mechanism and nature of stress. For example, in the seventeenth century, the word "stress" (originally derived from Latin) was used to mean hardship, straits, adversity or affliction (*Shorter Oxford Dictionary*, 1933) and was used in old French (*estrece*) to mean narrowness or oppression (*Shorter Oxford Dictionary*, 2007). By the eighteenth and nineteenth centuries, the use of the word "stress" had broadened to indicate "strain, pressure or strong effort". This was intended to include terms to describe the laws of physics and engineering, in addition to a person, or a person's organs and mental powers (Hinkle, 1973). Within the fields of physics, stress was used to refer to an object's resistance to external pressure. This model was adopted by the social sciences. However, as Cox (1985) pointed out, an engineering analogy is too simplistic. He said, "We have to accept some intervening psychological process which does mediate the outcome… stress has to be perceived and recognized by man [*sic*]. A machine, however, does not have to recognize the load or stress placed upon it."

Recent dictionary definition actually associates the word "stress" with disease. For example, the *Shorter Oxford Dictionary* (2007) describes stress as, "a condition or adverse circumstance that disturbs, or is likely to disturb, the normal physiological or psychological functioning of an individual". Medical dictionaries have included both a response-based and a stimulus-based approach to stress when providing guidance on definitions of stress. For example, *Stedman's Medical Dictionary* (2005, 28th edn) states:

1 Stress is the reactions of the body to forces of a deleterious nature, infections, and various abnormal states that tend to disturb its normal physiologic equilibrium.
2 In psychology, stress is a physical or psychological stimulus which, when impinging upon certain individuals, produces psychological strain or disequilibrium.

The *Encyclopaedia and Dictionary of Medicine, Nursing and Allied Health* (Miller–Keane, 2005, 7th edn) suggests that stress is:

the sum of all the non-specific biological phenomena elicited by adverse external influences including damage and defence.

Stress may be either physical or psychological, or both. Just as a bridge is structurally capable of adjusting to certain physical stresses, the human body and mind are normally able to adapt to the stresses of new situations. However, this ability has definite limits beyond which continued stress may cause a breakdown, although this limit varies from person to person...for example, peptic ulcers may result from prolonged nervous tension in response to real or imagined stresses in people who have a predisposition for ulcers.

However, within our conceptualization of stress, a person-environment fit model also acknowledges that "underload" as well as overload can be a stress agent. Levi (1987, 1998) takes account of this when he describes stress as a "poor-fit" – that is:

the interaction between, or misfit of, environmental opportunities and demands, and individual needs and abilities, and expectations, elicit reactions. When the fit is bad, when needs are not being met, or when abilities are over- or under-taxed, the organism reacts with various pathogenic mechanisms. These are cognitive, emotional, behavioral and/or physiological and under some conditions of intensity, frequency or duration, and in the presence or absence of certain interacting variables, they may lead to precursors of disease. (Levi, 1987)

This definition is consistent with a contemporary, interaction approach to the study of stress. Implicit in Levi's definition is the view that stress can have both positive and negative consequences. Therefore, a distinction must be made between stressors that promote a positive stress response and those that result in "distress": stress is inevitable, distress is not (Quick and Quick, 1984). This is most important in the work environment. Beehr and Newman (1978) acknowledge this and provide a working definition of job stress as:

a situation wherein job-related factors interact with a worker to change (that is, disrupt or enhance) his or her psychological and or physiological condition such that the person (that is, mind or body) is forced to deviate from normal functioning. (p. 670)

More recently, work stress has been operationally defined by the UK Health and Safety Executive as, "The adverse reaction people have to excessive pressures or other types of demand placed on them at work" (HSE, 2009).

THE ORIGINS OF STRESS RESEARCH

It is useful to review the various models of stress to help to explain the ways in which stress is perceived and operationalized. It is important to understand the origins and the evolution of the various models of stress, and how they have influenced our attempts to manage stress in the workplace.

It is clear that an either/or approach that considers either response or stimulus-based approaches is too simplistic to aid understanding of the complex nature of stress and the stress response. Clearly, a better model is needed for further research into the study of stress. Also, the broad application of the stress concept to medical, social and behavioral science research over the past sixty to seventy years has compounded the problem. Each discipline investigated and attempted to explain stress from its own unique perspective. The chapter now outlines the historical origins and the early approaches to the study of stress, leading to the consideration of an "interactive" model of stress.

A RESPONSE-BASED MODEL OF STRESS

As we have seen, when asked to provide alternative words to the term "stress" associations tend to be in terms of response-based meanings that take the form of strain, tension or pressure. The lay person readily identifies with the expressions, "being under stress" and "I feel very stressed", and can usually identify the manifestations of the stress response. Therefore, the response-based approach to understanding stress, in seeking to define an intangible phenomenon, views it as an "outcome". In research terminology, this is described as the "dependant variable", where the main conceptual domain is the manifestation of stress. Figure 3.1 illustrates a response-based model of stress.

The origins of response-based definitions of stress are found in medicine and are usually viewed from a physiological perspective. This is a logical stance for a discipline trained to diagnose and treat the symptoms, but not necessarily the cause, of the condition. For example, John Locke, the seventeenth-century physician and philosopher,

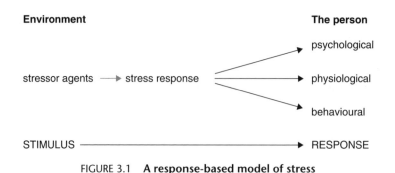

FIGURE 3.1 **A response-based model of stress**

proposed that intellectual functioning, emotion, muscle movement and the behavior of internal organs were the product of sensory experiences processed by the brain. From these early notions, the study of stress from a physiological perspective developed. Links were established between life experiences, emotions and the importance of hormonal and chemical actions in the body.

Thus, emotional stress as a causal factor in ischaemic heart disease was proposed by Claude Bernard as early as 1860. Osler (1910) later identified the high incidence of angina pectoris with the hectic pace of life among Jewish businessmen. In the 1930s, the psychoanalyst Franz Alexander and Frances Dunbar, a physician, reported on the relationship between personality patterns and constitutional tendencies to certain organic disorders: that is, they described a psychosomatic theory of disease (Warshaw, 1979). Claude Bernard was the first person to suggest the notion that the internal environment of a living organism must remain fairly constant despite exposure to external changes. This concept of stability or balance was later developed and described as "homeostasis" by Walter Cannon (1935). In systems theory, this would become known as "dynamic equilibrium", whereby the coordination of physiological processes maintains a steady state within the organism. The theory states that natural homeostatic mechanisms normally maintain a state of resistance, but are not able to cope with unusually heavy demands. Under homeostatic principles, it is acknowledged that there is a finite supply to meet demand.

The earliest report of a systematic study on the relationship between life events and bodily responses is probably attributed to Wolf and Wolff (1943, reported by McLean, 1979). Their observations and experiments with the patient, Tom, provided an opportunity to observe changes in stomach activity in response to stressful situations. These researchers were able to document the changes in blood flow, motility and secretions of the stomach in relation to feelings of frustration and conflict produced under experimental conditions. Sadness, self-reproach and discouragement were found to be associated with prolonged pallor of the stomach mucosa and a hypo-secretion of acid. Hostility and resentment were associated with a high increase in gastric secretion and acidity. From the results of this research, our understanding of the relationship between engorgement of the stomach lining, lowered resistance to psychological trauma and the incidence of gastric ulcers was formed. As McLean (1979) suggested, the study of Tom inaugurated the scientific study of psychosomatic medicine.

However, it is the work of Hans Selye in the 1930s and 1940s that really marked the beginning of a response-based approach to the study of stress. In 1936, Selye introduced the concept of stress-related illness in terms of a "general adaptation syndrome" (GAS). He suggested that, "stress is the non-specific response of the body to any demand made upon it" (Selye, 1956), and that all patients, whatever the disease, looked and felt sick. This general malaise was characterized by loss of motivation, appetite, weight and strength. Most of Selye's experiments were with animals, and so he was able to demonstrate internal physical degeneration and deterioration as a result of exposure to stress. According to Selye, "the apparent specificity of diseases of adaptation is ascribed to conditioning factors such as genetic predisposition, gender, learning experiences and diet, etc.". Response to stress was, therefore, deemed to be invariant to the nature of the stressor and followed a universal pattern. Four stages of response are described within the depiction of the GAS in Figure 3.2. The alarm reaction is the immediate psycho-physiological response and, at this time of initial shock, our resistance to the stressor is lowered (1). After the initial shock phase, the counter shock phase can be observed and resistance levels begin to increase (2). At this time, our defense mechanisms are activated, forming the reaction known as the "fight or flight response" (3) (Cannon, 1935). There is also an added phase that can result from prolonged and extreme adaptation, and which cannot be sustained without harm (4).

The "fight or flight" response prepares our body to take action. Increased sympathetic nervous system activity results in the secretion of catecholamines which, in turn, prepare the body for action. The internal physiological changes initiated by hormones provide us with energy from the metabolism of fat and glucose. This causes increased delivery

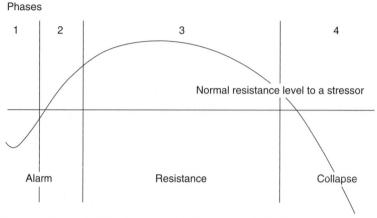

Phases

| 1 | 2 | 3 | 4 |

Normal resistance level to a stressor

Alarm   Resistance   Collapse

key   1 = Shock 2 = Countershock 3 = Resistance 4 = Collapse

FIGURE 3.2 **A depiction of the General Adaptation Syndrome (the "GAS")**

of oxygen (another energy source) to muscles through an increased number of red blood cells in the circulation, increased blood flow to the muscles, with reduced blood flow through the skin and the gut. So, our breathing becomes more rapid, the heart beats faster and our blood pressure increases. The spleen contracts and blood supplies are redirected from the skin and viscera to provide an improved blood supply to the brain and skeletal muscle. Glucose stored as glycogen in the liver is released to provide energy for muscular action, blood coagulation processes become enhanced, and the supply of blood lymphocytes is increased to combat the impact of injury and infection from wounds.

Table 3.1 illustrates the physiological changes experienced when we are in the alarm stage of the stress response. The table is provided to explain the effects we experience in response to stress. In summary, this includes:

- the release of adrenal hormones and free floating fatty acids
- lipid changes – for example, in cholesterol and triglyceride levels
- changes in various catecholamines – for example, thyroxin in urine and blood.

Thus, the actions of adrenaline, noradrenaline and cortisol combine to produce a variety of actions as part of the "fight or flight" response.

Stress, and the stress responses, in an evolutionary sense are good for us, and have been necessary for the development of our society.

TABLE 3.1 **The physiology of stress and the stress response**

Organ or tissue involved	Reaction
Lungs	Airways dilate and breathing becomes more rapid and deeper
Heart	Increased rate - the heart beats faster and harder; we can experience palpitations and chest pains
Legs/arms	An experience of muscle tension or tingling in the arms and legs as the electrical balance of the cells in the muscles undergoes change
Liver and fat tissue	Mobilization of glucose and fats for energy to fuel muscles
Brain	Increased mental activity to be alert for quick decision making
Skin and sweat glands	Increased sweating; hands and feet (extremities) often feel cold as blood supplies are diverted to the brain and muscles; hairs stand erect and we experience 'goose-pimples'
Salivary glands	Decreased flow of saliva; the mouth feels dry
Gut muscles	Gut activity is slowed; blood supply is reduced and we might experience indigestion or the feeling of a 'knotted' stomach because digestive processes stop or slow down
Spleen	Contracts and empties red blood cells into the circulation
Kidneys	Reduced urine formation
Ears	Hearing becomes more acute; people under extreme stress often report feeling very sensitive to noise
Eyes	Pupils dilate as an aid to keen vision; vision can become blurred if oxygenated blood is impeded in getting to the brain as blood vessels in the neck constrict
Blood	The action of cortisol produces an increased ability for blood clotting; the immune system is activated to prevent infection

Indeed, "social" Darwinism could be defined as the "promotion of the fittest", assuming that the individual survives the rat race in the first place (McCloy, 1995). The response to stress was meant to be both adaptive and vital for survival. In the past, we had simple choices to make: either to stand and fight an enemy, or to run away from a threatening and potentially dangerous situation. However, in contemporary society we face a dilemma because neither of these options is appropriate behavior in the workplace. In the work environment, there is limited opportunity to indulge in physical action and thereby dissipate the physiological effects that then become dominant and can cause distress. We cannot physically fight to escape workplace stress; but neither can we, without losing face, turn and run away from the situations that we must continue to meet, every day at work. Therefore, it is suggested that our bodies are continually primed to take actions that we are denied. Since many of us also lead increasingly sedentary lives at work and at home, we are denied both the aggression release and the physical activity necessary to quickly remove the build-up of hormone and chemical secretions. Fats released to fuel muscle actions are not used, and so we have elevated blood lipids. The fat deposits that are not used are likely to be stored on the lining of our arteries. This means that our blood pressure increases as the heart works harder to pump blood around the body through these smaller capillary openings. If one of the clots breaks away from the lining of an artery and finds its way to the heart or the brain, it will cause a stroke or a heart attack (thrombosis). Coronary heart disease can, therefore, be caused by indirect effects –namely, the stress-physiological consequences of sustained active distress on increase of blood pressure, on elevation of blood lipids and blood platelets, and on impaired glucose tolerance and related metabolic processes (Siegrist, 1997; Goldstein *et al.*, 2001). Studies have documented associations between high levels of psychosocial stress and the prevalence of hypertension, high levels of blood lipids not attributable to diet, and of high fibrinogen (a soluble protein in blood plasma, converted to fibrin by the action of the enzyme thrombin when the blood clots). In addition to diseases of the heart, we are also likely to suffer from ulcers, troubles with the gastrointestinal tract, asthma, colds and flu, and various skin conditions such as psoriasis, caused by exposure to mismanaged stress. These problems can be exacerbated because we often resort to using maladaptive stress coping strategies in response to stress rather than adaptive, positive stress management techniques.

In the third phase of the GAS, we observe resistance to a continued stressor, and where the adaptation response and/or return to equilibrium replaces the alarm reaction. If the alarm reaction is elicited too intensely or too frequently over an extended period of time, the energy required for adaptation becomes depleted, and the final stage of "exhaustion", collapse or death occurs. Resistance cannot continue indefinitely, even when given sufficient energy, because, as Selye says,

"Every biological activity causes wear and tear...and leaves some irreversible chemical scars which accumulate to constitute signs of ageing" (Selye, 1983).

Although the non-specificity concept of stress-related illness and the GAS model had far reaching influence and a significant impact on our understanding of stress, it has been challenged. Research indicates that responses to stimuli do not always follow the same pattern. They are, in fact, stimulus-specific and dependant on the type of hormonal secretion. For instance, anxiety-producing situations seem to be associated with the secretion of adrenaline (for example, waiting for an appointment with the dentist, or sitting and waiting for a written examination to commence). Responses to these experiences produce the feelings of fear and dread that make us want to just run away from the situation. Noradrenalin is released in response to aggression or challenge-evoking events, and these situations stir feelings of elation and excitement as we prepare to "fight" or take the plunge of the parachute sky-dive or bungee jump.

The GAS model makes no attempt to address the issue of psychological response to events, or that a response to a potential threat might, in turn, become the stimulus for a different response. It is acknowledged that this model is too simplistic. Whilst the framework of the GAS can explain our response to certain stressors, such as the physical effects of heat and cold, is not adequate to explain response to psychosocial stress (Christian and Lolas, 1985).

Kagan and Levi (1971) extended the response-based model of stress to incorporate psychosocial stimuli as causal factors in stress-related illness. Response to stress is viewed as the product of an interaction between the stimulus and the psychobiological program of the individual – that is, genetic predisposition and experience or learning. The term "interaction" is used in this instance to mean "the propensity to react in accordance with a certain pattern" (Kagan and Levi, 1971). Since their model also incorporates the concept of feedback, it cannot be considered a simple, stimulus-response model of stress. An additional problem associated with this approach is that stress is recognized as a generic term, which subsumes a large variety of manifestations (Pearlin *et al.*, 1981). Disagreement exists about the real manifestation of stress and the level in the organism or system that most clearly reflects the response. Pearlin asks, for example, whether the response is in the single cell, in an organ, or throughout the entire organism; is it biochemical, physiological or emotional functioning?

Is it at the endocrine, immunological, metabolic or cardiovascular level; or in particular diseases, physical and psychological? Resolution of this problem is not easy because the findings of replication research are likely to be confounded. Individuals adapt to any potential source of stress and so a response will vary over time (for example, in the assessment of noise on hearing and performance).

A STIMULUS-BASED MODEL OF STRESS

Historically, this approach, which links health and disease to certain conditions in the external environment, can be traced back to Hippocrates (fifth century BC). The Hippocratic physician believed that characteristics of health and disease were conditioned by the external environment (Goodell *et al.*, 1986). It is the belief that some external force impinges upon the organism in a disruptive manner. Indeed, it is also suggested that the word "stress" derives from the Latin word *stringere*, meaning "to bind tight". The stimulus-based psychological model of stress has its roots in physics and engineering, the analogy being that stress can be defined as a force exerted that results in a demand or load reaction that causes distortion. Both organic and inorganic substances have tolerance levels that, if exceeded, result in temporary or permanent damage. The aphorism, "It is the last straw that breaks the camel's back", is a view consistent with a stimulus-based model of stress. An individual is bombarded with stimuli in the environment, but just one more apparently minor or innocuous event can alter the balance between coping with the demand, and cause a breakdown in coping and of the system itself. Figure 3.3 illustrates this model of stress that treats a potential stressor as an independent variable that will cause a certain effect (that is, an outcome, or symptom).

Rapid industrialization provided an impetus for the increasing popularity of this particular model of stress. Much of the early research into blue-collar stress at work adopted a stimulus-based model when trying to identify sources of stress in the work environment. Considerable attention was paid to our actual physical working conditions and task circumstances, such as exposure to heat, cold, light levels and social density. Thus, workload conditions – either overload or underload – were explored and understood within this framework. (*Note*: The inverted "U" hypothesis is discussed in

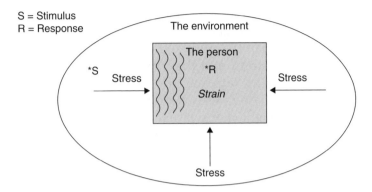

FIGURE 3.3   **A stimulus-based model of stress**

Chapter 4 in relation to workload as a source of stress.) However, it was realized that purely objective measures of environmental conditions are inadequate and do not fully explain the response to stress observed. Also, individual differences – including variability in tolerance levels, personality traits, past experiences (learning and training), needs, wants and expectations – seemed to account for the fact that two individuals exposed to exactly the same situation might react in completely different ways. A stimulus-response model of stress does not explain this and, thus, it is a major weakness of the model. In fact, Lazarus (1966) stated that no objective criterion was good enough to describe a situation as "stressful", only the person experiencing the event could do this.

Although this model does have limitations, it has some appeal in organizations seeking to identify common stressor themes or patterns of stress that might affect the majority of the workforce. However, rarely and ill-advisedly would any subsequent stress management intervention be carried out without exhaustive consultation with the personnel affected.

FROM STRESS TO WELL-BEING

Nevertheless, some organizations do use a response-based model of stress to guide their stress management program. They view the problems of stress as something inherent to the person, and this allows them to transfer responsibility to the individual. It means that they introduce a program that aims to help the employee cope with the stressor situation, but the organizations usually do nothing to remove or eliminate the origin of the stress. Other organizations favor a stimulus-based model of stress, and they attempt to manage the stress situation without taking into account the needs of the individual concerned. Both of these models have limitations and weaknesses. Industrialization brought many problems associated with physical and task-related sources of strain and pressure. Poor working conditions caused diseases such as tuberculosis and pneumonia that often led to early death. Legislation regarding health and safety requirements in the workplace resolved many of these unsatisfactory conditions. However, contemporary industrialization and new technology have brought different problems that have caused new forms of illness. These include, for example, upper body limb disorder, often known as repetitive strain injury (RSI), and psychological ill-health (for example, the problems of "sick building syndrome"), or increased accidents at work.

Despite these problems, our expectations for quality of life have brought a new meaning to the concept of health. It not only means an absence of disease or infirmity, but a satisfactory state of physical, mental and social well-being (WHO, 2010). Well-being is a dynamic state of mind, characterized by reasonable harmony between a worker's ability, needs, expectations, environmental demands and opportunities (Levi, 1987). As well as recognizing the potentially negative stressors, process and outcomes by referring to "stress", it is important to realize that optimizing performance, including in the workplace, is not simply about reducing pressures, but also about improving well-being. The World Health Organization believes that, "a healthy working environment is one in which there is not only an absence of harmful conditions, but an abundance of health promoting ones" (Leka *et al.*, 2007). Therefore, it is acknowledged that an interactive or transactional model of stress (one that considers the source or stressor, a perception of the situation or event and the response) is the most useful approach for providing a guideline for the study and management of stress, as well as the promotion of well-being. The emergence of Occupational Health Psychology is testament to movement towards psychologically healthy workplaces (Macik-Frey *et al.*, 2009), based on the premise that organizational well-being is continuous, rather than a static goal (Adkins, 2000).

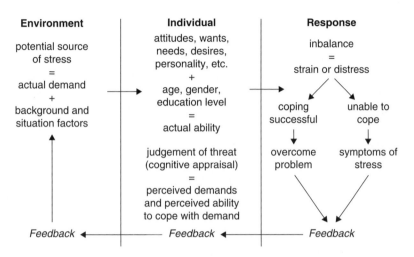

FIGURE 3.4   **Stress perception: an interactive model of stress**

AN INTERACTIVE MODEL OF STRESS

An interactive model of stress incorporates both the response-based and the stimulus-based models of stress. Figure 3.4 provides an illustration of the way in which stress is perceived and how a response is subsequently modified by individual differences. There are five key characteristics associated with this model of stress:

1 **Cognitive appraisal:** Stress is regarded as a subjective experience contingent upon the perception of a situation or event – that is, "stress is not simply out there in the environment" (Lazarus, 1966). As Shakespeare's Hamlet, says, "There is nothing good or bad, but thinking makes it so".

2 **Experience:** The way a situation or event is perceived depends upon familiarity with the circumstances, previous exposure to the event, learning, education and training (that is, the individual's actual ability). Related to this is the concept of success or failure in coping with the demand on previous occasions. Therefore, conditioning is an important part of an interactive model of stress.

3 **Demand:** Pressure or demand is the product of actual demands, perceived demands, actual ability and perceived ability to meet that demand. Needs, desires and the immediate level of arousal will all influence the way in which a demand is perceived.

4 **Interpersonal influence**: A potential source of stress does not exist in a social vacuum. The presence or absence of other people or work colleagues will influence our perception of stress. Thus, background and situational factors will influence the subjective experience of stress, our response and the coping behavior used. The presence or absence of other people can have both a positive and negative influence. For example, the presence of work colleagues can be a source of distraction, irritation or unwanted arousal. Conversely, the presence of work colleagues can also provide a support network that helps to boost confidence and levels of self-esteem, provide confirmation of values and a sense of personal identity and self-worth. Through the process of vicarious learning, increased awareness and an understanding of potential consequences can also be gained.

5 **A state of stress**: This is acknowledged as an imbalance or mismatch between the perceived "demand" and the perception of one's ability to meet that demand. The processes that follow are the coping process and the consequences of applying the coping strategy. Therefore, the importance of feedback at all levels is specified in this model of stress. Successful coping restores any imbalance, whereas unsuccessful coping results in the manifestation of symptoms of exposure to stress. The response might produce either short-term stress manifestations in the form of maladaptive coping strategies (such as, "light-up another cigarette"; "need alcohol", or "take a sleeping pill"), or long-term effects (such as heart disease, certain forms of cancer or ulcers). Obviously, it is acknowledged that the short-term consequences of exposure to stress and maladaptive coping strategies can also be causal factors in the aetiology of these long-term diseases (for example, the link between cigarette smoking and lung cancer). Thus, a method of coping with a source of stress can ultimately become the source of stress itself!

Within this model of stress, an accident at work can be both a short-term and a long-term manifestation of exposure to stress (having both a direct and indirect impact on behavior). McGrath (1976) states that a source of stress must be perceived and interpreted by the individual. It is also necessary to perceive that the potential consequences of successful coping are more desirable than the expected consequences of leaving a situation unaltered. For example, an individual who chooses to use palliatives as a coping strategy (perhaps as an "escape" from reality) views this type of short-term, immediate response as less costly or more personally desirable than trying to alter the demand. Of course, it might not be possible for them to alter the demand at the level of the individual concerned. This could happen, for example, if an individual were forced to work permanent night shifts because no alternative work schedule were available to him or her.

In summary, an interactive model of stress acknowledges that situations are not inherently stressful, but are potentially stressful, and it is necessary to take account of:

- the source of stress (stressor)
- the mediators or moderators of the stress response
- the manifestation of stress (strain).

One example of an interactive model of stress is known as "the person–environment fit" approach to understanding stress (French, 1973; Cooper, 1981). "Fit" is assessed in terms of the desired and actual levels of various job conditions. The main weakness of this model is that it infers some static situation whereas, in reality, response to stress is a dynamic process. However, the model is useful where certain personality traits are relatively stable. For example, Kahn et al., (1964) found that introverts under stress from role conflict will tend to reduce contact with other people and will further irritate work colleagues by appearing to be too independent. Role senders attempting to define the role will increase their efforts, thereby adding to the strain. This means that the introvert's coping strategy of defensive withdrawal is ultimately maladaptive. An understanding of such differences between introverts and extroverts can help to avoid potentially stressful inter-personal conflict situations. Kahn et al. also noted that "rigid" personality types tended to avoid conflict. They rely on compulsive work habits and show increased dependence on authority figures when under threat. "Flexible" people, however, are more likely to respond to a conflict situation by complying with work demands and seeking support from peers and subordinates. This compliance strategy can lead to work overload problems. Also, reliance on those of equal or lower status does not help to resolve the stressor situation because it is often the boss or superior who sets out the work expectation that is the source of stress. Thus, the "rigid" and the "flexible" personality types create very different problems in the workplace in response to stress, and could ultimately be more suited to some work environment more than others.

The role of personality in how the characteristics of a workplace impact on the individual has been extended and further popularized by the Effort–Reward Imbalance Model (Siegrist *et al.*, 1986). This suggests that poorer health outcomes are more likely where the employee experiences a mismatch between their efforts (when high) and rewards (when low). Similarly, the model predicts that those who demonstrate "overcommitment" to their work will be negatively affected, while those who have the combination of both effort–reward imbalance and overcommitment will be worse off. Research points to the adverse potency of the mismatch between efforts and rewards, while the other two scenarios have gathered either mixed or little evidence to support them (van Vegchel *et al.*, 2005). One or more of Siegrist's (1997) examples of imbalance are likely to strike a chord:

> Stressful experience associated with high effort results from the absence of an appropriate reward, either in terms of esteem, money, career opportunities and job security. Having a demanding but unstable job, achieving at a high level without being offered promotion prospects, or receiving an inadequate wage in comparison to one's efforts or qualifications, are examples of "toxic" psychosocial experience at work which adversely affects cardiovascular health.

STRESS: MYTH, REALITY OR SCAPEGOAT?

As we have seen, a variety of models has been offered in an attempt to increase our understanding of the nature of stress. The most recent "transactional" models of stress are indicative of the complexity of the concept. In reality, however, models still tend to oversimplify the problem to the extent that the issue of stress can seem to become trivialized. As Schuler (1980) says, "it is too all encompassing a phenomenon, too large to investigate". Yet, this has not deterred interest into the topic. However, this high level of interest and popularity is not always positive. Indeed, incorrect usage of the word "stress" is common, and it is now used interchangeably to refer to a state or condition, a symptom, or the cause of a state or a symptom. There are problems in defining and interpreting the word "stress", and whether, indeed, such a thing exists. We have asked, should the word "stress" be used at all! The words "stress", "pressure" and "strain" are readily used in an interchangeable way to describe feelings, emotions or situations. The lay person seems quite able to identify with the concept of stress and has an appetite to know more. This need is served too eagerly by the press and media. Without a doubt, certain individuals hope to make a quick profit from "being stressed" at work.

This situation creates problems for us in the effective management of stress because stress is often wrongly blamed for *all* our ills. It is now seen as the cause of *all* our problems. It has become a "whipping boy" and it is certainly misunderstood, leading some to question if it is a useful concept at all and others to criticize those who suggest there is a lack of consensus (Jones and Bright, 2001). Many of us continue to view stress only in negative terms, or even prefer to deny that any problem exists. Prevalence of this view is likely to be detrimental to the effective management of stress in the work environment because it is synonymous with not coping. One outcome is that staff will tend to hide their work problems and health condition until they become victims of exposure to stress. What they really need is encouragement to try actively and positively to manage the stressors and strains that are an inevitable part of modern day living and working.

So, it is vital that we acknowledge that *not all forms of stress are bad*. Hans Selye, the acknowledged "father" of stress research, said that the only person without stress was a dead person. By this, Selye meant that stress is an inevitable part of being alive, and should be viewed as "stimulation to growth and development...it is challenge and variety, it is the spice of life". Hans Selye used the word "stress" to describe a state of arousal in the nervous system. So, it is any stimulus, event or demand impacting on the sensory nervous system, with "eustress" referring to the positive buzz we can get from work when we successfully meet its challenges. When an imbalance exists between a perceived demand (that is, the stimulus) and our perceived ability to meet that demand, then we will experience a state of stress (that is, distress or pressure). Stress, therefore, is unwanted pressure and is manifest when we feel that a situation is out of our control, or when we feel unable to cope with the event. It is a subjective experience that is "in the eye of the beholder". An understanding of this explains why, in a given situation, one person might be highly distressed whereas another seems to prosper and thrive.

In organizational life, it is likely that we are now denied a natural outlet and expression of the stress response since we cannot "fight" or "flee". We are physiologically primed to take actions that are inappropriate, and the sedentary nature of the job further exacerbates this problem. Whilst, in the first instance, our response to stress is physiological, complex emotional and behavioral reactions also take place. These can lead to potentially damaging health outcomes. Understanding the nature of stress in these terms helps us to think positively and proactively about stress, instead of taking a defensive, self-blaming stance. It implies that each of us, at various times during our life, might be vulnerable to stress.

ADAPTIVE VERSUS MALADAPTIVE WAYS OF COPING WITH STRESS

Since it is mismanaged stress that is damaging in its consequences, it is apparent that we need to manage a potentially stressful situation in an active and positive manner. It is important to do this without resorting to maladaptive ways of coping. By this we mean avoiding:

- excessive use of alcohol or nicotine
- dependence on other drugs – such as tranquillizers, sleeping pills, "pep" pills and caffeine
- being tired all the time, so failing to take adequate levels of exercise or engaging in fulfilling social and recreational activities
- indulgence in "comfort" eating because we feel sorry for ourselves – especially when we binge on those foods high in sugars and fats that have empty calories and with low or poor nutritional value
- procrastination – putting off dealing with a situation because it is threatening or difficult: this usually causes the situation to escalate and leads to even larger problems to tackle
- becoming angry and aggressive with ourselves and others – this is a particularly damaging strategy if we persist in "bottling our anger up inside". A quietly seething time-bomb becomes dangerous and unstable, and can cause irreparable damage when a situation finally leads to a major eruption or explosion that is completely out of control.

All of these maladaptive coping strategies render us *less fit* to cope with the demand. Members of an organization are unlikely to come forward and deal with problems that exist within an organization if there is a fear of being identified and labeled as a "non-coper". Research evidence is clear: mismanaged stress arising from certain conditions and situations in the workplace, or at home, is likely to have an adverse impact on performance, health, well-being and quality of life.

Implicit in a contemporary approach to understanding the manifestations of stress are the assumptions that stress is a subjective experience, and that the outcomes or symptoms of distress can be physical, psychological, or behavioral. This means that establishing causation is difficult, because the relationships between exposure to stress and ill-health are not simple. Factors to consider include:

- the aetiology of disease
- subjectivity of response to stress and illness
- unwillingness to accept a situation, or actually denying the real reasons for one's plight
- inability to recognize the difficulties we are in when in a state of distress (that is, unwell, anxious, depressed).

These are just some of the reasons why it is difficult to identify the root cause of a problem.

Before we review various sources of stress in Chapter 4, it is useful to acknowledge how and why change is a significant and pervasive source of stress. It is considered at this point because of the major impact it can have on organizational life and has some effect on all the other stressor categories.

CHANGE AS A SOURCE OF STRESS

Research evidence indicates that a wide variety of workplace conditions causes stress, strain or pressure that are associated with a wide range of physical and psychological ill-health problems. However, for many people at work the changing nature of the work environment is a potent source of stress and pressure. For others, the challenges are routes to promoting self-efficacy and well-being. This balance must be managed in a positive way, if we are to remain both healthy and productive. Clearly, constant change has become the dominant theme of organizational life and this pattern seems likely to continue. While we endeavor to meet the demands associated with predictable life event changes, we must continue to face the endless reshaping of our work structure and climate, embedded in the changing nature of society.

Change, it is said, brings progress and improvement to our quality of life, and stimulation and variety that relieve us from boredom. So, why would we wish to make changes for the worse? It seems that our work environment has become a world of rapid, discontinuous change that requires us to live in a state of transience and impermanence. The situation is potentially damaging because energy is needed and expended by constant adaptation to stimulation from the external environment. In this way, "change" becomes a powerful stressor agent because it necessitates adaptation, whether it is perceived as a negative or positive experience. Whether we welcome the change, fear it, or actively try to resist it, adaptation or adjustment requires energy (Selye, 1956). Samuel Johnson, quoting Richard Hooker, suggested that, "Change is not made without inconvenience, even from worse to better". In Selye's view, impairment of function and structural change are wholly, or in part, linked to adaptation to stimulation, or as he described it, "arousal". He concluded, our energy resources are not infinite, and so breakdown of the system, in part or total, will ultimately occur. Exposure to a continued state of arousal will result in wear and tear on the body that, in the extreme, leads to exhaustion, collapse, and finally death of the system. It we accept this theory, we can concur with Hans Selye's hypothesis that the only person without stress is a dead person! Of course, we are not in the position to test his hypothesis and are happy not to have this opportunity. Instead, we prefer to accept Selye's view that stress need not be all bad news and, where appropriately managed, can represent "stimulation to growth and development...challenge and variety...the spice of life".

However, too often we try to cope with the demands of exposure to change by resorting to maladaptive ways of coping: that is, we drink alcohol because we believe it gives us confidence or helps us to sleep or relax; we drink a great deal of strong coffee to gain the "buzz" necessary to sustain long hours of working without a break; we smoke cigarettes to calm our nerves or take the place of meals that we must "skip" because of time pressures; we use various pills and potions to ensure sleep or to "pep" ourselves up; we eat "comfort" foods, particularly sugars and fats with low or poor nutritional value. These forms of coping render us less fit to cope with the demands of change and, in the long term, actually become the source of stress, when the addiction exacerbates the problem.

Studies of employees response to organizational restructuring have long emphasized the negative effects that might be manifest, and these include, "worry", "uncertainty", "job insecurity", "decreased job satisfaction, organizational commitment, trust in the company" and intention to quit (Schweiger and DeNisi, 1991). Nevertheless, "Change is here to stay" is the old adage whose truth permeates all our lives (Cooper, Cooper and Eaker, 1988). In the 1500s, Machiavelli recognized the perilous nature of change and, in the nineteenth century, Darwin formalized the significance of adaptation for our survival. Thus, it would appear that exposure to "change" as a source of stress is an inevitable part of modern day living and working. One key to surviving is to have some level of control over it, perceived or real, which, in Gandhi's words, enables us "to be the change you wish to see". Unless we effectively manage the prevalent form of workplace stress, it can result in adverse and costly outcomes for employees and the organization. In Chapter 4, we will examine the ways that "change" permeates organizational life to become a source of stress.

CHAPTER 4

UNDERSTANDING THE NATURE OF STRESS: ORGANIZATIONAL HOT SPOTS

The interactive model of stress described in Chapter 3 specifies that we need to identify, measure and understand three separate issues:

- sources of stress (that is, the stressors) that exist in the environment
- the moderators or mediators of the stress response (that is, those individual differences that shape our response to stress);
- outcomes or the manifestations of exposure to a source of stress, including strain.

Outcomes, or symptoms of exposure to stress, have already been discussed in Chapters 1 and 2. These can be either individual or organizational outcomes. The issue of moderators and mediators of the stress response are considered in Chapter 6, which describes the process of conducting a stress audit, or risk assessment. Since an understanding of the nature of stress is a vital part of an organizational approach to stress management, it is necessary to identify and measure the main sources of stress in the workplace. Therefore, in this chapter we review potential sources of stress, or "stressors", in terms of the "hot spot" issues identified in contemporary organizations. The hot spots coincide with the UK Health and Safety Executive's management standards on stress (HSE, 2004b), which form the basis for assessing organizations in relation to improving well-being at work. It is not surprising that this structure bears similarity to previous models of job characteristics (for example, Cooper and Marshall, 1978; Karasek and Theorell, 1990) and, for the purposes of this book, some of the related issues also touched on in Chapter 1 are examined in greater depth. The hot spots

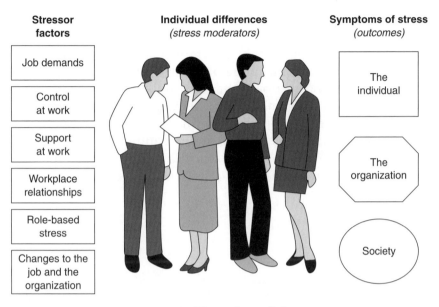

| Stressor factors | Individual differences *(stress moderators)* | Symptoms of stress *(outcomes)* |

Stressor factors:
- Job demands
- Control at work
- Support at work
- Workplace relationships
- Role-based stress
- Changes to the job and the organization

Symptoms of stress (outcomes):
- The individual
- The organization
- Society

FIGURE 4.1 **Dimensions of stress**

are classified in terms of six different stressor categories (see Figure 4.1):

- **Job demands**: These include workloads, working hours, shift systems, juggling work-life balance and demands emanating from the physical work environment.
- **Control at work**: This covers the way we work, the role of consultation and improving skills.
- **Support at work**: This refers to methods of supporting employees through management practices, including styles of behavior and feedback, as well as via organizational policies. This includes the concept of the psychological contract.
- **Workplace relationships**: These extend to include relationships with co-workers and line managers, encompassing expectations of behavior at work.
- **Role-based stress**: This includes stressors such as role conflict, role ambiguity and responsibility for the safety of others.
- **Changes to the job and the organization**: This examines how change is managed and its impact on employees.

HOT SPOTS: JOB DEMANDS

■ **Workload**: Without a doubt, the most talked about hot spot in the work environment is the amount we have to do, whether it involves work overload, the need to work long hours, shift working, managing others, or juggling work and home life. These sources of pressure exist within a work environment that exerts physical demands and often requires us to work with rapidly developing computerized technology (these topics are discussed in Chapter 5). In this section, the demands of the job are considered.

Stress and workload

Before we examine the issue of work overload further, it is necessary to acknowledge that both overload and underload are potential sources of stress in the workplace. As discussed in Chapter 3, Hans Selye believed a certain level of arousal (a stimulus) is needed for optimal performance. In this "optimal" state, we are likely to feel creative, calm and highly motivated to do the job well. When a level of arousal exceeds our ability to meet the demand placed upon us, we experience feelings of "burnout", exhaustion and, ultimately, collapse. This phenomenon can be explained in terms of a simple "underload/overload inverted 'U' illustration" (see Figure 4.2). If we do not feel challenged or stimulated by the job, or do not believe that our contribution is valued, it is possible that we will experience feelings of apathy, boredom, poor morale, and a lack of self-worth. Ultimately, such employees may "vote with their feet" and stay away from work, whilst complaining that they are "sick of the job" rather than feeling physically unwell.

It is apparent that a significant change for many of us at work is in the *volume of workload* and the level of demand placed upon each of us. It usually means having too much rather than too little work to do – although, as we have noted, both of these are potential sources of strain. Aided by rapid technological development, many organizations have "streamlined, downsized, or right-sized" in order to continue to meet increasing competition from home and foreign markets. Therefore, it is likely that there are now fewer employees, but engaged in more work. Thus, a high level of demand appears to be a common problem for

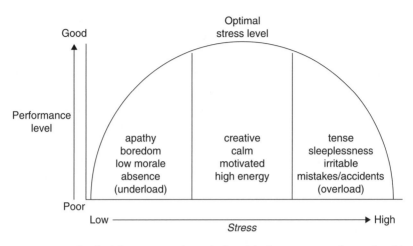

FIGURE 4.2 **Optimizing stress: the relationship between work overload/ underload, performance and health**

many people working in contemporary organizations, resulting in some or many of the following:

- simply having too much to do in the time allowed
- unrealistic time and deadline pressures that lead to long working hours
- spiraling production demands and responsibilities
- a fast pace of work that is often controlled by others or machines
- the challenging levels of work difficulty
- the lack, or uneven distribution, of resources available
- fluctuations in the form of peaks and troughs in work demand also creating uncertainty, which can also be stressful.

Within these demands, it is important to make an additional distinction at this point, in that "qualitative" load differs from "quantitative" load. Quantitative overload occurs when the employee is given too many tasks to complete in a specified period of time. Qualitative overload occurs when the individual does not feel capable of doing the prescribed task. Similarly, quantitative underload means long periods without being occupied; and qualitative underload means the task does not utilize the skills, ability or potential of the worker (French and Caplan, 1973). Both work overload and underload can result from an irregular flow of work that is outside the control of the employee. This problem is no longer confined to paced assembly line workers, since many occupations face restrictions that are caused by climatic conditions, seasonal variation and market fluctuation. However, the proliferation of call centers and the Taylorist approach of reducing human interaction to scripted phone conversations have translated some of the negatives of assembly line work into the service sector. Lack of control over the pace of work is also manifest in the unpredictability within certain occupations, such as air traffic controllers, fire fighters, the ambulance service, pilots and anesthetists – who must all deal with periods of inactivity and the need to spring into action on demand or when a crisis happens.

Quantitative overload

Various studies have shown that both physical and mental overloads are potent sources of stress in the workplace. Working under time pressures in order to meet deadlines is also an independent source of stress, and stress levels begin to rise as these deadlines draw near. French and Caplan (1973) observed an association between objective, quantitative overload and cigarette-smoking, a risk factor for coronary heart disease and certain cancers. Among British tax inspectors, both quantitative and qualitative overloads predicted levels of anxiety and depression (Cooper and Roden, 1985). Many blue-collar workers feel overloaded because the pace of work is too high. Rate of working has been shown to be a significant factor in the health of this occupational group, especially when the employee is unable to control the pace (Frankenhauser and Johansson, 1986). A seven-year study of quantitative workload in 2,465 bus drivers showed that working routes on which the traffic was of higher intensity could double the risk of heart attacks among employees (Netterstrom and Juel, 1988). Studies of the experiences of call center workers has shed further light on how our bodies can react to the amount of work we have to do. Employees with heavier workloads are more likely to report musculoskeletal disorders (Sprigg *et al.*, 2007). Consideration has been given to whether this is due to physical and biomechanical reasons, reasoning that musculoskeletal problems in the upper body and back can be attributed to spending long periods of time in one position, while risk of injury for the arms and hands is linked to repetitive overuse (Crawford *et al.*, 2005). However, the role of psychological factors in musculoskeletal disorders has been underestimated, but is entirely logical. For example, higher workloads contribute significantly to employees' experience of job strain which, in turn, has physical consequences, such as maintaining a tense posture (Sprigg *et al.*, 2007). Sprigg *et al.*'s study of 936 call center employees from 22 workplaces confirmed that, for every added unit of workload, workers had a 44 percent increase in the odds of experiencing upper body and lower back difficulties, as well as a 64 percent rise in the estimated chance of suffering musculoskeletal arm problems. Furthermore, our personal disposition to view job characteristics optimistically or pessimistically can prove highly influential in their impact on employee well-being. For those with a pessimistic style, levels of anxiety and depression are most elevated when work demands are high and levels of autonomy are low, and tend to be greater than those experienced by optimists (Totterdell *et al.*, 2006).

Qualitative overload

There is evidence to suggest that qualitative overload as a source of stress is linked to low levels of self-esteem among white collar workers. However, it is also likely that qualitative overload might be experienced by blue collar workers who are promoted into supervisory positions on the grounds of superior performance, but who have no past experience in the supervision of other people. This good, reliable employee is rewarded with a promotion, but faces considerable stress because the skills to do the new job are lacking. This is likely not due to a failure to engage with the job but is, rather, a product of not yet having the necessary skills to carry the job out effectively which, in turn, can predict the individual's level of job performance, as has been found in an army officer training corps (Britt *et al.*, 2006).

Within the job itself, the perception that a task is beyond the competencies of the individual can mean they are less likely to use systems, including those that might be necessary to carry out the job. One example of this was found among graduate accountants' reluctance to utilize new computer software (Pennington *et al.*, 2006).

Quantitative underload

Simply not having enough to do could affect psychological well-being. As Figure 4.2 shows, this type of underload, known as "rust out", leads to boredom and apathy. Boredom in the daily routine, as a result of too little to do, can result in inattentiveness. This is potentially dangerous, if the employee fails to respond appropriately in an emergency (Davidson and Veno, 1980). This lack of stimulation might be more hazardous at night, when the individual must adjust to the change in sleep pattern but does not have enough work to do to keep alert (Poulton, 1978). Work underload was identified as a significant source of stress among crane operators. Boredom and a lack of challenge were both significant predictors of job dissatisfaction, anxiety and depression among this group (Cooper and Kelly, 1984).

Qualitative underload

This appears to be more commonly reported than an overload condition, and is damaging because the individual is not given an opportunity to use acquired skills and abilities, or to develop potential. The individual is likely to feel that he or she is not getting anywhere and is powerless to show their talent. Thus, a "rust out" condition will exist. The resurgence of this phenomenon is evident in the working conditions of skilled migrant workers, who experience poorer psychological health alongside limited opportunities to use employment-related skills, which can also coincide with reduced earnings (Dean and Wilson, 2009). It is important to remember that this situation will be perceived as stressful, if the needs and expectations of the individual are not met. However, the long-term psychological toll can mean that under-employment of skills is as damaging as unemployment, and has been found to be disproportionately prevalent among migrants from culturally distant locations (Antoniou and Dalla, 2009).

Among native-born employees, previous research has suggested that new graduate recruits are likely to suffer from qualitative underload when starting their first full-time job after leaving university life. They enter the world of work with high expectations that are not realized, and this form of stress becomes manifest as job dissatisfaction and poor job motivation (Hall, 1976). Many individuals in this situation will quickly want to move on to another organization that appears to be offering what they are seeking from a job, although the economic climate might not mean this is practicable. This is the situation facing skilled migrant workers, and is fuelled by unrealistic job previews. It is very costly to organizations in terms of recruitment and initial training costs, and the individual is scarred by a bad experience at the beginning of his or her career.

Long hours of work

Greater workloads tend to mean raised working hours, as employees stay at work to fulfill the demands of the job. This can impact on workers' health, as well as home life. Long since the proposal of a ten-hour working day at the Manchester Quarter Sessions in 1784 (Federation of European Employers, 2005a), the UK has gained a reputation for having the longest average working week in western Europe. However, the adoption of a more Americanized approach to working times by European Union nations, such as Poland, means that the average UK working week of 44.8 hours is high, but only 1.1 hours higher than the EU average (Federation of European Employers, 2005b). While 20.1 percent of UK employees are working more than 45 hours per week (6 million), this proportion is lower than that of the USA, Australia and Japan (CIPD, 2009b). In the USA between 1976 and 1993, men and women increased their average annual working hours by 233 and 100 hours, respectively (Bureau of Labor Statistics, 1997), with 76.6 percent of employees working over 40 hours per week, compared with over 87 percent of the working populations of the Czech Republic, Hungary and Slovakia, who work similar hours (ILO, 2007).

The link between long working days and premature death led the esteemed *British Medical Journal* to suggest that "Overwork can kill" (Michie and Cockcroft, 1996). Furthermore, there is an established link between high workloads and coronary heart disease, based on observations that 25 percent of patients suffering with it had been working two jobs and that 46 percent had been working at least 60 hours each week (Russek and Zolman, 1958). A review of 21 studies into the effects of working hours on health concluded that there was a significant association between overall health, including physiological and psychological health symptoms and hours of work (Sparks *et al.*, 1997). Quantitative analysis of 12 further studies supported these findings. However, the type of job will moderate these health outcomes. For example, the impact of long hours of work might be greater for jobs that require attention (for example, driving), or repetitive work. It also seems that a certain amount of physical activity at work can protect the individual from coronary heart disease, although excessive physical demands can lead to exhaustion, injuries and poor health. These findings are the more alarming for the realization that 25 percent of UK employees also work in a second job to supplement their incomes (BBC, 2006). Furthermore, "presenteeism", where staff stay longer at work so as to be seen of value to the organization, helps to create an impression of "committed" employees. However, as was discussed in Chapter 1, this can mean costs to the organization that are higher than those due to absenteeism! Indeed, times of economic recession tend to accentuate this type of behavior.

The Pacific Rim economies host the longest working week (ILO, 2007), with Singaporean and South Korean employees spending 46 hours in the workplace each week (*The Standard*, 2005a, b). However, pressure from both unions and government has seen the institution of a five-day week in South Korea, as well as moves in Japan to ensure that its employees take their full holiday entitlement to balance the routine of long hours of overtime and to help combat the falling birth rate! The frequency of *karoshi* (death from overwork) has led to a series of legal cases in Japan; in China, overwhelmed by the pressures of an increasingly competitive society, there is a rise in self-inflicted deaths among those aged between 20 and 35 dwelling in cities, where suicide is the fifth most common cause of death (*The Guardian*, 2005a). On a brighter note, the leisure and retail industries have begun to burgeon in some of the cities of southern India dominated by information technology, and similar outcomes are anticipated in Malaysia, where the Saturday morning shift worked by its one million civil servants has been abolished (*The Standard*, 2005).

Juggling the work–life balance

The need to work long hours has other negative consequences, in that the individual consequently spends less time in social relationships. It means that the benefits of social support as a buffer in a stressful job are reduced. It can also cause strain in his or her relationship with a spouse or partner, thereby creating work-to-family stress. Nevertheless, it should be acknowledged that some individuals regard work and working long hours as a psychological haven and a way of escape from the pressures of home and family or an unsatisfactory personal relationship. Distress only exists when demand exceeds or fails to satisfy abilities or expectations (real or perceived). Also, we may decide to accept a stressful situation for a given period of time because the "pay off" is highly desired. Unfortunately, we often fail to balance the true costs and the gains, and thus become a casualty of exposure to mismanaged stress at work.

Home is at least as important as work for 71 percent of UK managers , but they continue to put in long hours, despite also believing that these are having an adverse effect on the relationships with their partner (72 percent) and/or children (77 percent) (Worrall and Cooper, 2001). Strain-based conflict is brought on by the spillover of negative emotions from work to home (WFC) or family to work (FWC), bringing with it a range of outcomes for either the work or home domain. Difficulties at home could see the employee under-performing at work, making errors and failing to meet expectations (Frone, 2003), while domestic strains caused by problems at work have been shown to contribute to burnout for nurses and engineers (Bacharach *et al.*, 1991) and to poor psychological health for politicians (Weinberg and Cooper, 2003). In the longer term, this can mean increased rates of depression, greater alcohol consumption (Noor, 2002), and more coronary heart disease (Haynes *et al.*, 1984). Cooper and Sutherland (1991) found that chief executive officers (CEOs) across Europe also experienced "work spillover" problems that adversely affected their home and social lives. This survey of 118 CEOs found that two thirds worked nearly 12 hours each day; some up to 16 hours a day. Almost all of them worked at the weekends, thus restricting time spent with the family. The top sources of stress were work overload, time pressures and deadlines, work-related travel and working long hours. Many of these senior executives seemed to realize the potentially damaging consequences of their lifestyle, and 25 percent believed that they were at substantial risk of job burnout (physical and emotional exhaustion); an even greater proportion of executives perceived themselves to be at high risk from heart disease (especially the younger CEOs). From the results of this survey, it was clear that these individuals were questioning their lifestyle, and many were actively thinking about quitting "life at the top".

Research into stress in organizations is painting a more complete picture where both work and non-work factors are assessed. Indeed, it is not possible to obtain a complete stress profile by looking only at sources of stress in the workplace. Thus, we must consider the interface that exists between work, home and social life. This includes the personal life events that might have an effect upon performance, efficiency, well-being and adjustment at work (Bhagat, 1983). Concerns within the family; life crises; financial difficulties; conflicting personal and company beliefs; and the conflict between organizational, family and social demands are examples of potential stressors that might spill over into the individual's work domain. Research evidence suggests that job and life satisfactions are influenced by the demands and conflicts of home and family life. It would appear that negative life changes, such as divorce or bereavement are related to lower levels of satisfaction with supervision, pay and the work itself. Positive life changes are associated with satisfaction about promotional opportunities.

In a study of the objectively assessed experiences of UK National Health Service staff, employees diagnosed with anxiety and depressive disorders were compared with same-sex and age-matched colleagues working in the same job role. They were found to have a significantly greater number of objectively stressful situations both inside and outside of work: a situation that affected 70 percent of those with psychological ill health compared with 28 percent of those enjoying positive mental health (Weinberg and Creed, 2000). Lack of management support was the single greatest work-based predictor of minor psychiatric disorder, while employees carrying a very heavy workload were twice as likely to experience an episode of minor psychiatric disorder (Weinberg and Creed, 2000). Phelan *et al.*'s (1991) study of 1870 employees at Westinghaus Electrical Corporation also highlighted the importance of both work and non-work factors in employee well-being. During a period of organizational change, the key predictors for depression (which affected 27.2 percent of those participating in the study) included negative work events and a lack of feeling valued by the organization, along with a personal or family history of depression, past psychiatric history in the employee's spouse and strain in the marital relationship.

Various factors can affect the relationship between work and family, and family and work. The job itself may elicit and reinforce certain styles of behavior (including personality traits). For example, the Type A behavior disposition (the need for power or position) can cause conflict in the home domain. The aggressive, controlling behavior that brings results, and even promotion, in the work environment might not be welcome at home! Also, the individual who feels thwarted and disillusioned because his or her promotion expectations have not been met might exhibit "revenge" behavior at home. Probably, it is the only place in which the individual can express feelings that are, by necessity, repressed at work. Job structure can place constraints upon the amount of time spent at home with family and friends. The need for more and more people to engage in shift work can also have an adverse impact on the quality of our social relationships. Indeed, the decision to accept a job and sustain it might be affected by our family commitments. For example, it has been observed that attitudes to working nightshifts were influenced by whether a spouse or partner could adjust to being alone at home at night. In similar ways, exposure to stress at work might have a spillover effect and adversely impact on one's family and personal life. The consequence of long working hours and overload conditions for family life can only be detrimental.

Work overload among managers

Some of the studies reported above illustrate the adverse impact of working long hours, and it appears that those employed as managers in the workplace, despite the assumption they have more control over their job, are also at risk. Whilst all employees have suffered the impact of change in employment patterns, Wood (1989) suggests that managers have acquired a "dual status". Thus, in theory, they are likely to have a permanent contract and access to an internal labor market of promotional opportunities; however, in practice, they often face redundancy or limited career prospects in their organizations. Their "dual status" (of being part of the reduced "core" of workers) creates a double burden, which is exacerbated by the long hours of working (Simpson, 1998). Managers' hours of working seem to have increased for two main reasons:

1 In the face of restructuring, new technology and the loss of key personnel, their workload is considerably increased. Studies of personnel in managerial positions suggest that many of these individuals, at all levels of the management structure, are increasingly exposed to working longer hours (although these are, on average, no higher in the UK than across the European Union) (CIPD, 2009b); a heavy volume of work; time pressures; difficult and demanding deadlines; and a lack of, or uneven, distribution of resources. Feldman (2002) recognized multi-level pressures accompanying the role played by personality, job characteristics and organizational and prevailing economic factors, including a fear of job cuts.
2 Since employers are unwilling to promise job security, many managers (and their subordinates) react to the insecurity and fear of redundancy by staying at the desk or workplace for longer periods of time. This is viewed as an attempt to demonstrate visible commitment

to the organization and the job itself (Scase and Goffee, 1989). Brockner *et al.*, (1993) described this behavior as part of a "survivor" syndrome that affects many managers who have experienced restructuring and downsizing of their organization. Characteristics of the survivor syndrome include heightened anxiety and decreased morale. According to Clarke (1994), this fear of being in line for redundancy drives the individual to work harder, and to be seen at work for longer periods of time. This means that they tend to arrive very early and stay very late into the evening. It is the work ethic of making sure that you are never first to leave the workplace! This dysfunctional outcome is more commonly known as "presenteeism" (Cooper 1996: 15). It means "being at work when you should be at home either because you are ill or because you are working such long hours that you are no longer effective".

Among a sample of managers who attended business schools, Simpson (1998) observed that long hours were worked for three reasons:

- the job demanded it – for example, sudden deadlines imposed one-off necessity, or a temporary phenomenon while new skills or procedures were being learnt
- restructuring had led to higher workloads because of loss of staff, or because of the demands of continual job changes
- managers who had been through restructuring were made to feel that they could only retain their position by working long hours as a way of demonstrating visible commitment to the job. Simpson also found that this was more likely to be a feature of male behavior, but they were more likely than the female managers to deny working longer hours than necessary.

Whilst personnel in managerial positions are under stress due to long hours of working, the blue collar and shop floor employees face the need to work long hours and a shift pattern that is imposed rather than chosen.

Shift work

The need to work for long hours is not restricted to personnel in management jobs in the organization. In order for companies to respond to demands for faster service and products, the need to operate a 24-hour per day operation is a reality for many organizations. Therefore, many employees in non-management jobs face the need to work shifts, including evening and night shifts, in addition to working extra hours and overtime in the downsized workplace. This is to facilitate the needs of industry to maximize the useful life of expensive technology and to increase profitability. Other companies are required to remain open around the clock because of the nature of their business. Increasingly, the world of business and industry resembles "the sleepless gorgon" described by Toffler (1970) in *Future Shock*. One in seven UK workers carries out their job between 9pm and 6am, and this is projected to increase to one in four by 2020 (Norgate, 2006).

Numerous different shift patterns have been identified. Singer (1985) reported 487 different shift work systems operating in Europe, including permanent, continuous and rotating patterns, some of which require night-shift working. Shift work described as "continuous" requires the employee to work at weekends, whereas "discontinuous" rosters typically require the individual to work a variety of shifts from Monday to Friday only. Whilst some individuals work a permanent shift (for example, "permanent nights"), the most common pattern of shift work is to rotate the hours of working. Indeed, Mitler (1992) reported that one third of the US labor market worked a rotating work schedule. A plethora of research evidence indicates that the consequences of shift work include physiological, psychological and performance-related outcomes. One startling claim suggests that working nightshifts could be equivalent to smoking twenty cigarettes each day, in terms of the potential cost to employee health, which has been equated to shortening life expectancy by ten years (Norgate, 2006). This is consistent with the finding that night work carries an increased risk of both cancer and heart disease (Arendt, 2010).

Typically, 10- or 12-hour shift rosters are the norm, and organizations work a four- or five-shift roster to facilitate this process. Overall, the number of annual hours worked remains the same, or even slightly fewer. Those who favor this work pattern enjoy the extra leisure time, long weekends, or "10-day breaks", and appear to be more satisfied with their job and work schedules. However, it means that many employees are required to work for, perhaps, 12 hours at a time, often engaged in work that is physically or mentally demanding. Thus, there is some evidence to suggest that the 12-hour compressed schedule can lead to lower performance. For example, Rosa *et al.* (1989) found performance decrements or increased errors of 187 per cent, compared with the same workers who had previously been on an eight-hour roster, even after seven months of adjustment time to the new shift pattern. Older employees, who are more susceptible to fatigue, appear to suffer most from these compressed work schedules and appear to be less enthusiastic about this way of working. While some individuals prefer the compressed working week, others loathe it! It seems that, for certain individuals, the need to engage in shift work of any kind is unacceptable. Chapter 7 highlights methods for combating the challenges posed by shift work, referring to the UK HSE's guidance.

Nevertheless, evidence suggests that the need to work shifts can be a potent source of stress. Individuals are required to engage in work activity at a time of day when they should be sleeping. Conversely, they must try to sleep at the time of day when usually they would be active and alert. Typically, sleep, metabolism, temperature and the production of many hormones follow a 24-hour cycle (circadian rhythm). It is controlled by our biological clock. This is an endogenous "pacemaker" (Daus *et al.*, 1998). It works in combination with exogenous environmental cues (known as *zeitgebers* – for example, the day–night light cycle) to keep our bodies synchronized to a 24-hour cycle. When we reverse these natural tendencies by engaging in nocturnal shift work, the circadian system becomes disrupted and rhythms move out of phase. Thus, shift work has a biological and an emotional impact on the individual due to circadian rhythm disturbances to the sleep–wake cycle, body temperature and adrenaline excretion rhythm. It can affect neurophysical rhythms such as blood temperature, blood sugar levels, metabolic rate and mental efficiency (Monk and Tepas, 1985). For example, Cobb and Rose (1973) found that air traffic controllers had four times the prevalence of hypertension, and more cases of mild diabetes and peptic ulcers than a control group of US Air Force personnel that did not work shifts. In a study of the psychological impact of shift work, Sutherland and Cooper (1991b) found that personnel in the offshore oil and gas industry who worked longer "tours" (that is, the number of consecutive days spent offshore), of 14 rather than seven days, were more likely to report job dissatisfaction and a poorer level of mental well-being than their counterparts who only worked for seven days offshore at a time.

Worryingly, the disturbance of nocturnal sleep leads to daytime fatigue and sleepiness impairs motivation and vigilance, thereby affecting the performance level and safety of the individual (Hellesøy, 1985; Moore-Ede, 1993). Many night-shift workers report that they are able to take catnaps to help them catch up on sleep loss. However, a "sleep debt" can accumulate over a seven-day period, to the extent that the employee effectively loses the equivalent of at least one night's sleep. In fact, Mitler (1992) found that over 55 per cent of a sample of 1500 shift workers admitted to falling asleep on the job during a given week. Akerstedt (1988) reported that 11 per cent of locomotive engineers "dozed off" on most trips, while 59 per cent admitted to falling asleep at least once. Since individuals engaged in night-work or rotating shifts have reported lower levels of alertness, concentration and vigor, and higher levels of confusion and fatigue, it is not only the individual who is at risk. Customers and clients serviced by shift workers might also suffer negative consequences in terms of poor performance and mistakes. At risk are those individuals who must respond to monitors as part of the job. For example, this group includes intensive care nurses and nuclear power plant operators, or those who need a high level of concentration at critical times (such as paramedics, and operators in process plants where potentially hazardous materials and chemicals are being used).

The degree to which the individual can volunteer for shift work is obviously a factor in influencing research findings; however, many employees do not have any choice about the pattern of their hours of work. Apart from the potential impact on individual health, working the night-shift can also have negative consequences for social relationships. Shift workers have trouble maintaining friendships with those who do not share their work pattern. This, in turn, can lead to feelings of isolation, and often the pursuit of lone activities (Prossin, 1983; Sutherland and Cooper, 1991a). They do not have the energy or motivation to socialize with others who do not work shifts. Furthermore, the need to engage in shift work can cause strains within the family. It interferes with family time, and can have a negative impact on relationships with a spouse or children. The quality of a marriage or relationship might suffer when issues of jealousy and infidelity are a concern. However, not all shift workers complain about disruptions to family life or domestic problems (Barton and Folkard, 1991). Many report that they spend more time with their children and find it easier to attend school and family gatherings. They are also able to plan childcare in a more desirable and cost-effective way because one parent is usually at home (Skipper *et al.*, 1990).

HOT SPOTS: CONTROL AT WORK

■ **Control**: Employees should "have a say about the way they do their work" and "where possible have control over their pace of work" (HSE, 2004b). Consultation over working patterns and the timing of breaks is recommended and opportunities to develop new skills should be supported.

From this definition of control it can be seen that it tends to mean slightly different things, depending on which part of the job is under scrutiny. The same is true when considering control through-out the structure of an organization. When front-line employees are given more control over their work, it is often referred to as empowerment; when it is at the level of the work group it becomes autonomy; at the top executive tier, it is known as power. Not surprisingly, the subject of control in the workplace has been the focus of much research and organizational debate, the majority of which seems to show that empowering the workforce is good for both mental health (Sparks *et al.*, 2001) and performance (Leach *et al.*, 2003). The benefits of increasing employees' levels of control, via job redesign and greater involvement in decision making, are explored in Chapter 7.

Whilst it is important to consider levels of control at the individual or small group level, the idea of empowering individual staff members to carry out their job can be seen as a gamble for some managers. Indeed, the prospect of granting partial or complete autonomy to a group of workers would be more likely to induce high anxiety in a controlling manager. This largely depends on whether or not managers trust their workforce, and is boldly outlined by McGregor's (1960) X and Y theory. Theory X states that we should not really trust the employee because he or she really only wants to get away with doing the bare minimum; therefore, he or she should be monitored as closely as possible and, at best, manipulated in order to ensure they do any work. Theory Y takes a much more positive view of the employee as inherently able to take on control for their work: given the appropriate forms of motivation by the organization, excellent results are likely to be achieved. For example, the shift from the practice of Y to X has been a major factor in the "new managerialism" sweeping the higher education sector, where academic freedoms have been challenged and methods of working often imposed.

For most managers, there is recognition that a balance is required to ensure employee engagement in contributing to the goals of the organization or sector, which can in turn translate into improved business performance (CIPD, 2009a) and well-being. This type of engagement can be defined as "a positive attitude held by the employee towards the organization and its goals" (Robinson *et al.*, 2004: 408) and, clearly, the employer plays a key role in its development. The evolution of a reciprocal relationship based on trust is more likely to mean employees will go that extra mile for the organization and participate in discretionary behaviors – that is, activities for which they might not be paid but that highlight good citizenship, including willingness to train, involvement in social events, and so on. In this way, enhanced control can help employees become the competitive edge for any organization (MacLeod and Clarke, 2009). Towers Perrin-ISR's survey (2006) tracked and compared over 50 global companies with 664,000 employees for one year, and found that the financial performance of organizations in which staff members were highly engaged with their work reported a 19.2 percent improvement, compared with a 32.7 percent decrease in low-engagement corporations. Workers who are engaged with their job take fewer days sick leave: 2.69 days per year compared with 6.19 days for disengaged employees (Gallup, 2003, cited in Melcrum, 2005).

An early example of the success of this approach underpinned the success of Japanese economic expansion in the latter part of the twentieth century, as Deming's (1982) philosophy of "continuous improvement" empowered groups of workers to make decisions about improving the workplace. The concept of quality circles took off – the name given to voluntary meetings between employees to discuss how the job or the product might be improved. The processes that permit workers to take control over their work in groups represent an extension of empowering individuals to improve their own work tasks – for example, fixing their own machines and thereby increasing productivity (Jackson and Wall, 1991). Of course, individuals will differ on the level of control that best suits them in carrying out their particular job and this can, in turn, mediate the relationship between job autonomy and experiences of strain, such as emotional exhaustion (De Jonge and Schaufeli, 1998). However, overall there is a preponderance of studies that show the negative impacts of low levels of control on a range of employee outcomes, including well-being. These can include mental health (Dalgard *et al.*, 2009), anxiety (Totterdell *et al.*, 2006), depression

(Holman and Wall, 2002) and intention to quit (Grebner *et al.*, 2003). Alongside control at work, levels of workload feature as key components of the widely popular Job Strain Model (Karasek, 1979), which predicts poor psychological and physical health for employees experiencing high workloads in combination with low levels of decision making over their job. Numerous studies have shown that either of these factors in isolation can predict negative outcomes (de Lange *et al.*, 2003), with a smaller number demonstrating that both act together to produce a psychologically toxic cocktail of job characteristics (Totterdell *et al.*, 2006).

HOT SPOTS: SUPPORT AT WORK

■ **Support**: Encouragement, information and sponsorship should be provided by the organization to its workers, enshrined in policies that make support by managers (including constructive feedback and access to the necessary resources) and by colleagues the foundation for employee development and success.

As we have seen, the positive attitude of employees to their work and their employer is only one half of the equation when it comes to engaging staff in a psychological sense. The support that is not only provided, but is perceived to be provided by the organization is a major predictor of employee well-being. Paramount in this regard is the availability of management support; without it, the employee is at far greater risk of developing psychological health difficulties. In one study of NHS staff, employees from medical, nursing, administrative and ancillary occupations were three times more likely to experience an episode of minor psychiatric disorder (for example, depression, or anxiety) where there was a lack of support from their line manager (Weinberg and Creed, 2000). Similarly, in a Japanese electronics company, a longitudinal study of mental health in a range of work groups (including production, management, technology and research) found that the largest increase in risk of developing poor psychological health was among those reporting a poor relationship with their superior (Shigemi *et al.*, 2000). A large-scale review of healthcare and non-healthcare employees, in the UK and overseas, highlighted links between sickness absence and management style, and between psychological ill-health and unclear management (Michie and Williams, 2003). Taken together, these factors demonstrate the importance of clear and constructive working relationships between managers and the staff answerable to them.

Managers are expected to fulfill a range of obligations, from being the giver of helpful advice to the enactor of disciplinary proceedings. One of the strongest predictors of perceived organizational support is supervisory support and, the more the organization is seen as backing its staff, the less employees report strain (Rhoades and Eisenberger, 2002). Job satisfaction and positive mood are other positive outcomes from this perception of a fair exchange between employee and employer. For most managers, there is a balancing act between the needs of the organization (effectiveness, profit, keeping things legal and healthy) and the needs of the individual (reasonable workloads and deadlines, being made to feel valued, opportunities for training). Employees see the manager as espousing the values of the organization, but there is also the possibility that some individuals do not take naturally to being good managers. It also goes without saying that what might appear to be sound management to some can simultaneously be seen quite differently by those who are on the receiving end: some of the more memorable television comedy programs have featured characters with appalling management styles. It is not surprising to note that the fundamental key to positive leadership is "understanding how to engage people" (Higgs, 2005). This, in turn, requires a grasp of a range of the emotions, for as we have seen, it is these that matter to individuals. Therefore, it is not surprising that transformational leadership (Burns, 1978) is widely lauded in the relevant journals (Judge and Bono, 2000) and is the style most strongly linked with demonstrating emotional intelligence (Gardner and Stough, 2002). The key components of transformational leadership are:

- recognizing workers' abilities and encouraging their development
- facilitating others' ownership of actions and the thinking that precedes them
- shaping and sharing a positive vision that enthuses others
- charismatic qualities that gain respect, including taking responsibility, showing determination, sharing success and placing the needs of the group above the leader's own.

The literature confirms the importance of emotionally intelligent behavior, illustrated via transformational leadership, in contributing to a range of positive outcomes (Antoniou, 2005). The idea that good leaders and managers are born rather than trained is increasingly challenged, and it is likely that the mode of learning is the key to preparing individuals for successful leadership (Boyatzis, 2005). However, one of the growing challenges to positive relationships between managers and their staff is the increasingly remote nature of working, which separates employees via distances and technology (see Chapter 5). Related to this are increasingly important cultural considerations that can influence the success or otherwise of management. Geert Hofstede (1980, 2001) has led the way in analyzing what employees want across more than 70 countries, within the same multinational organization: IBM. In highlighting the assumptions about work made by over 116,000 people across the world, Hofstede has shown how an approach valued in one cultural context needs to be modified to work well in another. One of the four key dimensions his research identified was the varying degree to which employees in different cultures tolerate inequality in the distribution of power across the organization. Known as the power–distance dimension, this data showed that in India and France there was acceptance of a large interpersonal (not physical) gap between those in management and their subordinates, whereas, in Israel and Austria, there was an expectation that consultation would take place in a climate of equality, making disagreements a more acceptable and expected phenomenon. As part of a worldwide study (named GLOBE) of what employees look for in sound leaders, Brodbeck *et al.* (2000) again found cross-cultural differences. Not surprisingly, integrity, vision and inspiration were commonly expected; however, where western and southern Europe highly valued the characteristic of performance, Middle Eastern countries placed a strong emphasis on diplomacy (Abdalla and Al-Homoud, 2001).

On considering the level of support the employee receives from their employer, the psychological contract has attracted much attention. It constitutes the unwritten set of mutual expectations held by organizations and their employees, which can play a major role in determining attitudes and behavior in the workplace. Central to its understanding is the importance of fairness and trust (Guest *et al.*, 1996) and the dynamics of the transaction between employer and employees (Rousseau, 2003). Indeed, where organizational support is perceived to be reduced, it is likely that the psychological contract assumes even greater significance (Coyle-Shapiro and Conway, 2005). It is not surprising that the violation of the psychological contract can impact on a range of workplace behaviors (Turnley and Feldman, 2000), and it is acknowledged that, where the mutual set of obligations fails to be met by one party – most often the organization, this results in differences between what the employee expects and actually receives (Coyle-Shapiro and Conway, 2005). Violations usually come about as the result of broken promises, which can carry with them far more emotion than a simple mismatch in expectations. A diary study of managers' daily experiences revealed that 69 percent of the sample of 45 employees reported violations during one 10-day period, with an average of one broken promise per week (Conway et al., 1999). The negative impact of breaches in the psychological contract has also been documented, with both emotional exhaustion and job dissatisfaction recorded in financial sector workers (Gakovic and Tetrick, 2003). In a sample of over 800 managers involved in organizational change scenarios, links were found between psychological contract breaches and subsequent job performance (for example, dodging duties, wasting time), but violations were more strongly related to employees looking for another job and withholding organizational citizenship (for example, refusing to volunteer for extra duties, or failing to defend the image of the organization) (Turnley and Feldman, 2000).

The importance of support within the two-way relationship between the employee and their organization is aptly demonstrated. Further consideration of support from colleagues is given in the next section.

HOT SPOTS: WORKPLACE RELATIONSHIPS

- **Relationships**: Positive behaviors in the workplace should be reinforced by policies and procedures for reporting and dealing with unacceptable behaviors, such as bullying.

"The dynamics of organizational relationships are among the most frequently cited sources of intense emotion" (Waldron, 2000: 66). Here, strong emotions are to be found ranging through jealousy, desire, anger, passion and hate. Nevertheless, good relationships between work colleagues are considered a central factor in individual and organization health. Given their likely ups and downs, Stoic philosopher Marcus Aurelius suggested we prepare ourselves for the worst: "Remember to put yourself in mind every morning that before night it will be your luck to meet with some busy-body, with some ungrateful, abusive fellow, with some knavish, envious, or unsociable churl"! Positive modern theorists emphasize the strengths of emotional intelligence, building on Dale Carnegie's *How to Win Friends and Influence People*. Certainly, one cannot underestimate the significant impact on others created by our ability to listen and provide positive feedback, verbally or non-verbally, which help others by demonstrating a genuine interest in them and appreciation for their work or what they hold dear. An additional consequence is to make others feel good about you – although Carnegie is keen to point out this should be done for sound rather than devious motivation. In short, supportive emotions within a work setting can contribute to good morale, constructive feedback, empowerment and improved productivity.

The co-worker relationship is the most common form of social support, in which we carry out the same or a similar job role as others within the unit of the organization, perhaps sharing an office, working alongside others on a production line or communicating via more remote means. Whatever the setting, there is little doubt that such relationships are important, occupying a considerable proportion of our time at work, and involving job tasks and performance in common. As a consequence, it is vital that organizations take responsibility for promoting and rewarding good practice in human interaction, as well as acting appropriately where interpersonal behavior breaches codes of conduct. The introduction of Human Rights legislation in the UK in 2000 underlines one route by which redress can be sought, if organizations fail to act.

Unsurprisingly, the importance of social support from colleagues is seen as a positive factor for employee well-being, and a buffer against psychological strain (Stansfeld *et al.*, 1998). It is featured in the Job Strain Model (Karasek and Theorell, 1990) as a factor that can offset the negative impacts of high workloads and low levels of control at work. Social support can function in a number of ways: helping employees manage emotions more effectively and lead to improved problem solving; providing the motivation to persist against challenges at work (Warr, 2007); engendering a sense of identity, perhaps as part of a larger employee group (Wood, 2008). A study of coping strategies in a range of occupational groups (including nurses, teachers and church ministers) has highlighted that approaches to coping depend on the job in question; however, drawing on the emotional support of others, particularly in shared situations, is an important factor (Dewe and Guest, 1990). Similarly, a study of workers in the offshore oil and gas industry found that "teamwork" was rated as the most important quality in the job (Livy and Vant, 1979), where feelings of security and confidence were generated by the sense of belonging to a stable work crew.

However, working with others can also be one of the most stressful aspects of life, and many people find the need to express their frustrations. The canteen, or even the photocopying room, can provide safe havens for staff to express their discontent; but what happens in environments where there is no obvious safe place to share views with colleagues? The option of keeping things bottled up is open to all, but there can be implications for our emotional as well as physical well-being, such as poor psychological (Weinberg and Creed, 2000) and physical health (Snow *et al.*, 2003), including cardiovascular disease (Miguel-Tobal and Gonzalez-Ordi, 2005). Denying our emotions appears to be one action that carries certain risks, but the struggle to manage our emotions can produce variable results. Emotional intelligence – "an ability to recognize the meanings of emotions and their relationships, and to reason and problems solve on the basis of them" (Mayer *et al.*, 1999: 267) – highlights self-control as an important component, and research has shown that venting negative emotion by complaining to others can actually make us feel worse (Brown *et al*, 2005). Emotions can also prove contagious (Strazdins, 2002), if we identify with those feelings for long enough, either as part of a job or outside of work. This can result in a working group that has developed the habit of complaining negatively about things as a matter of course, rather than in response to specific issues. This does not mean we should not let others know how we feel, as the ability to communicate our emotions to others can be an integral aspect of coping. However, an awareness of how others' emotions can affect us, taking into account our own durability, is useful in informing how we cope.

The lack of supportive relationships or forming poor relationships with peers and colleagues are potential sources of stress. These can be most detrimental to psychological health, as well as affecting job performance by leading to low levels of trust and reduced interest in problem solving. However, some of us are required to work with "difficult" or abrasive personalities (Levinson, 1978), who simply fail to see a need to "oil the wheels" of amicable social exchange in the workplace. These achievement-oriented individuals might be stubborn, tactless, critical of the efforts of others or condescending about ideas. They need to be in control and tend to dominate meetings; they are self-opinionated, impatient with the efforts of others, confrontational, or distant and cold. Some abrasive people are only preoccupied with symbols of power and status and so drive themselves hard, regarding others simply as rivals. In the extreme, the inconsiderate colleague can become an intellectual bully or even physically violent. Remote working has the potential to emphasize such negative effects, as the isolated employee has limited opportunities to socialize with supportive co-workers, channels of communication with others are restricted, and the opportunity to develop strong social support networks might be denied if the employee is restricted to a workstation.

A recessionary climate, characterized by job insecurity and the use of contingent workers, is not likely to be conducive to good relationships at work. These circumstances often lead to divisiveness, rivalry and unhealthy competition for jobs; and poor interpersonal relations at work that are low in trust and supportiveness. Research has shown that mistrust is positively related to high role ambiguity, inadequate interpersonal communication between individuals and psychological strain in the form of low job satisfaction and decreased well-being (French and Caplan, 1973). These researchers found that supportive relationships at work mediated the effects of job strain on physical indicators of health, including cortisol levels, blood pressure, glucose levels and the number of cigarettes smoked.

Taking the breakdown of workplace relationships to an extreme, levels of violence in the workplace add another sinister dimension to stress in the workplace (Bulatao and VandenBos 1996; Cox and Leather, 1994). Whilst this includes violence between staff and towards members of staff from people on the outside of the organization, incidents of violence towards employees from colleagues are alarmingly apparent. Across the EU, an average of 5 percent of workers report being subjected to physical violence from co-workers or others, with higher than average levels in the Netherlands (10 percent), France and the UK (both 9 percent) (Eurofound, 2005b). Fear of occupational violence and exposure to crime is known to be a serious and widespread source of anxiety and worry, capable of having a negative impact on health (Nasar and Jones, 1997). It is not only physical assault that is damaging in its consequences; some form of post-trauma reaction, for example, can occur without any physical injury being sustained (Flannery, 1996). This can include simply being a witness to violent circumstances in the workplace. Unsurprisingly, research evidence suggests that fear of workplace violence is associated with anxiety, thoughts about leaving the organization, and searching for alternative employment.

Bullying appears to be widespread and occurs where "one or several individuals persistently over a period of time perceive themselves to be on the receiving end of negative actions from one or several persons, in a situation where the target of bullying has difficulty in defending him or herself against these actions" (Hoel and Cooper, 2000). Referred to as bullying in the UK and Ireland, it is known as "mobbing" in Germany and Scandinavia and "workplace harassment" in the US and Canada. As with harassment, bullying is defined largely as the impact of the behavior on the recipient. This is an area receiving increasing coverage in published research: the prevalence indicates the existence of a widespread problem. A national UK survey of over 5288 employees found that 10.5 percent were currently bullied (Hoel *et al.*, 2001) and that 49.4 percent of British employees had experienced or witnessed bullying at work in the previous five years (Hoel *et al.*, 2004). The most frequently occurring problems were for those employed in the prison, postal and teaching occupations (Hoel *et al.*, 2001), although it seems to be widespread regardless of organizational culture (Hauge *et al.*, 2007). Bullying affects men and women employees equally, although women perpetrators tend to be co-workers and the males are likely to be either co-workers or supervisors (Vartia and Hyyti, 2002). Three quarters of the perpetrators of bullying occupy managerial or supervisory roles compared with one third of colleagues, with men more likely to be bullied by a manager and women more likely to face bullying from colleagues (Hoel *et al.*, 2004). Within occupations, teachers report the highest level of difficulties with managers (86.4 percent), while health service (53.6 percent) and university employees (51.4 percent) are the most frequent targets of peer-bullying (Hoel *et al.*, 2004).

The impact is on both the physical and emotional well-being of the victims (Einarsen and Mikkelsen, 2003), and has also been found among those witnessing bullying (Hoel *et al.*, 2004). US findings shockingly record that 97 percent of Asian, Hispanic and African-American employees had experienced some form of bullying in the previous five years (Fox and Stallworth, 2005). It is suggested that bullies are "stress carriers" within the organization. Usually, they do not personally suffer from the effects of stress, but their behavior causes a great deal of stress for subordinates and colleagues alike. Thus, an employer must ensure that the dignity of the employee is upheld, and acknowledge that he or she has a right to be treated with respect. These findings are borne out by studies in other countries (Vartia and Hyyti, 2002).

The quality of interpersonal relationships at work is important, in that supportive relationships are less likely to create the pressures associated with rivalry, petty bickering and rumor mongering. It is also acknowledged that social support (in the form of group cohesion, interpersonal trust and a liking for one's supervisor) appears to contribute significantly to feelings about job stress and health. Whilst organizations cannot guarantee these more desirable outcomes, they can play a vital part in creating a climate and culture based on positive relationships, approving policies and events to support this approach.

HOT SPOTS: ROLE-BASED STRESS

- **Role**: Employees should be clearly informed about their function(s), and carrying out a role should not cause conflict for individuals charged with those responsibilities; where this does arise, systems should be in place to address role conflict.

Changes to job role structure are common as companies continually reinvent themselves and, as we have described, change itself can be stressful, especially if we try to resist it. Nevertheless, the impact of changes in the workplace can alter the nature of one's job role, causing role ambiguity or role conflict. This relates back to the concept of the psychological contract considered earlier in this chapter under the heading of "Support at work" (pp. 96–7), where mutual understanding of the expectations held by employers and employees alike is liable to shift.

Role conflict

Role conflict exists when an employee feels confused by opposing demands or incompatible goals surrounding the tasks connected with the job. Having to do tasks that are not perceived to be part of one's job role will also lead to stress associated with role conflict. For example, having to deal with the demands of meeting high (and perhaps unrealistic) production targets whilst satisfying product quality demand, or meeting production demands without compromising safety standards, can lead to stress caused by role conflict. Role conflict has been associated with employee-related outcomes such as absenteeism (Breaugh, 1981), job dissatisfaction and elevated blood pressure (Ivancevich and Matteson, 1980), as well as organizational outcomes including low performance of international joint business ventures (Mohr and Puck, 2007) and unethical behavior (Grover and Hui, 1994). Miles and Perreault (1976) identified four types of role conflict:

- **Person–role conflict:** The individual would like to do a task differently from that suggested by the job description.
- **Intrasender conflict:** This happens when a supervisor or manager communicates expectations that are incompatible – for example, the employee is given an assignment but without sufficient resources to complete the task.
- **Intersender conflict:** When an individual is asked to behave in such a manner that one person will be pleased with the results whilst another will not be satisfied, intersender role conflict occurs.
- **Role overload:** When the employee is assigned more work than can be effectively handled, the stress associated with role overload is experienced.

Role conflict is a potential problem for personnel working at organizational boundaries (Cooper and Marshall, 1978). It happens when job demands take the individual into contact with people external to the organization, or across functions or departments within the company. Thus, for example, trade union representatives and health and safety supervisors or representatives can experience conflict because they work at a boundary role in an organization. Trade union representatives pledge to help employees receive all the rights to which they are entitled, and to ensure the organization provides work conditions that adhere to the standards set by safety and health agencies. At the same time, they are required to meet their own job description demands, and the goals and objectives of the business. These interests are not always compatible.

Some supervisors or managers perform boundary-spanning roles that are more typically described as being "piggy in the middle". Margolis *et al.* (1974) found that personnel occupying this type of job were seven times more likely to develop ulcers than shop-floor workers. Personnel in managerial positions can experience the stress associated with role conflict when required to satisfy the policy demands of the company, in the knowledge that the actions required are not in the best interests of his or her staff. Studies have shown that some behavioral styles are better suited to dealing with conflict situations. For example, Tidd and Friedman (2002) found that individuals adopting active and positive approaches, whilst avoiding negative styles, benefited from reduced levels of role conflict.

Role ambiguity

Role ambiguity refers to the lack of clarity about one's role or the task demands at work. It occurs when an employee does not understand or realize the expectations and demands of the job, or the scope of the role. A lack of training or inadequate information can lead to role ambiguity. Research evidence has shown that role ambiguity at work has been associated with tension and fatigue; intention to quit or actually leaving a job; and high levels of anxiety, physical and psychological strain, and absenteeism. The stress arising from unclear objectives or goals can lead to job dissatisfaction, a lack of self-confidence, a lowered sense of self-esteem, depression and low work motivation, increased blood pressure and pulse rate, and intention to leave the job (Kahn *et al.*, 1964; French and Caplan, 1970; Margolis *et al.*, 1974)

A wide range of work situations can cause role ambiguity. For example, being in one's first job, promotion to a new position, a location transfer, having a new boss, or changes to the work structure or systems, can all create ambiguous work conditions (Ivancevich and Matteson, 1980). Some of these role changes are made by necessity, in response to organizational change, and not of choice. A move to a new type of industry or business exposes the individual to the unique technical language, colloquialism, jargon and workplace culture. Unless adequate job previews and induction training are provided, an employee is likely to be exposed to role ambiguity and perhaps is more vulnerable to error or accidents at work. Role ambiguity was found to be the most important predictor of stress among new nursing graduates during the first three months of employment, but this was superseded by role overload after one year in the job (Chang and Hancock, 2003).

Role conflict and role ambiguity situations are exacerbated when employees perceive a lack of managerial or supervisory support at work. In some jobs, this is perhaps unavoidable – for example, clergy report low job satisfaction when facing both role conflict and ambiguity

(Kemery, 2006). Significant downsizing of a workforce also impacts upon management grade personnel. They experience high workload demands, long hours of working, plus the realization that they might not be available to their employees when a need arises. These individuals might experience conflict between different role sets, such as the conflicting demands of the job and the home or social environments. Nevertheless, feeling unable to fulfill others' expectations of one's job role is now a commonly cited stressor experienced by personnel with responsibility for other people. However, there is also commercial pressure to run many business operations on a continuous 24-hour basis, thus stretching the demand on managerial staff, who still tend to work mainly day shifts. This compounds the problems associated with the lack of availability of one's supervisor or manager when needed. So, in addition to the problems associated with role conflict and role ambiguity, having "responsibility" is a potential source of stress at work. Pincherle (1972) also found that the level of one's responsibility in the organization was a predictor of coronary heart disease (CHD) risk factors among 1200 managers in the UK. Also, responsibility for people's safety and lives was a key factor in predicting risk of heart disease among air traffic controllers (Crump *et al.*, 1980). This potential source of stress is not confined to managerial or professional occupations, as crane drivers are aware of the risk of serious injury or a death to one of their colleagues if they make a mistake while working (Sutherland and Cooper, 1986). Outside the workplace, it is sobering to note that among registered nurses in the US, an increased risk of CHD has been linked with providing childcare for more than 21 hours each week and for at least nine hours each week for grandchildren (Lee *et al.*, 2003).

It is suggested that one of the impacts of rapidly developing new technology is to facilitate the ability to push responsibility for decision making lower down the organization. This means that a potential stressor problem will exist if the employee is untrained or lacks the experience to deal with the situation. Alternatively, the enthusiasm for technological costs to be curbed can come at a very high price to safety. Indeed, a move to change the culture of the organization by empowering the workforce and giving them more responsibility for decision making about their jobs requires careful planning. Having more control and a say about the things that affect us at work is recognized as a way of reducing stress at work, if the process is managed effectively. However, if the organization tries to make these changes towards an empowered model of working too swiftly, or in a way that is poorly managed, employees are likely to resist their newly ascribed level of responsibility. It is unrealistic to expect employees that are used to a "dependency" culture of "tell me what to do" to transfer quickly and successfully to a "let us together decide what to do" culture without full debate and adequate training. It is important that managers are also trained to delegate responsibility and manage effectively through an open process. These are important, if the change in culture to an empowered workforce is to be successful. In our experience, shop-floor employees are most likely to describe lack of trust as the strongest barrier in moving towards an empowered or interdependent culture and climate at work. As many shop-floor employees have told us, "They tell us we are empowered, but they still don't trust us to get on with the job!"

HOT SPOTS: CHANGES TO THE JOB AND THE ORGANIZATION

- **Change**: This should be carried out by engaging with and informing employees, providing opportunities for them to influence proposals for change. Furthermore, employees should be made aware of the potential outcomes of the change process, and training and support should be available to help them adjust.

We have already begun to describe the changing nature of industry, and the structure and climate of the organization as potential sources of stress at work. It is difficult to avoid some overlap between stressor categories since stressors rarely exist in isolation. Thus, the interactive and dynamic nature of stress must be acknowledged. The structure and climate of the organization determine the way it treats its people, whereby increased control and opportunity to participate have recognized benefits in terms of improved performance, lower staff turnover, improved levels of mental and physical well-being, and accident reduction (Sutherland and Cooper 1991b). Change is often ironically referred to as the constant feature of work and, while there can be little doubt that the impact of the shifting psychological contract has been clear, this is not simply due to change itself but, rather, to the way in which that change is managed (Giga and Cooper, 2003). Indeed, the mishandling of such situations has even drawn a directive from the European Parliament to oblige European employers to provide advance notice of any major organizational change (Giga and Cooper, 2003). The spate of suicides among staff during a period of proposed reorganization at France Telecom (whose company brand name is better known as Orange), including compulsory internal transfers (*The Guardian*, 2009b), reinforces the risks of ignoring the impact of change and the process by which it is introduced.

Whatever the political reality, change is always likely to send reverberations through an organization. It impacts employees in a number of ways, both through the change process and its outcome. Findings have illustrated the positive impact on workers' well-being when they are given some measure of control over their work environment during a period of uncertainty (Bordia *et al.*, 2004) and, similarly, change need not be negative where careful management of the process is exercised (Firns *et al.*, 2006). A large study of 8504 Swedish employees revealed clear benefits for the well-being of employees who had been involved in change processes rather than being on the receiving end of them, with those who participated experiencing half the rates of absenteeism and depression of non-participants (Karasek and Theorell, 1990).

However, employees might resist the offer to adopt a more participative style of working where they are skeptical about the reasons for the proposed changes to working practices. Where the changes are aimed at improving productivity, customer service, quality or safety, employees might feel that they are being put in place to gain competitive advantage. Levine (1990) suggests that employee support for a participative work climate is more likely to succeed when an industrial relations system is characterized by the presence of some form of profit, gain sharing or job security. Also, ways must be in place for the development of group cohesiveness together with some guarantee of individual rights; a workforce acclimatized to a dependency culture, used to being told what to do, cannot move easily or quickly to a condition of mutual dependence (control shared by mutual agreement), or to interdependence (characterized by flexibility, interchange of activities, joint decision making and sharing of control). In other words, the procedures for empowerment are as important as the outcomes for the success of the empowerment process. If management attempts to hand over control too quickly, or employees try to escape from being controlled when the authority figure will not relinquish control, the workforce can become counter-dependent (Cox and Makin, 1994). In these situations, there will be a "fight back" with acts of rebellion, such as a ban on overtime, strikes, sit-ins, or "work to rule" procedures. To avoid these problems, it is necessary to overcome the state of learned helplessness, low levels of confidence and lack of esteem that characterize the "dependent" workforce. This is important for success in changing to an empowerment model of working (McGrath, 1994). Also, an understanding of this concept explains how changes proposed as "stress reducers" can easily fail to achieve their goal.

An additional explanation for the resistance to change in the workplace is the strain linked to job insecurity. This has been associated with a high level of stress and anxiety (Jacobson, 1987). Workers feel anxious about the lack of certainty regarding when layoffs will occur and who will be affected by these changes associated with downsizing, mergers and acquisitions. Vahtera *et al.* (1997) found increased incidence of musculoskeletal disorders among staff that remained with the organization after cut-backs to Finnish local government structures. In such circumstances, job dissatisfaction, alternative job search and non-compliant job behaviors can be manifested as outcomes of exposure to the stress of job insecurity. These negative behaviors are costly to the organization and the individual. However, research evidence suggests that there are potential negative effects for the "survivors" of cutbacks in organizations. After the axe falls, the survivors often find themselves in a high workload situation, sometimes with much curtailment of their original job, and also reduced resources.

A sector-wide example of this eventuality is higher education, which has consistently registered some of the highest and most rapidly rising levels of strain, both among academic staff in Australia (Gillespie *et al.*, 2001) and in the UK. Almost 50 percent of a sample of 1100 university staff have seriously considered leaving and 69 percent reported their job as "stressful" (Kinman and Jones, 2004), even before projected cuts to UK public sector funding. In the re-engineered business, employees face the likelihood of their career reaching a plateau, and also interpersonal conflict as competition for the remaining jobs heightens. In this structure and climate, a culture of tension exists. Levels of creativity can also suffer because individuals might be too insecure to suggest radical or risky solutions to problems. The following effects of cutbacks in organizations have previously been documented:

- centralization: decisions are passed upward, participation decreases, control is emphasized;
- absence of long range planning: crises and short term needs drive out strategic planning;

- decrease in innovation: no experimentation, risk aversion and scepticism about non-core activities;
- scapegoating: leaders and/or groups of workers are blamed for the pain and uncertainty;
- resistance to change: conservatism and "turf protection" lead to the rejection of new alternatives;
- increased labour turnover: the most competent leave first, causing leadership anaemia;
- lowered morale; decreased effort and commitment: few needs are met and infighting is predominant;
- no slack: uncommitted resources are used to cover operating expenses;
- fragmented pluralism: emergence of special interest groups of a "political" nature;
- loss of credibility of senior management;
- non-prioritized cuts: attempts to ameliorate conflict lead to attempts to equalize cutbacks; across the board versus prioritized cuts;
- conflict: interpersonal conflict and "infighting"; competition for control predominates when resources are scarce (Cameron *et al.*, 1987).

Therefore, further changes proposed by management will be viewed skeptically in a climate of staff cutbacks. Lim (1996) suggests that support from colleagues and supervisors can help to buffer the individual against the effects of job insecurity, particularly for work-related outcomes such as job dissatisfaction, job search and non-compliant job behaviors. These include tardiness, absenteeism, job theft – including theft of time by leaving early, counter-productivity – such as putting less effort in at work, working slowly, spending time gossiping and in idle conversation instead of working. As Lim suggests, some individuals admitted engaging in counterproductive behaviors as a means of getting back at their organization because they were dissatisfied that the company had not assured them of secure jobs. This manifestation of the psychological contract shows its reciprocal nature, with employees acting to make their side of the bargain "feel fair" (Weinberg, 2009b).

A previous example has been provided by changes to the UK public sector over the last 25 years, particularly in health and social care, as heads of industry and policy makers "set in motion a revolution in the nature of the employment relationship the like of which they never imagined. For they have shattered the old psychological contract and failed to negotiate a new one" (Herriot and Pemberton, 1995: 58). Prior to this major shift, mutual expectations saw employees prepared to commit to the goals of public service, displaying conformity and loyalty, while trusting the employer to value their efforts and well-being (Herriot and Pemberton, 1995). In return, public organizations were able to offer job security, a career path, and the necessary training to cement this transaction. Changes fuelled by globalization, technological innovation and government ideology dismantled such assumptions, and created increasing reliance on economic considerations. It is not surprising to have seen research findings revealing very high levels of psychological strain among the affected occupational groups (Taylor *et al.*, 2004), more sick leave than in UK private sector jobs (CBI/AXA, 2006), as well as increased staff turnover and resulting skill shortages in such occupations as nursing (Scott, 2002) and social work (Huxley *et al.*, 2005).

Job insecurity will continue to be an issue of concern for the foreseeable future. Therefore, to the extent that job insecurity is shown to be detrimental to outcomes that are valued by employees as well as employers (Roskies and Louis-Guerin, 1990; Schweiger and Lee, 1993), organizations can play an important role in enhancing social support at work to assist individuals in coping with job insecurity. Without assessing emotions, all change risks failure, and the significance of use of emotionally intelligent approaches by employers leading such processes should not be underestimated (Scott-Ladd and Chan, 2004). To employees facing what are perceived as unacceptable violations of their psychological contract, Herriot and Pemberton (1995) offer three possible courses of action: "Get safe, get out or get even!" Any or all of these have clear implications for organizational behavior and well-being.

SUMMARY

Clearly, there are many potential sources of psychological strain. However, the management of stress in the work environment can only be successful when we understand the source(s) of pressure. The six aspects of the workplace highlighted in this chapter are the leading contenders recognized by the UK's Health and Safety Executive. Identification of the factors that have a negative impact on performance and well-being is an essential part of a stress management program. This is the objective of the stress audit described in Chapter 6. Before we describe the stress audit process, issues concerning stress and the developments in new technology as a part of the physical and psychological environment at work are reviewed in Chapter 5. These also have important implications for the changing face of the workplace.

CHAPTER 5

STRESS, NEW TECHNOLOGY AND THE PHYSICAL ENVIRONMENT

Rapid technological development in the work environment has exposed more of us to the need to work "with" and "for" computers at work. "Computer phobics" are still found in the workplace, but a great majority of us are now required to work with computers, in some way. It has become a part of daily work practice that also forms part of our wider physical working environment. Within work surroundings, employees are also exposed to the potential for distress caused by noise, vibration, extremes of temperature, inappropriate lighting levels and poor hygiene. In this section, issues related to new technology are considered first, followed by scrutiny of the impact of physical demands in the work environment on our well-being and functioning.

BRAVE NEW WORLD

Advances in computer technology have created dramatic changes in the work environment and our conditions of work. New technologies and computer-aided technology describe the processing hardware and software that transform information and materials (Majchrzak and Borys, 1998). Such technologies are found in service and manufacturing sectors everywhere. Since people "partner" these technologies, the potential for unique forms of stress exists in the workplace, in addition to the pressures and strains of living and working.

Typically, new technology might expose us to:

■ computerized communication tools such as email, internet, videoconferencing

- hand-held communication and storage devices, including mobile phones, blackberries and iPods
- computerized decision support systems
- computer information systems
- advanced manufacturing technology (AMT)
- computer aided design (CAD)
- computer aided manufacturing (CAM)
- computer integrated manufacturing (CIM)
- computer numerically controlled machining (CNC)
- flexible machining systems (FMS)
- mechanized product systems, such as conveyor belts or workstations (adapted from Majchrzak and Borys, 1998).

These new technologies and computer aided systems alter the ways that people perform their work. Ultimately, new technology is introduced to maximize performance potential and replace physical activity with cognitive activity. In theory, this leaves people to deal with important, unpredictable and random occurrences, while machines deal with repetitive, predictable and non-random activities. The intention is for "machines" to take over the mundane, boring and routine tasks. However, certain questions about technological advances and the drive to automate the work environment need to be addressed. For example:

- Has automation freed us from the drudgery of work?
- Have we been released from the shackles of alienating labor?
- Has new technology has created a stratified society, with a human elite commanding robotocized labor?
- Who is in control – human or machine?

The answers to these questions are complex and, from a humanistic perspective, are far from being satisfactory. Thus, it is likely that the potential for stress does exist in the workplace because we are not able to provide positive answers to these questions. However, the demands of new technology have created some instances where we have traded manual dexterity skills for cognitive skills, and greater levels of responsibility: 37 percent of EU workers use a (personal computer (PC) for significant proportions of their job and the work of 23 percent is determined by the use of machinery (Eurofound, 2005a). Whilst some jobs have become deskilled, others have become upgraded and more complex with the need to learn the use of the new technology, and the ever-evolving and developing universe of the computer. Clearly, skills have changed, but many jobs have also vanished. Some authors suggest that automation has left two main types of jobs. First, there are the low-skilled, operation jobs, while the others are described as, "high-skilled, planning, programming and maintenance type work". Across the EU, clear differences have emerged with some countries using information technology (IT) to a high degree alongside a low utilization of machinery (for example, Scandinavia, the Netherlands), while mainly southern and eastern European nations show the opposite balance of increased mechanization, but lower levels of IT use. "Work determined by machinery is characteristically more repetitive and monotonous, with less autonomy and is physically – and sometimes psychologically – more demanding" (Eurofound, 2005a: 45).

In pursuit of cutting human resource costs and maximizing output, employers continue to grapple with the white heat of technology, which back in the 1970s carried the promise of easier working lives, and the prospect of enhanced and plentiful leisure time. However, it appears that we are moving towards a catch-22 situation. Advanced manufacturing systems rely on skilled intervention for their operational performance. However, Bainbridge (1983) warned that human intervention is problematic when it comes to the monitoring and diagnosis of system errors, because machine "minders" are not routinely required to develop the necessary skills from observing automated machinery in action. Some key studies have provided counter-arguments, such as decreasing downtime via the knowledge enhancement of machine operators (see Jackson and Wall in Chapter 7). However, it is possible that with continuing advances in technology, a situation could develop in which there is a shortage of shop-floor or front-line operators with the capacity to control or override malfunctioning highly automated systems manually. The tragedies involving Toyota motor cars that became evident in 2010 might come to be seen in this light.

The economic appeal of utilizing new technology effectively and safely is clear to see. However, there is an additional attraction for those wishing to guarantee the quality of processes and outputs – that is, to retain as much control as possible over both. Some of these benefits are listed here:

- savings on the costs of recruiting and training people
- potential to reduce overheads by encouraging teleworking – where employees work remotely from the organization's site

- speeding up and standardizing the processes of the business – for example, automatic stock checking and ordering
- producing quality goods on a large scale
- improving communications – increasing speed, availability and frequency of contact
- monitoring performance;
- enhancing security.

While the changing nature of the workplace might cause skills to become obsolete, exposure to ever-changing equipment or systems can be threatening for the individual. Workers must adapt to each novel situation or condition, and engage in education and training in order to cope with the new demands. Training is vital, but the "leaner" workforce can experience pressure when trying to find time to attend training sessions. Difficulties also arise when trying to release colleagues for training, in addition to the time off needed for holidays and to cover periods of sickness absence. All of this must be accomplished while trying to maintain performance and production demands and standards. When de-skilling occurs (real or perceived), the employee can experience "qualitative underload" as a source of pressure. This is because he or she believes that the job no longer is a challenge, or that the job does not offer an opportunity to use and develop their abilities. Alternatively, it is possible that employees experience stress at work because they are required to become "multi-skilled", so that maximum use is made of the costly investment in new technology (that is, plant and equipment). In this case "qualitative overload" can become a source of stress. Alternatively, information overload can be experienced as the employee struggles "to cope with new computer technologies in a healthy manner" and succumbs to "technostress" (Aida *et al.*, 2007). Whichever situation prevails, the potential for human error is increased, along with the likelihood of a breakdown of machinery or accidents that are beyond the individual's capacity to prevent. When it comes to accounting for the reasons for these, there is the additional issue of sorting out who was actually in control – the employee or the technology?

All of these contribute to a different type of working experience, in which jobs are redesigned with negative effects on control over one's work; de-skilling, which can also impact badly on the individual's future employment prospects; and a range of outcomes for employees' physical and psychological health (Langan-Fox, 2005).

Of course, there is no reason why new technology should not bring benefits to the worker too. Depending on the job, there is the increased opportunity for flexibility, which can free the individual to telework, or carry out their job at times of day or night suiting their personal circumstances. In fact, individuals with high levels of conscientiousness, who are well-organized and work-focused, thrive better in this rather than a traditional work environment (Lamond *et al.*, 2003). The decreased need for physical effort was at one time viewed as positive, too. Defined as working from home with a PC, around 8 percent of EU employees undertake telework (Eurofound, 2005a). However, those engaged in working remotely from their office or organization face a range of potential challenges:

- blurring of the boundaries between work and non-work – for example, increased potential for both time and role conflict
- unpredictable working hours – a "waking" not a "working" week (Parker *et al.*, 2001)
- social isolation from colleagues – for example, minimized opportunities for informal discussion and gossip, missing out on new developments
- reliance on virtual communications, thereby risking an increased potential for misinterpretation of intended meanings
- increased expectations of what can be achieved in terms of pace and productivity – a new psychological contract, or even a re-negotiated real one
- invasion of privacy via electronic performance monitoring
- limited access to technological support
- sedentary work existence with accompanying health and fitness issues.

An additional source of stress observed in a rapidly changing work environment is having a boss or supervisor schooled in the "old" ways that prevailed before the technology was introduced. The new employee, trained in the latest methods and software skills, and probably qualified to a higher level in order to compete in a competitive job market, will experience overload stress (and possibly strain in relationships at work) if this job situation breeds contempt or, indeed, if the adequacy of supervision or management is questionable. Confidence and respect in the ability of those responsible for the efficient and safe operation of work are vital to good interpersonal relationships. However, as we have observed in Chapter 4, trust in those further down the managerial line does not always abound. Thus, the introduction of new technology might expose a supervisor to conflict and their own experience of qualitative overload.

In the next part of this chapter, we focus on the work that is "computer led", incorporating the trend towards electronic performance monitoring as a medium for communication and management, which exemplifies key challenges facing those organizations relying to a greater or lesser degree on new technology.

COMPUTER-BASED TECHNOLOGY

Advances in computer technology have radically changed our work environment in many ways. Manufacturing industries have witnessed the impact of technological changes due to automation for many decades. Since the Industrial Revolution, such changes have aimed to increase the amount of managerial control over production processes, reduce manpower requirements and labor costs in production jobs, and thereby reduce the cost of goods and increase profitability. Automation also aimed to reduce the level of physical and manual effort required by the work force. For example, robots do not become tired and robots do not strike! History has shown that changes towards a more automated work environment have been dramatic and turbulent, resulting in wildcat strikes, vandalism and violence, as workers resisted change and feared for the security of employment. These fears were not unfounded. The postwar manufacturing industry was characterized by a significant decrease in the number of people needed to operate machines and plant.

This trend continues as science and technology strive towards the fully-automated factory of the future. In 1988, Wright and Bourne suggested that advances in production engineering and computer science will result in "people-less production" by the year 2010. This did not happen, and with good reason, as other writers have offered caution and identified the restraining forces to prevent this becoming a reality. Nevertheless, the introduction of computer technology into the work environment has resulted in dramatic and sweeping change in human resource requirements and the nature of work. Large manufacturing plants already appear to be characterized by one common feature – a dearth of people! The number of personnel employed on production lines is minimal, and jobs are usually confined to the activities of production operators, seated at the console of computerized control panels. Their job is to monitor the machines, make decisions, and override malfunctioning highly-automated systems, while the equipment does the physical aspects of the task. Although we cannot classify all manufacturing industry in this simplistic way, it appears to be a trend. The stressful nature of underload has already been discussed in Chapter 4. However, there is a range of stress-related issues associated with automation and the use of computer technology in the work environment.

ELECTRONIC PERFORMANCE MONITORING

The introduction of computer technology and electronic monitoring has pervaded both the manufacturing and service sector at all occupational levels. While it is often assumed that the task and job demands associated with computer working are likely to result in stress, this need not be the case (Briner and Hockey, 1988) but, where it does, the negative impact on productivity is clear (Tarafdar *et al.*, 2007). Obviously, there is potential for stress to exist as information overload. Indeed, feelings of boredom might result in "rust out" or work underload conditions that can be stressful because the individual does not feel challenged or able to contribute at a cognitive level. However, these sources of stress are also found in non-computer based jobs. One of the keys is to involve the end user in the development phase of introducing new technology, which, in turn, can generate ownership and a sense of control (Weinberg and Cooper, 2007). Accordingly, the continued balance of control between employee and organization can be finely tuned to facilitate positive outcomes. The use of electronic performance monitoring (EPM) provides a salient example. Where employees view EPM as helpful in developing skills, there is greater positivity in their job attitudes and satisfaction, commitment to the organization and motivation to uphold their side of the psychological contract (Wells *et al.*, 2007). This underlines the importance of human resource practitioners taking care to help staff understand the role of EPM and providing feedback in a constructive manner. Where staff perceive EPM as shaping future behavior, their attitudes towards it (and, subsequently, the employment situation) are not as positive (Wells *et al.*, 2007). In addition, there has been concern that EPM can reduce employee privacy and raise workloads (Carayon, 1994). Technology can exert control, either at the machine or the system level, and the US Congress's Office of Technology Assessment (1987) defined the process of electronic work monitoring as, "the computerized collection, storage, analysis and reporting of information about employees' productive activities" (p. 27). Surveillance, regulation, control, and the reporting of processes, procedures and persons can all be achieved by computer monitoring. Real-time feedback can be provided that is instantaneous and objective. Therefore, computer control systems can be used to prevent internal theft and to enforce workplace rules, as well as monitor performance levels (Susser, 1988). The systems are designed and in place to monitor employees' performance or behavior unobtrusively, and performance measures include task completion rates, number of key strokes, or rate of errors. Computer work, such as data entry, is often paid on a key stroke basis. Consistent with this, the proportion of workers engaged in repetitive hand or arm movements for at least one quarter of their job grew in the five year period up to 2005, with almost two thirds of employees reporting this type of physical effort (Eurofound, 2005a).

The ethics and merits of using computers for surveillance have been the topic of much debate, not least in the guise of EPM. However, as Nebeker and Tatum (1993) have suggested, computer monitoring is not a unitary concept and can vary along certain dimensions, including:

- **Individual visibility:** This refers to the issue of monitoring of individuals versus groups of employees and the size of the group. Clearly, the impact of monitoring and the acceptance of it as an assessment of performance will be affected by this dimension.
- **Focus:** This refers to the behavioral focus of the monitoring – for example, a focus on activities or outcomes, or a focus on processes versus products.
- **Outcome control:** This concerns the issue of results monitoring and the degree to which the results have an effect on outcomes valued by the employees and how much it influences these outcomes.
- **Privacy:** This refers to the issues associated with access to the information collected – that is, is the information made public, seen only by the employee, or by management, or by both.
- **Timeliness:** This concerns the length of time between monitoring and information feedback.

- **Feedback medium:** Feedback can be given in real time, verbally in face-to-face communication or through computer generated reports. The medium used in feedback can be a determinant of credibility and reliability of the information received by the employee.
- **Tone:** This refers to the degree to which a monitoring system is designed to be "positive" versus "punitive".

The research evidence suggests that computer monitoring has both advantages and disadvantages. It permits management to set reasonable productivity goals, identify problems, price products and services, and reward high achieving employees (Sherizen, 1986). However on the other hand, it can lead to an emphasis on quantity to the detriment of work quality, resulting in job dissatisfaction and increased stress levels among the workforce (Harz, 1985). Increased time pressure, mood disturbance and musculoskeletal discomfort were all noted in an experimental study by Schleifer *et al.* (1996) that randomly allocated employees to EPM and non-EPM working conditions, providing evidence that basic job dimensions, including increased workload and reduced job control, contributed to employee experiences of psychological and physical strain. In this regard, employees can feel that their productivity levels had gone up, but that they are now working for the same pay (Irving *et al.*, 1986). Schleifer *et al.* recommended that production expectations are linked to workers' skills and abilities.

One of the main oppositions to computer monitoring is that it is an invasion of privacy. Research evidence indicates that other various deleterious effects might exist as low morale and poor health outcomes. The former can result from an adverse impact on team working, whereby reductions in employees' contact with co-workers and line managers are the potentially negative effects of computer monitoring. VDT users complain that they are lonelier at work and have less opportunity to develop social support networks. Performance monitoring, and the high level of information available to employees at the workstation terminal, reduces opportunities to move around the workplace in order to collect this material and, at the same time, engage in social contact (Aiello, 1993). The benefits of social support and supportive organizational climate as moderators of stress in the EPM work environment (Alder, 2001), and in directly reducing the perception of stress and pressure at work, were highlighted in the previous chapter. Therefore, the observed higher incidence of stress-related illnesses might be linked to the resulting decrease in social support in the work environment.

A variety of ill-health symptoms have been reported following the introduction of workplace monitoring. For example, Aeillo (1993) found that VDT workers were not as satisfied with their jobs as they had been, and described a greater number of physical symptoms, including eyestrain, headaches and musculoskeletal discomfort; effects that appear to manifest widely in call centers after four years (Lin *et al.*, 2009). In addition, VDT workers were more likely to feel irritable, anxious and depressed. Monitored workers can experience an increased amount of control over their activities and a lack of discretion in the job. As we have already observed, a lack of autonomy and discretion in a high-demand work condition translates into job strain, and is associated with reduced psychological and physical well-being. This is confirmed in applications of Karasek and Theorell's (1990) Job Strain Model to the work of information systems personnel (Love *et al.*, 2007). The organizational costs of this can be high if the "controlled" employee responds by behaving in undesirable ways, such as sabotage, withdrawal and diminished citizenship behavior (Kidwell and Bennett, 1994). These potential sources of challenge for those in a supervisory capacity are heightened by the need for them to actually spend time carrying out the monitoring process.

Given the commitment of organizations to ensure that costs are controlled, and that their initial investments in computers and accompanying software are protected, it is likely that EPM is not destined for immediate departure. However, it might not be the concept that is the problem, but, as with many other technological innovations impacting on the way we work, it is how we manage the interface between people and machines that counts. It is worth noting that research evidence has highlighted a number of factors that can facilitate the acceptance and success of computer-based work monitoring:

1 Managers should communicate the role and purpose of the computer monitoring system to employees in an effective way. Employees need to understand who will be monitored, why, what information is to be collected, and the purpose for which it is to be used.
2 Technological changes are often introduced without effective consultation with the workforce. Sometimes a new system or method is actually not fit for the purpose and it means that the employee is exposed to a new and unfamiliar work routine, thus creating a potentially stressful situation. The same will apply to the introduction of computer-based monitoring. It is suggested that resistance

to such a system will be lower, and acceptance is likely to be more positive, when employees are given the opportunity to take part in the design, setting up and implementation of computer-based performance monitoring (Aiello, 1993).

3 It is suggested that decisions about performance levels should be set in consultation with workers and in a flexible way (Long, 1984). This is key to the acceptance of new technology and change, and enhancing the quality of employees' work lives. This, of course, assumes that employees actually know that they are being monitored. Clearly, some organizations use surveillance devices without the knowledge or consent of the work force (Blinsky, 1991)!

4 Increasing the perception of job control helps to minimize the impact of high job demands and reduce levels of stress. Creating a sense of ownership and personal control over a computer-based monitoring system and process would reduce the stress associated with the introduction of this type of management control system. Acceptance of, and satisfaction with, new technology is related to "a sense of achievement" (Kaye and Sutton, 1985) and autonomy (Mankin et al., 1984). In relation to new technology, job control can be exercised at three levels (Sainfort, 1990).

- instrumental level – that is, feedback and control over pace, which corresponds to the task being performed by the employee
- conceptual level – that is, decision latitude, control over how tasks are carried out and work is scheduled, which involves conceptualization and cognitive processes
- organizational level – that is, participation in decision making and employee involvement.

Carayon (1993) suggests that computer-based monitoring systems have the potential to increase or decrease employee job control. For example, a monitoring system might be used to provide feedback to help workers gain instrumental control over a task. However, systems also have the potential to decrease levels of autonomy and decision making (conceptual control), so must be handled properly to ensure that this does not lead to negative outcomes and rejection of the monitoring system:

1 Perceived fairness of the system is a factor that plays a large part in determining affective reactions to workplace control (Kidwell and Bennett, 1994). Fairness judgments affect employee attitudes,

such as satisfaction as well as supervisor evaluation (Alexander and Ruderman, 1987; Lind and Tyler, 1988).

2 It is important that a system does not collect information that is unrelated to job performance. Employees must feel that their most important and appropriate tasks are being measured fairly, and that comparison of their performance with reasonable standards is being made (Aiello, 1993). If surveillance is made of non-work activities, such as bathroom trips, problems are likely because employees will feel that this is an invasion of their privacy. Therefore, EPM should be accurate, flexible, compatible with employees' moral and ethical values, and be based on collaborative design with the workers being monitored (Kidwell and Bennett, 1994).

As a guiding principle, Carayon (1993) states:

a system that collects data only on outcome quantity (completeness) or that overemphasises quantity at the expense of quality (change in relevant measure of performance) can be more stressful than a system that measures group performance as opposed to individual performance (unit of measure). A system that gathers a lot of detailed information on worker performance (intensiveness) can be more stressful than one that collects performance data infrequently (frequency) or continuously (continuousness) at predictable intervals (regularity). (p. 388)

Some authors believe that, if computer monitoring is managed and handled properly, it will not create the problems feared by its opponents. As Eisenman (1986) found, workers did not report concerns for a monitoring initiative because they had adapted to it, and had learned to minimize any of the possible negative effects of performance monitoring. Also, the perception existed that they were buffered from it by their supervisors. Nebeker and Tatum (1993) believe that organizations need to concern themselves with three main issues in the introduction and implementation of computer-based monitoring in the work environment:

- quality of working life – such as stress and health
- political rights of employees – such as rights of privacy, individual due process and legislative action
- economics – concerning the debate over monitoring and productivity.

Therefore, we must ask if "quantity" at any cost is truly our objective. Decisions need to be made about the role of "quality of work", "worker satisfaction", and the costs of stress in the work environment. We need to accept that these are important factors to be included in the calculation of the "real bottom line" in business profitability.

THE DEMANDS OF THE PHYSICAL ENVIRONMENT

In addition to the task demands of the job as a source of stress, it is important to consider the demands associated with the physical nature of the environment at work. These include the distress caused by noise and vibration, extremes of temperature, lighting, and hygiene factors, including levels of physical comfort. Many of these potential sources of stress were the focus of attention for early researchers who investigated the links between the physical conditions of the workplace and productivity levels (Munsterberg, 1913; Roethlisberger and Dickson, 1939). The significance of the relationships between emotional and social factors, performance and health was identified in these early studies. However, the work of Roethlisberger and Dickson, 1939, in the famous Hawthorne Studies, identified the significance and importance of "subjective reactivity" as a response in these conditions. They correctly identified the weakness of using only objective measures of these factors, and forced subsequent researchers to acknowledge that, "stress is in the eye of the beholder". While the early studies of stress at work attempted to identify the work conditions that were optimal for performance and productivity, Kornhauser (1965) found that unpleasant work conditions, the necessity to work at a fast pace, expend a great deal of physical effort, and work excessive and inconvenient hours were associated with poor mental health. Since then, research has continued to suggest that there is a need to consider poor physical environment as a source of strain in the workplace.

Piotrkowski et al. (1992) conducted a survey for the National Institute for Occupational Safety and Health (NIOSH) in the USA. This was a comprehensive study of the relationship of working conditions with health and well-being among women office workers, in the context of women's dual roles as employees and family members. Data was collected from 625 respondents in this study of both the public and private sectors. The results from questionnaire, interview and ergonomic data indicate that a poor organizational climate, lack of job control, excessive workload, interpersonal tension *and* a poor physical environment were related to greater strain. The European Foundation for the Improvement of Living and Working Conditions (Eurofound) survey (2005) found that stressful physical environments (characterized by noise, polluted air, heat, cold and vibration), carrying heavy loads, and working in painful or tiring positions continue to provide challenges to employee health. Across 25 EU member states, 20 percent of workers are exposed to breathing in smoke, powder or fumes, while almost 50 percent endure painful or tiring positions for at least one quarter of their time at work. Exposure to noise and vibrations has risen since 2000 and, in the following sections, these issues are considered, together with temperature (heat, cold, ventilation), hygiene and exposure to danger and hazard, as potential sources of stress in the physical work environment.

Noise

Whilst language and communication enrich human culture, "acoustic noise" – defined as "unwanted sound" (Jones, 1983) – can be a source of stress. Two health hazards are linked with exposure to noise in the environment: first, the risk of occupational deafness; second, that, as a source of stress, noise increases a person's level of arousal and might cause some psychological imbalance. Exposure to noise can also impede hearing ability and cause a situation to become dangerous if a "wanted" sound is not heard. For example, an accident can occur if warning sounds are not audible (Poulton, 1978). The extent to which noise, as a source of stress, can cause an increased level of arousal and a psychological imbalance is still debated. Ivancevich and Matteson (1980) suggest that excessive noise (of approximately 80 decibels, on a recurring, prolonged basis) can cause stress. The noise from a pneumatic chipper is measured at around 130 decibels. Our pain threshold is 140 decibels (Oborne, 1994), whereas 70 decibels is normal conversational speech and a bedroom at night is measured at 30 decibels. However, noise operates less as a stressor in situations where it is excessive but expected, rather than in those circumstances where it is unpredictable or unexpected. This helps to make noise the top environmental challenge in open plan offices, where speech acts as the principal distraction, due to its unpredictability, loudness and content (Hongisto *et al.*, 2008). Phones, footsteps and other activities follow in the unofficial hierarchy of distracting noise, whereas we become accustomed more easily to noise produced by ventilation, traffic and computers. Considered in this way, it becomes clear how speech can prove detrimental to concentration and cognitive performance in such a setting. However, there are jobs where it is imperative to listen to the speech of others and working in the burgeoning call centre industry has been linked with increased incidence of both tinnitus and a hoarse or painful throat (Lin *et al.*, 2009).

However, it also appears that personality characteristics mediate the response to noise as a source of stress. Belojevi *et al.* (1997) suggest that those at risk from noise are those who are more often characterized by anxiety. Although noise can be expressed in objective, physical terms according to its intensity, variability, frequency, predictability and control, reaction to noise is ultimately a subjective experience. Exposure to noise is associated with reported fatigue, headaches, irritability and poor concentration. Behavioral consequences include reduced performance, lowered productivity levels and accident occurrence. It is also possible that there is some adverse impact on our social behavior. Exposure to noise can reduce our willingness to help other people, and increase levels of hostility and overt aggression towards those people around us. Thus, when exposed to noise, we exhibit a more extreme or negative attitude towards others (Jones, 1983). This will lead to poor relationships in the workplace as a consequence of imposed isolation due to excessive noise, or the need to wear hearing protection.

Nevertheless, the main psychosocial impact of "noise" and other physical environmental demands is to reduce worker tolerance to other stressors, and to adversely affect the level of worker motivation (Smith *et al.*, 1978). These forms of stress in the workplace are known as "noise factors", since they take up the attention of the individual and limit capacity to attend to task-relevant information (Hockey, 1972). This explains why a large-scale review of the impact of office design on employees found "strong evidence that working in open workplaces reduces privacy and job satisfaction", suggesting that this type of work environment also increases demands on cognitive factors and leads to deteriorations in employees' interpersonal relations (De Croon *et al.*, 2005). However, noise as a harmful source of stress is reported by many groups of blue collar workers. For example, those in the UK steel industry (Kelly and Cooper, 1981) and personnel working on offshore drilling rigs and platforms report noise as a potent source of stress (Hellesøy, 1985; Sutherland and Cooper, 1986, 1991b). Indeed, unpleasant working conditions due to noise were associated with job dissatisfaction among offshore workers. Cohen (1974, 1976) observed an increased rate of accidents in noisy working areas, particularly among the younger and the less experienced employees. The introduction of hearing protection among these employees produced a significant reduction in the frequency of accident occurrence.

In summary, therefore, the impact of noise is a cause for concern for the following reasons:

- a narrowed focus of attention, which has detrimental effects on performance of complex tasks.
- noise that is unpredictable and uncontrollable reduces one's overall perception of control over the environment. This is often accompanied by a depressed mood and a decrease in motivation to initiate new response. This is described as "learned helplessness".
- research evidence suggests that performance remains impaired after exposure to noise, which reduces tolerance to everyday frustrations.
- physiological arousal to noise includes increased blood pressure and other stress related hormones (adrenalin and cortisol).
- exposure to noise levels of 85 decibels (or greater) at work for three to five years is associated with an increased prevalence of a variety of specific non-auditory diseases – such as cardiovascular disorders, gastrointestinal complaints, and infectious diseases. Disease prevalence seems to be greater when the noise is unpredictable or intermittent (Welch, 1979).
- exposure to noise is associated with a variety of negative, behavioral outcomes including a reduction in helping behavior, and a more extreme or negative attitude towards other people. Thus, there are implications for impoverished relationships and team working in a noisy work environment.
- call centre employees with over two years' length of service have a significantly raised risk of tinnitus. More than four years service is strongly associated with discomfort in all areas of the body (Lin *et al.*, 2009).

Vibration

Sound, at the low end of the range, is felt as vibration. Noise below 16Hz is described as infrasound, as this can be produced by any pulsating or throbbing piece of equipment (such as ventilation systems). The experience of driving on rough ground (for example, tractor drivers) can cause vibration levels that might lead to structural damage to the body, over time (Rosegger and Rosegger, 1960). The drivers in this survey, exposed to the vibration of driving a vehicle over a long period of time, complained of spinal disorders in the lumbar and thoracic regions of the body, as well as stomach complaints.

The health hazards of exposure to "vibration" at the high frequency end of the range include loss of balance and fatigue; numbness or clumsiness of the fingers; and possible damage to bones, muscles and joints, and the condition known as "white finger". It is acknowledged as a source of stress that results in elevated catecholamine levels and alterations to psychological and neurological functioning (Wilkinson, 1969; Selye, 1976). The vibration of rotary or impacting machines (for example, road drills and chain saws) that cause vibrations to transfer from physical objects to the body might lead to performance deterioration. In addition, the "annoyance" factor can also contribute to some psychological imbalance. Personnel working in the steel casting industry (Kelly and Cooper, 1981) and the offshore oil and gas industries (Sutherland and Cooper, 1986, 1991b) are exposed to vibration as a source of stress. Although these individuals claim "you get used to it", unpleasant working conditions due to vibration and disturbance in the living quarters were rated as significant stressors in the offshore working environment. The long-term impact of exposure to vibration is known to include damage to hands and fingers, as well as chronic back pain (HSE, 2010a).

Temperature, ventilation and lighting

Inadequate illumination is an obvious contributory factor in accident occurrence. Thus, the aims of a good lighting system are to facilitate performance of the job, to ensure that the work can be carried out safely, and to assist in creating a pleasant environment (McKenna, 1994). Poor lighting, the flicker of fluorescent lights, or glare, lead to eye strain, damaged vision, visual fatigue, headache, tension and frustration. Also, the job is likely to be more difficult and time-consuming to complete (Poulton, 1978). However, the findings from the Hawthorne Studies (Roethlisberger and Dickson, 1939) indicate that creating a pleasant environment, one that that facilitates performance and promotes safety, is not a simple matter of the objective measurement of lighting levels in the workplace. Architects have tried to combat the problems of illumination and "glare" by designing the "windowless" workplace, and rely on artificial lighting. However, in one study of a windowless office environment, while there were very few complaints about the quality of the artificial lighting, 90 per cent of employees who worked on their own expressed dissatisfaction about the absence of windows. They complained about the lack of a view, daylight, poor ventilation, and a lack of awareness about the state of the weather (Ruys, 1970).

Ramsey (1983) states that physiological response to thermal conditions varies greatly between workers and within the same individual from one occasion to the next. Attitudinal and physical problems arise because the factory environment is characterized and described by workers as too hot, too cold, too stuffy, too draughty, and so on (Smith et al., 1978). Manual dexterity can be reduced in a cold environment. This might be a factor in accident causation – due most likely to reduced sensitivity, slowed movement and interference from protective clothing, rather than from the loss of impaired cognitive ability (Surry, 1968). However, work that requires critical decision making and fine discrimination, and performance needing fast or skilled actions might also be adversely affected by exposure to thermal stress. Thus, the subjective perception of thermal comfort is all-important. It seems, also, that an inability to control one's physical work environment personally could also be a key factor in the perception of thermal discomfort. For example, Ramsey (1983) observed an association between "comfort" and an individual's performance on perceptual motor tasks.

Noise, fumes and the heat were the most commonly reported problems for casters in the steel industry (Kelly and Cooper, 1981). In the Norwegian offshore oil and gas environment, draughts, uncomfortable temperatures and the dry air were perceived as sources of environmental stress (Hellesøy, 1985). However, it was also noted that workers were more likely to complain about overheated work conditions (25 per cent of respondents) than the cold (12 per cent of respondents). The general effect of working in overheated conditions is a negative reaction to one's surroundings, and this can result in a lowered tolerance to other stressors and lead to a reduction in worker motivation.

A combination of the above environmental factors has been implicated in the existence of "sick building syndrome" (SBS), which itself has achieved some notoriety, not least for its rather imprecise definition (symptoms include nausea, headaches, and so on). However, a large-scale survey of UK civil servants has highlighted the significant contribution of psychological, and not physical, factors to explaining the prevalence of the problems associated with SBS. Taking into account airborne bacteria, dust, light bulb temperature and relative humidity, Marmot *et al.* (2006) found that high workloads, low levels of social support, and control over one's physical environment were the key predictors of employee health. This provides further confirmation of the importance of factors identified as contributors to job strain at work.

Hygiene

A clean and orderly place of work is important for both hygiene and safety reasons, and it is acknowledged that, as housekeeping standards in the workplace improve, the level of accidents is likely to decrease. Poor hygiene standards are likely to cause poor health or disease, and have an adverse impact on the level of morale of the workforce. Shostack (1980) reports blue collar grievances about the often neglected working conditions and the double standards that exist in industry. The all-glass, lavish "front offices" and headquarters accommodation are compared with the noise, lack of windows and air conditioning in dirty and poorly maintained factories and workshops. Likewise, workers in the steel industry described their dirty, dusty conditions, the poor accommodation provided for rest periods and the lack of lavatory facilities nearby (Kelly and Cooper, 1981). These features of the physical work environment were rated as key sources of stress among steel casting crews. In a dirty work environment, it is more likely that employees are exposed to the inhalation of dust and vapors from inefficiently stored chemical-based products. In addition to good housekeeping standards, employees must also be provided with the correct protective clothing and apparatus, and also actively encouraged to use them.

Exposure to danger and hazard

Various occupational groups are exposed to physical dangers at work. While police officers, prison service personnel, fire fighters, mine workers and military personnel face obvious physical dangers and potential harm as part of the job, other workers are also exposed to physical hazards at work. These include a variety of customer service and clerical workers who, by virtue of their job, have to face and deal with aggressive and sometimes violent clients, customers and criminal offenders. Thus, many building societies and housing departments now offer training in dealing with physical assault and abuse incidents. Others provide a counseling service for those who have become victims of these frightening situations and who suffer psychological trauma as a result.

The risks and hazards to blue collar workers tend to be different, in that the hazard arises from exposure to the dangers of plant, machinery, chemicals and so on. Inhalations of certain vapors, gases and dust are potential hazards in the workplace. Although strict controls are in place, incidents leading to injury do occur, and businesses continue to be prosecuted by the UK Health and Safety Executive (HSE) for breach of the rules and regulations. Despite the recognized dangers of substances such as asbestos, some companies are found negligent of providing adequate protection to their own staff and, indeed, members of the public who later return to use the building – including a school, in one case.

Failure to protect workers while using potentially hazardous machinery, or an inability to provide safe systems of work also leads to prosecution. Each month, the HSE provides a bulletin report on these incidents and the fines imposed. Clearly, it indicates that the work environment for the blue collar employee still poses dangers, hazards and risk to life. For example, organizations are still being fined £1000s for inadequate guarding of machinery and equipment, or omitting to provide adequate training to operate machinery. The failure to provide safe systems of work can result in injuries ranging from serious internal injuries to amputation while operating or cleaning machinery, or even the death of an employee when structures collapse or are in disrepair. Fines are often levied against the guilty party, and where death has occurred custodial sentences for manslaughter have been handed down.

CHAPTER 6

CONDUCTING A STRESS AUDIT

We have argued for an organizational approach to the management of stress, but also acknowledge that a successful stress management package will need to operate from more than one level. Indeed, a number of stress researchers have pointed out that stress control can be successful only if it is tackled at the level of the individual *and* the organization (Giga *et al.*, 2003). Therefore:

- we should operate at an organizational level to prevent or limit stress where this is a possible and reasonably practicable solution (Elkin and Rosch, 1990).
- we can work with individuals, teams or groups, to educate and train employees to cope more effectively with sources of stress that cannot be removed from the job. However, we need to ensure that the weaknesses of this approach are overcome.
- we must also have in place strategies to deal with employees who "fall through the net" to become victims of exposure to stress, since no organizational intervention is likely to be perfect or foolproof. Individuals are complex and unique, and so they vary in their response to stress. Therefore, a stress management solution for one individual will not suit all employees or occupational groups.

This holistic, organizational approach to stress management is discussed fully in Chapter 7. At this point, we must ask how we choose the best course of action. Many options are available for the management of stress. Some of these initiatives are complex, time-consuming to implement, potentially disruptive and sometimes costly. Few organizations would be prepared to commit themselves to change, and an extensive organizational developmental program, without justification of its necessity, and a means of evaluating the effectiveness of the initiative. Similarly, the provision of, for example, counseling services or an exercise fitness facility without first consulting with employees (on the need for these particular methods of stress control, an assessment of the potential usefulness of them, and the perceived benefits to be gained) might otherwise be a waste of organizational resources. In order to identify a course of action, we need to identify:

- whether a potential problem exists
- whether the cause of the problem can be identified – whether it is stress related
- who is affected by the situation
- what employees need in place to overcome the problem or potential problem.

In order to understand the nature of stress and to design an appropriate stress management program, we suggest that it is necessary to conduct a stress audit or psychological risk assessment.

In order to implement an effective stress control program, it is necessary to identify and measure the sources of stress that exist in the workplace. These should include the sources of stress that spill over from home and family life to act as barriers to performance effectiveness and well-being. This process is known as "conducting a stress audit". It can also be referred to as "a psychological risk assessment". Human resources personnel and health and safety managers are familiar with the system and practice of conducting risk assessments, since this is a legal workplace requirement. A psychological risk assessment is quite similar in many ways, but some of the tools and methods are somewhat different.

Until we can identify sources of stress, known as "stressors", it is unlikely that our stress management activities will be focused or successful. Clarification of the term "stress", an understanding of the potential sources of stress in our environment, and recognition of our response to stress are all vital steps in the effective management of stress. Since it is likely that different groups will experience different problems, and research findings are variable, it is important that a stress audit identifies specific problems, as well as high risk, vulnerable workers. We need to ask why some individuals handle difficult situations and thrive in a demanding environment, while others clearly do not prosper, or even survive. Research evidence suggests that this "tailored" approach, which aims to increase our understanding of human behavior in the workplace, has many potential benefits for the organization. Improved productivity, good health, and safety performance are just some of these benefits. The ultimate advantage can be an important determinant of business success in a highly competitive business climate.

THE STRESS AUDIT PROCESS

Under the terms of our definition of stress, any situation or condition is potentially stressful, and so it is necessary to distinguish between positive and negative pressures in the workplace. To identify the action to be taken is it vital in order to diagnose the problem accurately. Therefore, we must ask: what, who, where, why, when and how? This is the essential function of the stress audit. However, it must be conducted in a systematic and objective way.

Benefits of a stress audit

The benefits of a stress audit are:

- As a diagnostic instrument it is a proactive, rather than a reactive, approach to the management of stress at work.
- A stress audit aims to identify organizational and individual strengths and weaknesses in a similar manner to that of an appraisal or an analysis of training and development needs. Therefore, it helps the organization to target scarce budgetary and time resources.
- The audit enables us to identify both target and strategy for stress management actions. These can be classified under three headings. First, primary prevention, which is a stressor-directed strategy that aims either to eliminate or to minimize the source of stress. Next, is the classification known as secondary prevention. This is a response-directed strategy that aims to help the individual or group respond to the source of stress in an appropriate and effective manner. Finally, the tertiary stress management strategies are "symptom-directed" initiatives that are intended to treat victims of exposure to mismanaged stress.
- A diagnostic stress audit provides a baseline measure from which to evaluate subsequent interventions.

■ The action of conducting a stress audit helps to make "stress" a respectable topic for discussion in the workplace. By using a stress audit to understand workplace stress problems and the perceptions of employees to both problems and possible solutions, it is likely that resistance to change, associated with the subsequent introduction of stress management interventions, will be reduced. Employee participation and involvement in a well-conducted stress audit will help to reduce any threat or fear associated with potentially sensitive stress-related issues in the workplace. It is important that feedback of the results of the stress audit is provided to employees. The mechanism for this and the scope of the feedback should be decided and mutually agreed by all parties involved before the process begins. This includes management, the employees taking part and those conducting the audit.

Components of a stress audit: What should be measured?

Essentially, there are five key components to the stress audit process. The focus of such an audit can vary, given existing areas for concern; however, by adopting a broad approach in the first instance, a model of occupational stress that is relevant to the workplace in question can be developed – for example, the model developed by the UK's Health and Safety Executive (HSE) described in Chapter 4.

1 **Identifying sources of stress**: First, we need to identify and measure the sources of stress that exist. In research terms, these are called "independent variables". The HSE model emphasizes demands, control, support, roles, relationship and the management of change and has its own 35-item Management Standards Indicator Tool that aims to assess these (HSE, 2009a). However, other well-known stress audit tools, such as ASSET (A Shortened Stress Evaluation Tool; Faragher et al., 2004), are specifically designed to act as a relatively brief screening instrument for identifying "problem" areas within an organization. The authors recommend that its length aids cost-effectiveness by allowing managers to focus on those areas requiring intervention, but also recognize the role for more detailed follow-up. In this way, information can be obtained that will say more about the difficulties experienced by individual staff. ASSET explores employees' job perceptions and potential sources of stress: relationships at work, overload, control,

job security, resources and communication, work-life balance, pay and benefits, employee attitudes and commitment to the organization, and perceived organizational support, as well as symptoms of physical and psychological strain.

2 **Strain-related outcomes**: Measures of stress outcomes include performance indicators such as quality or customer complaints. Measures such as sickness absence levels, physical symptoms of ill health, accident rates, job satisfaction levels, labor turnover rates, and levels of anxiety or depression are also "outcome" measures. In effect, these are the "symptoms" of exposure to the experience of stress and, in research terms, they are described as "dependent variables". For example, we might be interested in understanding the impact of hours of work (the potential source of stress) on levels of depression or job satisfaction.

3 **Individual differences**: Identification and measurement of the individual differences that can moderate or mediate the stress response. These include a wide variety of individual differences that act to shape our response to exposure to stress, such as:
- biographical and demographic differences – for example, gender, race, occupation, education level, and socio-economic status
- physical condition – for example, levels of fitness and health, life stage, diet and eating habits, exercise activity, sleep patterns, relaxation activities, hobbies or interests
- Personality traits and behavioral characteristics – for example, extroversion, neuroticism, need for achievement or power, internality versus externality (perceived degree of control), tolerance for ambiguity, Type A Coronary Prone behavior pattern, needs, values. This list is not exhaustive, and many more examples could be included. However, it begins to explain the diversity of individual differences as outcomes and symptoms observed in response to the experience of stress. It helps us to understand why people respond in such varied ways to a common source of stress. Indeed, we can say, "one person's meat is another person's poison". This, of course, makes it difficult for the decision makers in an organization to plan a holistic stress management strategy. Nevertheless, it is possible to identify the key stressors that appear to act to have a negative impact on the majority of the group, team or department. Then, an informed decision on the most viable and acceptable method for stress control can be made.

4 **Predictors of stress**: Identification of stressor predictors of the outcome measures, that is, the dependent variables. In simple terms, this means that we use a technique (regression analysis) that will identify the factors most strongly associated with a given outcome measure. For example, in a stress audit conducted among general practitioners in the UK (Sutherland, 1995) it was observed that the strongest predictors of levels of depression were:

- the high level of demand in the job itself and patients' expectations of the doctors
- the stress associated with trying to balance work and home life demands
- low use of social support as a strategy for coping with the experience of stressful situations and conditions.

Thus, the strategies recommended for stress control among general practitioners were to:

- initiate a campaign to educate the general public about the role of the general practitioner, particularly with respect to night calls and locum duties.
- increase levels of social support by having regular meetings after surgery hours, and extending these sessions into a social gathering that included partners and spouses.

Both of these recommendations were successfully implemented to great effect by one large general practice group in the South-West of England. They included general practitioners, practice managers, nurses and administrative staff in these sessions. The meetings were used to solve problems and plan future strategies. Opportunity for resolving role conflict situations, which were previously rife, were especially welcomed by the group, and the initiative was deemed to be a great success.

5 **Staff attitudes**: Ascertaining and measuring staff attitudes to the options available for the management of stress – that is, acknowledging and understanding what employees need and want in place in order to remove the stressor barriers to their effectiveness, productivity, health and satisfaction at work. In this part of the audit process, it is important to ensure that employee expectations remain realistic about the options and potential for the management of a stressful situation. If unrealistic expectations are raised but not realized, it is likely that the stressor problem can become exacerbated. This appears to be one area that most threatens the human resources management group and deters them from

embarking on a stress audit. It is often referred to as, "opening a can of worms" but finding that "you can do nothing about the situation". Again, much of this problem can be avoided before the audit process begins. Clear and consistent communications about the remit and scope of the audit are essential. One large pharmaceutical company avoided potential problems by setting up multilevel teams to discuss the audit findings and to identify potential solutions. Possible methods of controlling a source of stress were considered by using a SWOT analysis (Ansoff, 1969). Thus, the strengths, weaknesses, opportunities and threats that faced the group and organization were listed and used in the decision making process.

Stress audit instruments

A wide variety of techniques and measures are available for use when conducting a stress audit. These include arranging focus group discussion sessions, conducting one-to-one or group interviews, the completion of stress logs or diaries, the use of critical incident techniques, and the administration of questionnaires. Certain standardized measures are available, and these have the advantage of providing normative data comparisons. The use of computerized testing has simplified this procedure considerably, although care must still be taken to ensure that the assessment tool has been developed in accordance with recognized test procedures.

One extensively used instrument is ASSET, which is increasingly used as a brief assessment of stress in the workplace and is the successor to the Occupational Stress Indicator (Cooper, Sloan and Williams, 1988). Based on models of stress (see Chapter 3) and borrowing from the positive psychology movement, ASSET includes measures of both the positive and negative aspects of the workplace:

- strengths as well as sources of pressure with respect to the job itself, including balanced workload, a sense of control within the job role, job security, interpersonal relationships, levels of resource to carry out the job and work-life balance interface
- individual personality characteristics linked to effective behavior at work, as well as intrinsic and extrinsic motivators – such as a sense of purpose, and acceptable pay and benefits

■ measures of the individual and organizational symptoms stress – covering psychological well-being, productivity, attachment to the organization, levels of engagement, motivation and commitment (RobertsonCooper, 2007).

By using a coding system in the administration process, a stress audit measure can be used anonymously, and the data can be collected and analyzed without breaching confidentiality which, in turn, helps to ensure honesty in reporting. A highly effective stress audit tool can be used in conjunction with a stressor item bank designed specifically for a given occupational group. For example, in a study of occupational stress in the social services, the audit was the main instrument of measurement and was supported by a stressor item bank developed through in-depth interview sessions conducted with social workers and home help staff (Bradley and Sutherland, 1995).

Other similar measures include, The Generic Job Stress Questionnaire which was developed in the US by the National Institute for Occupational Safety and Health (NIOSH, 2008). This instrument makes an assessment of different job stressors, in addition to providing measures of reactions to job strain. It is designed to be modular so that organizations can select individual scales with known reliability and validity.

While the questionnaires described provide a comprehensive tool for use in the stress audit process, there is a plethora of diagnostic instruments available to measure specific variables. Researchers are likely to select from an enormous battery of self-completion measures in order to design their own audit packages. The General Health Questionnaire (GHQ), which has been widely used in studies of workplace well-being, is available in many versions and lengths – for example, GHQ-12 (Goldberg and Williams, 1988). It is suitable for assessing psychological health inside and outside of work, however Warr's Job-Related Well-Being Scale (1996, in Mullarkey *et al.*, 1999) has been specifically designed for use in organizations, and is also a popular choice of audit instrument (it has both six- and 12-item versions). This assesses employee well-being along two axes, one extending from anxiety to contentment and the other from depression to enthusiasm. In addition, the 15-item job satisfaction scale measure (Warr *et al.*, 1979) has been widely used to explore employees' views of key aspects of the workplace, and is quick and simple to administer. A huge selection of single variable measures is described in the literature for the purpose of measuring both dependent and independent variables.

O'Driscoll and Cooper (1994) recommend the use of a "critical incident analysis" as a method of identifying stress and stress-coping processes in work settings. This technique was first described by Flanagan (1954). Essentially, the process consists of asking individuals to describe stressful transactions in terms of three elements:

- the antecedents or circumstances in which the stress occurred
- their response in that situation, together with the responses of other people
- the consequences of both their own and other individuals' behavior.

We also use this method in our "stress log" (see Appendix). Individuals are asked to describe the most stressful experience of the day, what happened, what they did in the situation, the other people involved and, on reflection what they might have done differently. The critical incident technique can be used in an interview situation to ask individuals to describe the job-related events that they believe to have placed demands upon them or caused them difficulties. It is important that the individual is encouraged to be specific and non-emotive about the incident. For example, "reprimanded by my supervisor for being late for work – felt angry all day" is too general a description of stress and not sufficiently specific. "My day was disrupted because I was reprimanded by my supervisor for arriving late for work; my alarm did not go off", is a specific and non-emotive description of the event. It assists the individual in eliminating this particular source of stress in the future, either by ensuring that the alarm clock does work, or by the purchase of a new one! It is also necessary to establish how the employee coped with the reprimand and responded to this situation. Clearly, a negative reaction is one that results in an argument with the supervisor. It is not an appropriate coping behavior. Behaving in a disruptive manner for the remainder of the work shift is also likely to be equally damaging in its consequences. Therefore, in the final stage of this process, the individual is asked how they felt about the consequences of their behavior in response to the situation. It is important that the interviewer does not try to judge or evaluate the individual's coping process until the process of stress identification is completed. When the employee has described a series of such incidents, the analysis will reveal specific stressors, behaviors and consequences, in addition to coping style trends and preferences. This technique can be used to identify key sources of stress among a particular occupational group, team or for a specific individual in the organization.

It is important for the organization to consider what information is already available from existing company records, to support the findings from self-report data obtained from questionnaire instruments, stress logs, or critical incident analysis. These might include, for example, sickness absence records, accident reports, grievance records, labor turnover figures and the cost of compensation claims.

Some companies have incorporated a psychological risk assessment into employee medical examinations. Typically, personnel from the occupational health department or an external organization will conduct this part of the program. While the employee is waiting to see a doctor or nurse, they might be required to complete an online version of a stress audit tool. This offers the advantage of computer scoring and the facility of producing a stress profile immediately on completion of the questionnaire. The data are stored and used to produce in-house, company norms. These can be compared with either the general population scores or some similar occupational group. Consultants are also often employed to assist with the audit that is being managed and directed by either a personnel director or a human resources group. There are, of course, pros and cons for both of these approaches.

CONDUCTING A STRESS AUDIT: WHO DOES IT?

An audit conducted by personnel internal to the organization gains benefit because it is carried out by those individuals who already know much about the business. Unfortunately, this can also mean that the research results can be distorted. This is not deliberate, but due to the preconceived notions of the individuals involved. These perceptual distortions or errors are caused by stereotyping, the halo effect, perceptual defense and projection:

■ **Stereotyping**: This is the tendency to ascribe positive or negative characteristics to a person on the basis of a general categorization and perceived similarities. Therefore, the perception might be based on certain expectations, rather than on the recognition of that person as an individual. It is a means of simplifying the process of perception and making judgments of other people. We can base our stereotypes on many factors, including nationality, occupation, age, physical state, gender, education, social status or politics. For example, occupation, "all accountants are boring"; social status, "all unemployed people are lazy".

- **Halo effect**: This is the process by which the perception of a person is formulated on the basis of one favorable or unfavorable trait or impression. Thus, the effect tends to shut out other relevant characteristics of the person. For example, a single trait (such as good attendance or timekeeping) might become the main emphasis for judgment of overall competence and performance, rather than other considerations (such as the quantity or quality of work).
- **Perceptual defense**: This is the tendency to screen out certain stimuli that are disturbing or threatening. Thus, we select information that is supportive of our point of view and choose to ignore less favorable information.
- **Projection**: This is the tendency for people to project their own feelings, characteristics and motives on to their perception of other people. Thus, judgment of other people is likely to be favorable when they have characteristics in common with the perceiver. However, it also means that projection will result in the exaggeration of undesirable traits in others that they fail to recognize in themselves.

On a practical note, we must also consider whether internally employed personnel fulfill the following requirements:

- Do they have enough time to conduct a potentially lengthy and time-consuming project? It is vital that those involved are able to demonstrate their commitment to the project overtly and actively. If the audit is not seen to be a priority activity, then it is unlikely that the workforce will take it seriously and the rate of participation will be too low to provide meaningful and valid results.
- Do they have the appropriate skills and qualifications to do the audit?
- Can they be objective and remain discreet in order to guarantee confidentiality?
- Is there likely to be any risk of breach of ethics?
- Do they have the trust and respect of the staff that are being audited?

- Is there a possibility that they might be influenced, directly or indirectly, by other stakeholders or "politicians" within the company? Pressure from powerful others can result in information being withheld, omitted, or distorted, thereby corrupting the results of the audit or risk assessment.

The use of an external body to conduct the stress audit will overcome many of the concerns expressed, particularly those associated with the issues of objectivity and confidentiality. However, these individuals will know little about the company initially. Thus, they will need to spend time becoming familiar with the culture and climate of the organization. Also, it is likely that the costs are certain to be higher. The use of computers for the administration, scoring and interpretation of audit instruments has helped many companies to be almost self-sufficient in the stress audit process. However, many still prefer to use external agencies in a nominal way in order to add credibility and objectivity to the audit exercise. Audit data analysis can be a lengthy procedure, since the results should identify differences – for example, between departments, job grades, gender, age, length of service, location, and so on. This will ensure that the required stress control actions are targeted specifically where they are needed in order to be successful and cost effective.

INTEGRATING A STRESS AUDIT INTO CURRENT RISK ASSESSMENT PROCESSES

We have already advised that it is important to identify data already available within the organization and to integrate this into the risk assessment process. Ideally, a stress audit should not become a "stand alone" exercise within the company. Indeed, it is also worth considering whether the term "stress audit" is to be used, given that the word "stress" still has negative connotations in the workplace. This is partly the reason for the increasing popularity of the phrase "well-being". Whereas a "stress audit" might be perceived as a threat to both managers and staff, a survey of employee well-being suggests a rather more positive spin. If employees greet the audit with suspicion and suspect some other "real" purpose, they will feel threatened. They will also feel that they are being blamed for not coping with stress and will try to overcome this by denying that any stress-related problems exist. Typically, in this situation, employees will try to emulate swans, who glide serenely on the surface of a smooth lake, appearing to be calm and in control. However, just like a swan, all the frantic activity remains hidden beneath the surface! This is similar, in certain respects, to the problems encountered when conducting performance appraisals. Thus, it is now acknowledged that, to be effective, it is necessary to conduct separate appraisals for the purpose of employee development and training, and for purposes intended for promotion and pay awards assessment. Ultimately, the objective of a stress audit is to optimize the performance and health (that is, the well-being and quality of life) of employees, so why not describe it as that and avoid using the word "stress" in such a high-profile way.

STRESS AUDIT CASE STUDIES

In the final stress section of this chapter, we describe three different stress audits, demonstrating their use and potential for heralding positive changes at work. The first spearheaded a business case for improving employee well-being and producing a culture change in a UK County Council and has been recognized as a "Beacon of Excellence" by the Health and Safety Commission.

Tackling stress at Somerset County Council

Early in the millennium, the UK government initiated "Best Value" reviews to ensure compliance with standards of service in its public sector organizations. Naturally, such policy-led changes impacted on employees' working practices and conditions. Somerset County Council has approximately 17,000 staff, and was experiencing considerable costs due to sickness absence, totaling in the region of £3.7 million in 2001/02. Concerned about the mounting likelihood of litigation in relation to stress, the Council commissioned an audit to identify the potential sources, location and severity of stress in its workforce (RobertsonCooper, 2007). The ASSET was used but, prior to taking baseline measures, important political steps were taken to ensure that commitment from top-level management was established, and that the Quality of Working Life (QWL) initiative was incorporated in the Council's "People Strategy". The stress audit formed the basis for developing a stress prevention strategy, accompanied by an action plan that highlighted "aims, responsibilities, resources and time frames for resolving any problems identified across the organization". The QWL project team comprised representatives from all the principal stakeholders, which ensured that managers, trades unions and employees were able to contribute to the action plan. This resulted in a range of interventions at different levels of Somerset County Council. Initiatives aimed at individual employees included skills training to help staff deal with critical incidents such as conflict and aggression from members of the public, while, at a group level, managers received training to manage their own and their team members' stress more effectively. At a strategic level, training for managers and staff in the use and deployment of performance review systems sought to encourage increased effectiveness without producing stress at work.

At the outset of the project, average sickness absence levels were 10.8 days per year for each employee. After three years, this dropped to an average of 7.2 days. Over this time, the Council's "People Strategy" had also become embedded within the culture of the organization and a total of £4.2m was saved in sickness absence costs (bearing in mind the intervention cost of £510,000). As a consequence, there were reduced costs for Somerset Council's Occupational Health and Counselling provision, improved staff retention rates and the satisfaction of ensuring not simply compliance with legislation, but also achieving government sickness absence targets. Peter Rowe, Head of Human Resources at the Council, said:

> We have achieved cost saving of over 1 million per annum. We had assumed that we would need to employ more staff, but realized it would have made the problem worse.

Improving well-being at Kent Police

Employing approximately 6200 officers, stationed at over twenty locations, Kent Police has developed the goal of ensuring high levels of well-being and performance among its employees. A 2003 survey conducted using the ASSET confirmed the need for improved levels of well-being as stress, poor health and fitness were identified as main contributors to absenteeism. It was found that line managers were not best positioned to identify the symptoms of stress and, furthermore,

145

did not always have the necessary capacity to help staff cope. At the time of the initial survey, levels of perceived support from the organization were lower than in other police forces, a finding that was consistent with higher reporting of resourcing and communication issues. In addition, stress-related hot spots were identified that included the Control Room Call Centre, Crime Investigation, the Custody Suite, IT and Special Operations.

Based on the findings of this baseline survey, the consulting organization proposed recommendations, and a working party from Kent Police was appointed to produce an action plan for integration into ongoing change initiatives (RobertsonCooper, 2007). A number of interventions were launched, incorporating the psychological screening of staff in areas that involved highly sensitive work, such as child protection, as well as the implementation of a new attendance management program and the introduction of "well person" checks. The new attendance program trained managers to identify trigger points for stress and absenteeism, and provided a framework for highlighting potential issues before problems developed. The W8wise@work campaign helped Kent Police to provide its employees with advice on diet and fitness, as well as raise awareness over key health issues, offering "Health MOTs" to staff.

Two years after the first stress audit, a follow-up survey found that the previously identified barriers to well-being had decreased, employees perceived greater support from the organization, the organization noted increased levels of commitment from its staff, improved levels of psychological and physical health were reported, and there had been a 25 percent drop in sickness absence. The reduction in the costs of absenteeism to the police force were equivalent to three more working days per year per employee (18,600), leading Kent Police to share its experience of best practice with other UK Forces.

Creating a business case for staff support at Salford University

Changes in the university sector in the UK and elsewhere have transformed the job of lecturers in the higher education sector. Increased levels of psychological strain had been noted in national surveys, and the conduct of an in-house stress audit at the University of Salford, which employs approximately 2600 staff, aimed to find out whether the organization was following the national trend and whether there was a case for extending its staff counseling service. The provision of a face-to-face counseling service had been previously established; however, at the time of the survey, this was limited in the number of sessions that could be offered: the option of joining a telephone-based Employee Assistance Program (EAP) was under consideration. Having gained the agreement of the senior management team and trades union representatives, the member of staff conducting the audit circulated a brief questionnaire, which included the General Health Questionnaire (GHQ-12), an assessment of working conditions (Objective Measure of the Workplace Environment) (Weinberg and Creed, 2000) and a measure of non-work life events.

A response rate of 41 percent of the 1078 surveys randomly distributed across all parts of the University provided a sample of 445 university employees for the stress audit. The results showed that Salford University was experiencing the same high levels of psychological strain as other higher education institutions, with hot spots identified as those areas facing cuts in resourcing. At the level of the individual employee, further analysis showed that a mix of work and non-work related challenges predicted high levels of psychological strain. These included organizational change, job promotion difficulties, problems with work colleagues, and lack of support from managers, as well as personal life events, such as the end of a close partner relationship in the last year and difficulties with a friendship (Weinberg, 2002). Although the last two issues were beyond the remit of the employer to address, there was a recognition that, naturally, such issues would cause affected employees considerable distress which, in turn, would impact on absence and well-being. Given the range of issues highlighted and the levels of psychological strain identified, the University took the decision to buy into the telephone-based EAP. This extended the provision of counseling, as well as advice on a range of life challenges, to all employees at any time of the day or night. Five years after the introduction of the EAP, a staff experience survey put the University in the top quartile of the UK public sector for overall satisfaction with pay and benefits.

On a smaller scale, the GHQ-12 was used again to evaluate the face-to-face counseling provision offered by Salford University (Weinberg, 2009a). Comparison of scores on this measure, obtained from 47 employees completing the GHQ-12 before and after utilizing the service, revealed a statistically significant drop in psychological strain, from high levels of distress to within the expected range by the end of their course of sessions. Clare McFarlane, the University's senior counselor said:

> Many employees find it extremely helpful to talk to someone who understands the nature of working in a modern university setting. As a counsellor it was also great to have some objective feedback on the impact of the service we offer.

THE STRESS AUDIT: SUMMARY OF STEPS

In the final part of this chapter, we provide an outline for the steps to be taken when conducting an audit. While the example used is a rather formal process, it should be remembered that an audit can also be undertaken in an informal, small-scale manner. Whatever method is used, two key points are worth emphasis:

1 Is the audit valid?
   - Is it measuring what you want it to measure?
   - Does it have face validity among the people taking part? They will not take part in the audit if they do not have confidence in those conducting the audit, or the measures being used.
2 Is the audit reliable?
   - If you repeated the survey, would you get the same results?
   - Is the sample size large enough to provide confidence about the findings of the survey?

Steps in the stress audit process

The process we suggest includes:

Deciding on a title for the project: for example, "Optimizing Employee Well-being and Performance in the Workplace"

Aims and objectives of the audit:

1 To conduct a stress audit in workplace "X" to identify:
   - the levels of stress currently operating compared with similar occupational groups

- sources of stress within the sample population, and to observe differences between the various groups according to job type, function, location, and so on
- individual groups at risk – that is, to examine biographical, demographic, personality and behavioral style differences in response to stress.

This would highlight potential stress problems that might exist within the organization.

2 To develop an organizational stressor item bank specific to workplace "X".
3 To investigate staff attitudes to a variety of stress management interventions.
4 To make recommendations as to appropriate organizational and individual initiatives as part of a stress management strategy within the workplace.

Procedure

1 Identify the sample; it must be representative of the workforce and large enough to ensure confidence about the findings of the survey.
2 Method.

Phase I: Planning

(A) Assign a project manager or coordinator to liaise with the consultants (if external to the organization). This individual (or small team of people) will be the first-line contact for all queries and questions, and all matters concerning the audit logistics – for example, the sample identification, planning of workshops or focus groups, the provision of absence, accident or health records, and the like.

(B) Design and circulate a pre-audit letter to all staff involved and all others on a need-to-know basis – that is, to introduce and explain the project, and the role of the consultants, if used. This should include:

Why?
Who?
What and how?
When?
Answers to questions you might ask

Phase II: Qualitative data collection

Stress logs or diaries, critical incident data, interviews, and focus group discussions can be used to collect information. These data should be collected from a randomly selected, representative sample of the workforce. Workshops or focus groups of 10–14 people usually involve half-day sessions. It is common to use a two-phased approach:

- one week prior to workshop attendance, employees are required to maintain a daily stress log, to be used by the individual in the workshop discussion sessions
- attend half-day focus group discussion sessions to identify sources of stress, and facilitators and inhibitors of performance and productivity at work.

Outcomes

(a) A stressor item bank specific to Workplace "X".
(b) Qualitative data to assist in the interpretation of the larger-scale questionnaire survey.

Note: It is important to assure attendees that any individual information divulged by participants during this stage of data collection would remain confidential. In other words, comments would be reported but not attributed to a specific participant.

Phase III: Quantitative data collection

- Questionnaire design is based on the findings from the qualitative data
- The measures – for example, a questionnaire package might include:
    (i) a covering letter with instructions for completion and return; a return envelope;
    (ii) the stress audit tool;
    (iii) a stressor item bank relevant to Company "X" ;
    (iv) biographical/career demographics data;
    (v) health behaviors – including sickness absence information, accidents, cigarette-smoking, alcohol consumption, exercise habits and general health information;
    (vi) attitudes to stress control interventions

- Time to complete, dependent on the choice of measure – for example, approximately 15–20 minutes for ASSET
- Questionnaire distribution and return.

The questionnaire could be distributed to: all staff; a 50 per cent sample of staff; or a randomly selected, representative sample. Many organizations usually distribute the questionnaire in their internal mail system and provide central collection points for completed documents. It is important that staff are provided with an envelope that can be sealed. Ways of maximizing the rate of return should be considered. For example, staff might be allowed to complete their questionnaire during a team briefing session. In some organizations, the occupational health personnel have organized group administration of the questionnaire.

Note: We recommend that the survey remains anonymous; guaranteeing anonymity and confidentiality would help to achieve a high response rate. If it is required to provide staff feedback, a confidential coding system could be used for the retrieval of individual or group results.

Phase IV: Statistical analysis

Data analysis usually involves:

- computer analysis – possibly using the Statistical Package for the Social Sciences (SPSS)
- analysis to include:
  - *descriptive statistics*: comparison of results to be made between personnel, relevant subgroups and normative data – for example, by job grade, function, location, age, gender, and so on.
  - *factor analysis*: to identify common patterns and stressor themes
  - *multiple regression*: to identify predictors and possible causal relationships between stressors and stress outcomes
  - *bivariate analysis*: to examine differences in findings between various subgroups in the work force.

Phase V: Interpretation of the results and recommendations

This stage of the process involves:
- preparation and presentation of a report
- feedback of results to staff.

A report should provide a psychological health profile of employees within Workplace "X", comparative with normative data and relevant population comparisons where possible. Comparisons between subgroups should be provided. The report should identify patterns of reported sources of stress and make recommendations for further action strategies at the individual, group and/or organizational level. The audit should also provide a base line measure from which to evaluate any subsequent intervention.

Consultants usually provide a presentation of the results to management or a "stress management steering group".

It is vital that feedback of the results of the audit, and the recommendations, are made available to the people who took part in the survey. This can be done either by providing access to the report, or during presentation sessions – for example, during team briefing.

Phase VI

Implementation of stress control initiatives; monitoring and evaluation.

CONCLUSION

The benefits of conducting a stress audit are that it enables us to understand individual vulnerability or risk. This means that we can implement effective development programs or "change" initiatives that will remove or reduce these risks. Certain sources of stress would respond to organizational change (for example, a change to the structure such as work-shift patterns, job characteristics or team working), and these will be discussed in Chapter 7. Nevertheless, raising awareness by a thorough analysis of the work environment is a sound basis from which to inform action and evaluate effectiveness in the management of stress. This is what we mean by "optimizing performance and health in the workplace". Those organizations that recognize the high costs of mismanaged stress in the workplace, and seek to achieve enhanced levels of effectiveness and the well-being of their employees, need to adopt an integrated approach to stress management. A stress audit guides this process.

CHAPTER 7

OPTIONS FOR THE MANAGEMENT OF STRESS IN THE WORKPLACE: AN ORGANIZATIONAL APPROACH

We have now considered all the necessary issues in respect of the first two "A"s in our "Triple A" approach to the management of stress: AWARENESS and ANALYSIS. To achieve this, we have examined the stress process, explained its origins, given definitions of stress, and provided a model of stress to guide the process of analysis. In order to complete the process of analysis, a means of identification and measurement of stress at work has been described. This is the "stress audit". The objective of this type of psychological risk assessment is to enable the organization to optimize the performance and health of the workforce. This is achieved by eliminating or minimizing sources of stress that are damaging in their consequences. Thereby, we are acknowledging the maxim "healthy work force – healthy organization" (Davies and Teasdale, 1994), and promoting the World Health Organization (WHO) statement that "a healthy working environment is one in which there is not only an absence of harmful conditions but an abundance of Health Promoting ones" (Leka *et al.*, 2007). In this instance, we use the word "health" in its widest sense, to mean not merely the absence of physical and psychological diseases, but to describe feelings of well-being, happiness and satisfaction. Indeed, it is about obtaining a "good quality of life". Research findings highlight the nature of stress in the workplace in terms of potential "hot spot" issues (see Chapter 4). Thus, the steps described so far are necessary to guide and inform the ACTION phase of the stress management process. This is the final "A" in our Triple A approach to stress management. "Action" is the subject of our final chapter.

The objective of this chapter is to present an organizational strategy for stress management in the workplace. It acknowledges the importance of both preventive and curative approaches to the management of stress. A wide variety of options is available for the management of stress at work and, as we have seen, there is not just one problem; neither is there just one solution! Increasingly, public and private sector organizations are acknowledging the unacceptable costs of stress by providing stress management programs for employees in an attempt to combat the problem of stress. However, these stress prevention activities in Europe have tended to be confined to large organizations employing more than 500 employees (Wynn and Clarkin, 1992), although there have been attempts to demonstrate their effectiveness using small samples of employees (Randall *et al.*, 2005). Thus, it remains a challenge for human resource professionals and organizational psychologists to find ways of extending the scope of stress management activities into both medium-sized and small companies. Typically, this type of program teaches the individual to cope with stress, rather than tackle the problem at source (Ivancevich *et al.*, 1990). Therefore, the approach is described as "reactive", rather than "proactive", because it seeks to cure the symptoms of exposure to stress, rather than to prevent a stress problem from arising. Typically, stress management courses are often introduced into the workplace as a reaction, in response to a perceived problem or negative situation within the organization (for example, to combat a high level of absenteeism or accidents at work). Other stress management initiatives, such as the use of a counseling service or an employee assistance program (EAP) seek to "cure" the symptoms of exposure to stress. However, this is a potentially negative and harmful situation: it supposes that distressed victims of exposure to mismanaged stress are either at work and behaving in ineffective, non-productive ways; or they are absent from their job, thereby causing extra strains and pressures on the remaining work colleagues or team. Both of these situations are undesirable and costly for the employer and employees.

The type of stress control program that focuses on the individual places the onus and burden for change on the employee. Thus, the message is loud and clear. It is saying, "You do not seem to be able to handle the stress and pressure of your job or life circumstances, so we will help you to cope more effectively". While these aims might be well-intentioned and honorable, the underlying message to the employee also implies that, "We (the organization) are not going to change the way we do things around here. You must learn to cope with the situation!" Although this approach to stress control has a certain appeal to organizations, it has also been suggested that stress control can only be really successful if it is tackled at the level of the individual and the organization (Giga *et al.*, 2003). While good, well-controlled evaluation studies are scarce, there is evidence to indicate that the approach which focuses solely on the individual to address the management of stress has certain weaknesses (Murphy, 1996; Bunce, 1997):

■ Such interventions might only produce effects that are present for shorter time periods, but decline thereafter. Furthermore, the positive impact of an intervention could be generic rather than specific, with alternative types of program having different outcomes. It is not known to what extent the success of a course is due to the characteristics of the facilitator and, additionally, the absence of a standardized guide to any techniques used makes it hard to pinpoint the effective aspect of this kind of intervention. It might not be surprising that programs that utilize more than one approach tend to have a greater positive impact.

■ Organizations seem to be prepared to spend precious and limited budgets on a stress management course or stress management training initiatives, but do not know how great is the demand for the course or program, or who should attend. This decision should be made on the basis of a training needs analysis. However, such courses are offered on a voluntary attendance basis; those who take part tend to feel motivated to do so, either because they are prone to health worries or, less often, are already experiencing some level of distress. For example, Conrad (1987) found that volunteer participants in worksite wellness programs appear to be somewhat healthier and more concerned with fitness and health matters than non-participants. Participants were also less likely to be cigarette-smokers, less likely to have been in hospital in the previous five years, and tended to spend more time exercising than non-participants. Therefore, it is possible that many of those individuals who really do need to attend these types of training session will sometimes try to avoid taking part. This happens sometimes because they are in a state of denial about their stress-related problems, or perhaps they simply prefer to choose to avoid bad news about their health. As Brodsky (1987) has pointed out, individuals might not be aware that they are under stress. Often, they do not wish anyone else to find out that they are not coping with a situation at work or at home. Some employees actually fear that the results of their stress profile will end up on personnel records held by the company and will be used as a screening tool when the organization decides to "downsize" once again, or to block them from any further promotion opportunities. Thus, the intended program does not reach the employees who are deemed to be at risk for disease and disability (Conrad, 1987).

- Training packages and courses are offered, but rarely does the organization know whether it is obtaining any return on its investment. While training institutions tend to evaluate their courses, this is rarely done in a structured way. This is because the programs are not evaluated beyond the "reaction level" of the participants (Houtman and Kompier, 1995), or because they do not incorporate a control group with which to compare outcomes. Surprisingly, evaluation information is not always made available for the company that paid for the course. It would seem that organizations tend to accept the effectiveness of such training packages as an act of faith, and so the impact is not assessed. However, there are ongoing efforts to demonstrate the efficacy of interventions; some have already shown the positive impacts of initiatives enhancing both employees' coping and problem-solving skills in comparison with those awaiting training (Bond and Bunce, 2000).

- The strategy of waiting for an employee to become a victim of stress before taking action is a high-risk and potentially high-cost strategy for the organization, from both legal and insurance perspectives (Earnshaw and Cooper, 1994). The law emphasizes that each case will be considered on its merits, and that employers should be proactive in safeguarding the well-being of their employees (*Barber* v. *Somerset County Council*).

A TRIPARTITE MODEL FOR STRESS MANAGEMENT

An organizational approach to stress control has three separate levels. This means we need to:

- identify and eliminate or minimize stressful situations
- teach the individual to cope with stress
- help those individuals that have become victims of exposure to stress.

Research evidence suggests that stress-related problems are complex. Both the organization and individual employees, perhaps working in a team or work group, should be encouraged to manage stress actively in order to eliminate or minimize the stressor problem at source. Therefore, it is recommended that stress in the workplace should be addressed by adopting a tripartite approach consisting of:

- **Primary-level stress management**: This type of strategy or intervention is *stressor directed*, in that it eliminates, reduces or controls a source of stress. The aim is to prevent stress at work.
- **Secondary-level stress management**: These interventions are *response directed*, in that they help individual employees or groups of workers to recognize their response to stress and the symptoms of stress. Thereby, they can respond in a way that is not harmful to themselves or to the organization. Thus, the aim is to develop stress resistance and adaptive coping strategies through education and training.
- **Tertiary-level stress management**: These forms of intervention are *symptom directed*. The objective is to assist in the cure and rehabilitation of stressed and distressed employees.

    Within each of these levels it is also possible to direct the focus on either the:
    ○ individual
    ○ team or work group
    ○ organization.

Figure 7.1 illustrates this integrated model of stress management. Using an onion as our metaphor, we would describe stress management in the workplace as "peeling an onion". The organization exists within its "universe" and is thereby exposed to many different factors. Peel off this layer and you find the organization, exposed to changes and pressures imposed by the global economy, financial constraints, international politics, and legal requirements. All of these, and more, influence the fortunes of the business and the decisions it must make. To survive, and to be successful and effective, the organization must be AWARE of the potential stress problems that might exist to impact adversely upon performance, productivity and the well-being of its work force. From an ANALYSIS or diagnosis, ACTION is possible at primary, secondary or tertiary level. A description of each of the levels of stress management, with examples of strategies and interventions, is now given.

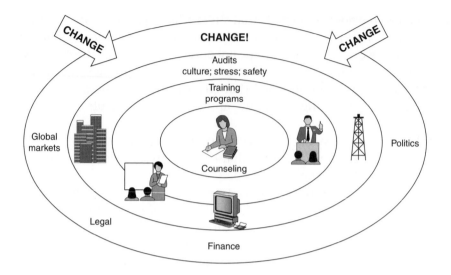

FIGURE 7.1 **An integrated model of stress management**

PRIMARY LEVEL STRESS MANAGEMENT INTERVENTIONS

A more commonly used term for this type of stress management strategy is "organizational-level interventions" (Giga *et al.*, 2003). Essentially, these "stressor directed" strategies for the reduction or elimination of stress in the workplace can be categorized in three ways:

- changes in the macro environment – that is, organizational culture and leadership, physical work conditions and workload, safety climate, career development programs and bullying at work
- change in the micro environment – that is, systems and task redesign, alternative work arrangements, shift working, and communication exercises such as role negotiation
- improving perceptions of worker control; increasing opportunities for decision making.

Changes in the macro-environment

In this section, we consider the issues of organizational culture, management coaching and coping, work overload conditions, safety climate, career development programs and bullying at work.

Organizational culture

Building a supportive and open climate and culture, and ensuring that the style of management is compatible with the goals and aims of the organization, are important in the reduction of stress at work. It also means developing a culture that encourages staff to be more supportive of each other. This appears to be a key feature of those organizations considered by their workers as "The Best Companies to Work For" (*Sunday Times*, 2009), where employees are more likely to feel engaged in their work and committed to managers and employers that lead by positive example and that value the opinions, as well as non-work lives, of those working for them. "Good leadership has the largest influence on employee engagement", according to Peter Bradon, who coordinates the research that informs the *Sunday Times* surveys, which have been running since 2001 and, in 2009, gathered data from 200,842 employees from 738 companies (*Sunday Times*, 2009). In the top 10 percent of companies earning a place on this influential list of good employers, 94.9 percent of workers agreed that "the leader of this organization runs this organization on sound moral principles". Clearly, this facilitates team working and good interpersonal relationships in the workplace as a whole. It is also likely to be an important stress reduction and prevention mechanism in instances where external forces deter us from eliminating certain sources of pressure and strain in the workplace – for example, the need to work night shifts. Employee perceptions of the organization – and, in turn, factors affecting individual well-being – are highly influenced by the justice of the behaviors witnessed at work on a daily basis, and particularly by the level of support provided by the organization (Rhoades and Eisenberger, 2002).

An assessment of organization culture guides the process of culture change. Similarly, the use of psychometric measures to understand the appropriateness of "management style" and its role as a source of stress in the workplace might be necessary, and underpins an effective approach to management coaching, which is considered later on. Thus, use of this type of intervention to reduce the stress associated with poor leadership or supervision would also incorporate the next level of stress management action: secondary-level intervention. This assessment might reveal, for example, a need for management retraining, and/or improved recruitment or selection procedures.

Literature on the impact of mergers and acquisitions suggests that more action is necessary to reduce the stress associated with

159

this business venture. Blake and Mouton (1984) used an "interface conflict-solving model" to facilitate the acquisition process between an American company and an acquired British organization. The top teams of both organizations engaged in meetings during which they shared perceptions about their concerns and questions. From this, a successful operating model emerged. Data collected two years later indicated that this business venture had been a success and that no senior personnel had left the organization. Realistic merger previews (also known as "a communications program") have also been used to facilitate the merger process and to reduce negative impact. Typically, this means that several kinds of information are provided to employees on how the merger will affect them. This includes answers to questions concerning lay-offs, transfers, promotions and demotions, changes in jobs, pay, and benefits. Schweiger and DeNisi (1991) observed the negative affects of a merger announcement in a light manufacturing plant. This included a decrease in job satisfaction, global stress, absenteeism, perceived uncertainty, a decrease in commitment and perceptions of trustworthiness, honesty and caring. Compared with the control plant, where no merger preview process was used, the negative effects of the merger were reduced in the experimental plant, both immediately and at the end of the follow-up period four months later. Thus, newsletters, access to a telephone hotline, and meetings are all needed to transmit merger preview information in order to reduce the negative impact of this type of major change in the work environment. The potential negative affects tend to focus on perceptions of job insecurity. Annual survey data of 10,000 US employees that compared 1985–88 with 2005 found that this was the top-rated concern in both periods (Kenexa Research Institute, 2007). In addition, the negative impact of mergers and acquisitions on job satisfaction had actually lessened but the intent to quit had increased, confirming that clarity of vision and a communicated plan remain high priorities in a changing organizational context.

Management coaching and coping

While the role of leadership is highly influential in determining employee attitudes and performance outcomes, the behavior of immediate line managers can prove pivotal in the well-being of employees: 76 percent of UK managers find that they have found that their interpersonal skills are more important than their positional authority alone

(Worrall and Cooper, 2001). Given the prevalence of change in the working world, managers' roles both inside and outside the organization are ever-more demanding, and the quality and quantity of support they offer to employees are key issues. It is acknowledged that control is important for individual well-being, and it can be determined by how much autonomy can be devolved or retained by line managers. Furthermore, the availability of support from a line manager has been shown to be a major predictor of employees' psychological health (Gilbreath and Benson, 2004; Shigemi *et al.*, 2000; Weinberg and Creed, 2000), and the gathering pace of management coaching suggests that organizations and managers alike are recognizing the pressure to be ever-more flexible to the demands of employees and their companies. In order to respond to these imperatives, managers might find the need for intensive training that relates to their daily experiences of working. This can be provided by coaching programs that assess their behavior and provide detailed and personalized feedback that can be incorporated into their managerial styles. This is a more intensive and, potentially, more effective intervention than that achieved through periodic workshop attendance. Given that the skill of managing others is often assumed, like driving, to be inbuilt, coaching helps to train individuals on the job, and monitors their progress.

The starting point, which can be through a 360-degree feedback exercise, helps to establish a baseline of managers' behavior in relation to their own managers, colleagues, clients and those under their direct supervision. Key behaviors include leadership and organizational qualities, communication skills, interpersonal sensitivity and resilience. It is unsurprising that managers' behavior can impact so significantly on the staff reporting to them, and there are positive indicators of the benefits of coaching programs, not simply on the managers, but also on the employees for whom they are responsible. A range of interventions in the UK National Health Service (Borrill *et al.*, 1998) showed that training in relation to key managerial behaviors including "creating a team environment", "integrity and respect" and "presenting and providing feedback" preceded improvements in both managers' and staff levels of well-being. Similarly, a case-control study of a coaching intervention in a UK university found decreases in psychological strain among participating managers, and improved experiences of personal development and job promotion prospects among staff for whom they were responsible, with accompanying decreases in time conflict and problems due to role change (Weinberg, 2008).

The promotion of increasing numbers of individuals who possess greater emotional capabilities, alongside designated job skills, can only contribute to the right climate for shaping factors such as tight timescales, which currently challenge managers to maintain good practice. Management in the *Sunday Times* Top 100 Companies is not simply about reaching common goals; it is also about optimizing the process for reaching those goals. In other words, workers are saying it is no longer sufficient or acceptable to use any means to justify the ends; instead, organizations should behave in a way that guarantees cooperation and collaboration. The adaptability to utilize these competencies in a range of contexts is likely to predict managerial success.

Globalization has highlighted cross-cultural differences in working practices: it is interesting to note national variation in the coping strategies utilized in the workplace, with Bulgarian managers more likely to employ both objective and planning strategies for coping, as well as seeking help and using non-work resources, than managers from the UK, US and India (Bernin *et al.*, 2003). Cultural differences in leadership style are also highly relevant to change scenarios with Middle Eastern countries prioritizing aspects of managerial process, such as diplomacy, over the performance outcomes, which seem more highly prized in western and southern Europe (Abdalla and Al-Homoud, 2001).

Work overload

It is acknowledged that work overload is a potent source of stress in contemporary organizations and this has been enshrined in the social chapter of the European Union Treaty within the Working Time Directive, which stipulates a maximum 48-hour working week, with provision for exemptions. A healthy approach to workload is further underlined by the UK's Health and Safety Executive (HSE) guidelines for the management of stress, which emphasize "adequate and achievable demands in relation to the hours of work" (HSE, 2004b). A high workload leads to long hours of working, either as paid or unpaid overtime, as well as a high level of sustained intensity. The consequences of overwork are potentially fatal. Indeed, "death from overwork" (*karoshi*) and "suicide due to overwork" (*karojisatsu*) are commonplace in Japan, where 28.1 percent of the population regularly work more than 50-hour weeks (Hiyama and Yoshihara, 2008).

The extension of the 48-hour ceiling to UK medical doctors has necessitated considerable readjustment in the NHS, but there remains a need to follow guidelines provided for minimizing the negative impact of shift working in other sectors. The re-analysis of staffing levels and an improved (real) costing of the impact of downsizing, or job and task redesign are also recommended to help reduce work overload stress. Some organizations have found that their enthusiasm for downsizing has been too zealous, and a subsequent cost–benefit analysis has proven the reinstatement of certain jobs to be the most effective management strategy. The marked increase in the working hours of university staff (both in the UK and Australia) found organizations in the early Noughties unprepared to deal with the consequences, which have coincided with the introduction of funding cuts. Given the known physical and psychological toll of long working hours, it is imperative that employers act in accordance with the best interests of their workers and the law.

In a work overload condition, it is important to ensure that employees are not stressed by the physical conditions of their work environment. In addition to being a source of stress in their own right, these also take up the attention capacity of the individual, and so the employee is more vulnerable to workplace stress. Kornhauser's (1965) classic study of the motor industry found that unpleasant working conditions, the necessity to work rapidly, to expend a great deal of effort, and to work excessive and inconvenient hours were related to poor mental health. The work environment must provide satisfying physical conditions; a clean and orderly place of work is important for both safety and hygiene reasons. This has implications for the morale of the workforce, especially in an environment where the work situation is acknowledged as hazardous. The comparatively comfortable physical surroundings of the modern call center might not appear to raise the same challenges, but the time and motion issues that applied to the early motor industry have reappeared in this context, where employees have little control over their work and the pace at which it is conducted (Holman, 2002). This carries with it both a physical and psychological price, as the relationship between higher employee workloads and musculoskeletal disorders is accounted for by individuals' experiences of job-related strain (Sprigg *et al.*, 2007).

Clearly, many of the opportunities for the prevention of stress associated with the physical demands of working exist at the design stage, and, of course, in the provision of adequate personal protection equipment. With the will of the employer, there is scope for negotiating schedules of work, which, as part of the process, can empower and engage employees and, as an outcome, can enhance performance, as was found in a pilot exercise carried out by Marks & Spencer (Miller, 1994). This gave staff the responsibility for determining their work rotas and incorporating a variety of tasks within their shifts, resulting in improved levels of job satisfaction. Subsequently, a high profile has been given to case studies from private sector organizations that proactively addressed the issue of a culture of long working hours in 2004/05. Accenture, the global management and IT consulting giant, previously renowned for its macho approach to the job, removed the opt-out from the Working Time Directive from its induction packs, introduced a "time off in lieu" system and made under-reporting of working hours a disciplinary offence. BT's adoption of home-working in the 1980s has progressed to an "anytime, anywhere" approach that is practiced by 73,000 (75 percent) of its employees. Including flexible, nomadic and annualized working hours, BT built its initiative on trust in its staff. The company estimates it has saved £5–6 million in productive time and claims this has broken the presenteeism culture. PricewaterhouseCoopers' introduction (in 2001) of support for employees wanting to work flexibly or take career breaks has led to a 92 percent return of staff following maternity leave (previously 40 percent in 1998) and a 92 percent agreement rate for requests to flexible working.

However, many places of work are modified and adapted to meet the needs of industry and economic fluctuations and, thus, might not always provide optimal conditions for the workforce. In the modern work environment, complaints are often about the lack of personal control, not simply over working hours, but also over physical work conditions. Whenever possible, the practice of more open discussion and debate about the issues that directly affect working conditions should be encouraged. This includes the arrangements made for rest and lunch breaks. The work environment should be perceived as comfortable and safe; therefore, a high standard of hygiene and cleanliness is also desirable.

Safety climate: minimizing the impact of working in dangerous or hazardous conditions

Many individuals are exposed to certain dangers and hazardous conditions at work. In countries where health and safety legislation is strongly established, one might expect the number of accidents at work to be minimized yet, in the UK alone, 241 fatalities and 141,350 injuries were reported among workers in one year, with 6 million days lost due to injury (HSE, 2007). It is clear that, while a risk assessment allows us to control and minimize threats to employees, some jobs still have inherent or perceived dangers. For example, the safety of helicopter travel was identified as one of the top ten sources of stress by offshore oil and gas workers (Sutherland and Cooper, 1991b). It was associated with poor mental health among contractor person-nel working offshore. Also, among Norwegian offshore workers, more than one third reported that they felt unsafe about the transportation of people by helicopter (Hellesøy,1985). Sunde (1983, cited in Hellesøy, 1985) indicated that the perceived risk associated with helicopter travel was the most common reason cited for resignation from offshore employment in Norway. This action is very costly to the industry in terms of selection, recruitment and training. Nevertheless, helicopter travel is a reality that must be faced by these workers, since we do not yet have any means of "beaming people through space". However, education about the nature of the risk and safety performance might help to overcome any irrational fears that are held. These tend to be magnified during the inevitable and intensive media coverage of a helicopter incident offshore that would probably go unreported in other industries.

In quite a different context, and contrary to public expectations due to the lower profile accorded to their situation, nursing staff can experience more non-fatal accidents than in many other industries, including construction, due to back injuries sustained while lifting and moving patients, as well as needle-stick incidents involving contaminated as well as clean needles. However, a distinction can be drawn between individual accidents that "occur in circumstances where the hazards are close to people and the defences are limited or non-existent" and "organizational accidents...that happen to complex systems that have defences-in-depth" (Reason, 1998). The importance of addressing both is clearly evident, and is aided by seeking to understand the reasons for terrible events such as those at the Chernobyl nuclear reactor, the Piper Alpha oil rig, the *Herald of Free Enterprise* and numerous transport crashes. Through the study of these it has become clear that gaps in the defenses which would otherwise prevent such disasters, due to errors and contraventions in working practices, have combined with not anticipating every potential scenario, to create breaches of the safety systems. This "Swiss cheese" model (Reason, 1998) highlights the processes by which active and latent failures in the systems align to create the conditions for accidents to happen.

Physical and psychological safety is a basic human need (Maslow, 1970), and having a predictable and non-threatening environment is fundamental to this need. However, the importance of non-technical factors in designing protocols that decrease the chance of accidents occurring can be underestimated. Key issues include vigilance, quality of communication and team coordination (Flin, 2009), and at the individual level are recognized as, "the cognitive, social and personal resource skills that complement technical skills, and contribute to safe and efficient task performance" (Flin et al., 2008: 1). For organizations and occupational groups, it is recommended that analyses of non-technical aspects of work behavior are carried out: these can be summarized under the following headings (Flin, 2009):

- situation awareness – for example, problems maintaining attention to the task
- decision making – that is, recognizing and considering problems and options, followed by choosing, implementing and evaluating these options
- teamwork – that is, effective two-way communication, support, coordination and conflict resolution
- leadership – for example, determining goals, influencing processes, adhering to standards
- managing stress – for example, identifying symptoms, consequences and coping strategies
- coping with fatigue – for example, recognizing symptoms and effects, managing fatigue.

Following on from action to analyze the challenges to each of the above categories, safer working environments can be promoted in relation to the following goals (Hellesøy, 1985):

- being able to prevent critical situations arising
- being able to recognize unsafe or dangerous situations before they develop further and while the situation is still under control of the individual

- avoidance of the worst consequences of an accident, if a critical situation has developed
- being able to reduce the consequences of an unavoidable incident by emergency training and contingency planning.

Clearly, there are some job situations where these are difficult to achieve, such as working within a war zone or battleground setting; however, three components of safety orientated behaviors are important, particularly as they can prevent a crisis becoming a disaster. These include knowledge, behavior (skills, routine, practice and motivation), and material and organizational support (that is, training, resources and facilities necessary to be prepared for contingencies). As Hellesøy *et al.* states, "for a safety measure to be effective, it is essential that these components mutually support each other and whenever possible, they should be included as natural components in the production system itself". The efficacy of material and organizational support depends on a trustworthy system of reporting errors. For example, doctors are more likely to report incidents where this is done locally within the organization and forms part of the medical processes for continued improvement (Waring, 2004). In this way, an increased sense of ownership can lead to improved confidence in the efficacy of the system, promotion of a team approach and meaningful steps to prevent further problems. The Swiss cheese model, which has become the leading approach for investigating medical errors ... emphasizes the importance of a "just culture in which the line between acceptable and unacceptable behavior is clearly drawn and understood" (Reason, 1998).

Realistic and reliable *knowledge* is needed about a work environment, the organization, technology, the job itself, and the systems and practices. Raising an awareness about work activities, and helping employees to understand what is happening and why, is particularly important in potentially dangerous situations. It is necessary to understand perceptions of risk and safety in order to plan safety policies, to "market" safety, and design safety measures and training programs. It is important to know how safe personnel feel about potential sources of risk, and to ensure that they have a realistic and "healthy" perception of "real" risk in their work environment. This means that we must ask whether the subjective experience of risk matches the reality of the situation. A state of stress will usually exist if there is a mismatch between real and perceived expectations.

Although denial is often used as a coping mechanism among people working in high risk occupations, it is vital to ensure that this does not prevent the individual from taking part in the training and drills necessary for effective working. A poor understanding about the risks of, for example, fire or explosion, and a lack of confidence about evacuation facilities, might dwell on the mind of employees. This can have an adverse affect on performance, productivity and safety behaviors. Confidence in and about the availability and effectiveness of equipment and medical help needed during these incidents is crucial to safety needs. Indeed, the perception that an organization is "only paying lip service" to safety is likely to be a significant source of stress among shop-floor workers employed at the "sharp end" of the business. Organizational commitment to safety, compliance with legal requirements and safety rules, and an ongoing training program are integral components of safety oriented behavior, because they have an effect on the attitudes and behaviors of the workforce. Training to be effective in the work environment is an important part of minimizing the deleterious impact of perceived hazard and risk to safety at work. It is also effective in reducing the stress of role ambiguity. Thus, the issue of training as a method of stress management is discussed separately in the section on secondary-level strategies.

Career development programs and the psychological contract

Fear of job loss and threat of redundancy are common features of contemporary working life. Perceived or real, pay and job status inequity, lack of job security or limited potential for future career development are sources of stress. In times of instability, poor work conditions are tolerated, and employees endure long hours and arduous conditions. This does not happen without personal and organizational costs. Fear of job loss and insecurity in times of high unemployment adversely affect both the individual and the organization. A keen, competitive job market can threaten the quality of co-worker relationships at a time when social support is of particular importance. Indeed, the stress of insecurity that can be alleviated by supportive working relationships might be broken down if the workforce perceives that competition is necessary in order to retain a job. Personnel might also stay in a job that is unsuitable or disliked because no suitable alternative for change exists. This results in costs to the organization due to poor productivity or performance and, indeed, presenteeism. Limited career opportunity can be demotivating and frustrating (Warr, 2007). This can cause negative behaviors, directed at the organization, the system of authority, colleagues at work or the family. Perceived inequity of reward or compensation can have adverse consequences for the individual and commerce. In exchange for effort, skill, tenure and education, a person expects pay, recognition and advancement (Adams, 1965). These unwritten expectations constitute the psychological contract that exists between employees and organizations. Perceived inequity might lead to disruptive performance, poor morale, psychological distress, and lowered tolerance to other stressors (Turnley and Feldman, 2000). There is a tendency for personnel to resolve inequity by attempting to increase the magnitude of attained outcomes – for example, requesting pay rises or making demands about the environment – as the perceived injustice also assumes greater significance (Coyle-Shapiro and Conway, 2005). Although it is difficult to manage this source of pressure in the workplace when it has become ingrained in the organizational climate and culture, it is possible to take certain steps to minimize the problem by ensuring that personnel have realistic expectations about career and reward prospects. This can be achieved in two main ways:

■ **Provision of realistic and honest job descriptions**: If terms and conditions are discussed openly at the time of selection and recruitment, the individual can make an informed choice about selecting into this situation.

■ **Reduction of uncertainty and ambiguity by appraisal interview**: It is also possible to reduce the stress associated with uncertainty and ambiguity about the future and career potential through the mechanism of the appraisal interview. This is usually conducted on a one-to-one basis with an immediate boss or supervisor. However, this type of appraisal interview, which is used to discuss career opportunities and training and development needs, should be kept quite separate from any pay review discussions. An individual is unlikely to reveal any weaknesses and training needs if he or she perceives that it will detrimentally affect a pending pay award.

Often, employees will need to accept that a change the direction of their career is inevitable. Organizations should be willing and prepared to facilitate this process by:

- providing career development appraisal, including the use of self-assessment tools and psychological testing
- offering individual counseling by internal staff or external services
- providing retraining opportunities
- providing assistance in job search, and training in skills such as producing a curriculum vitae and interviewing
- offering access to job placement services, such as "outplacement".

This process is important, because the stress of the job-loss situation will be exacerbated when the individual realizes that the termination of long-term employment requires adjustment to a major life-events change. This might happen at a time when learning something new seems to take longer, energy is scarcer, opportunities are fewer, and the threat of competition from younger job applicants is daunting. Thus, the individual is most vulnerable at a time when they might face rejection and fear of rejection. Both circumstances are damaging to morale, self-esteem and confidence (Black Report, 2008).

Bullying at work

Bullying can be a form of misuse of power and involves a person in authority bullying those below him or her (see Chapter 4). However, it can also occur when an individual or a group of individuals bullies or picks on a peer or co-worker. It is suggested that bullying at work might be more evident at work because:

- of an extremely competitive work environment, job insecurity and fear for one's job
- organizational change and uncertainty are created when organizations restructure and become "leaner and meaner"; the accompanying insecurities often generate bullying behavior
- excessive workload and demand, impossible targets and deadlines cause strain and pressure.

An authoritarian culture, poor work relationships, and a lack of clear codes of acceptable behaviors are all conditions that foster a climate in which bullying is likely to occur. Bullying is often confused with strong management, and so becomes condoned and part of the culture of the organization. Bullying can often be insidious and subtle, and so the victim has no witnesses. If there are witnesses, they are often afraid of supporting a victim. The victim is usually afraid of complaining for fear of not being believed and of the bullying getting worse.

Bullying as a form of misuse of power can take many forms such as:

- excessive supervision and criticism; monitoring every action; overruling the person's authority
- using terror tactics, open aggression, threats, shouting and abuse
- humiliation and ridicule; belittling efforts in front of other people
- setting impossible objectives or changing the "goal posts" without telling the person or consulting with them
- withholding information that the person needs to do the job effectively; removing whole areas of work responsibility and reducing a job to routine, low-skill activities
- ostracizing and marginalizing the individual by dealing only through a third party; excluding the individual from discussions, meetings and decisions that they need to be part of to do their job
- spreading malicious rumors
- refusing reasonable requests for leave or training
- blocking promotion.

One of the first steps for the organization is to raise awareness of bullying through the use of newsletters, posters and meetings. All staff must be aware of what constitutes bullying and made to understand that the organization will take action again bullying behavior. This means that the organization must have an agreed policy on bullying, which can be part of the health and safety policy. This must state clearly what is unacceptable behavior and the sanctions that will be imposed if people go beyond the bounds of acceptability. Although there is no single Act of Parliament dealing with bullying, UK equality at work legislation makes it possible for statutory steps to be taken to redress injustice (see Chapter 2). In relation to gender, the amendment of the Sex Discrimination Act (2008) further prohibits harassment within the organization, as well as failure to protect employees from it at the hands of clients and customers.

ACAS (Arbitration, Conciliation and Advisory Service, 2006) states that an organizational policy promoting Dignity at Work should include:

- a clear definition of bullying and examples of the forms it takes
- a statement that bullying is unacceptable behavior, will not be tolerated at any level of the organization, and can result in dismissal
- how bullying and harassment are addressed by existing legislation
- examples of positive behavior expected from employees
- reference to the commitment of the employer to updated legislation on equality in the workplace
- details of the relevant organizational processes, including timescales and contactable individuals, and how these fit with the statements of the organization's values, ethics and social responsibilities.

Employees should also receive guidance on the steps to be taken if they are a victim of bullying. This must include a guarantee of confidentiality, and confirmation that anyone complaining of bullying will not victimized. Usually, complaints are dealt with in conjunction with both counseling and mediation services. In some organizations, a helpline, a helpdesk, employee assistance programs, face-to-face counseling, and the occupational health service all play some role in dealing with bullying in the workplace. Ultimately, the process will depend on whether the victim is making a formal or an informal complaint. It is useful if people are advised to keep a written record of bullying behavior, since a one-off occurrence is not likely to be treated as anything more than an outburst from another person at work. Therefore, the victim should:

- log all incidents and include dates, times, details of the behavior and the names of any witnesses present. It is important that the individual sticks to the facts, but, at the same time, records his or her feelings at the time, and the response made.
- make sure you know the exact nature of your responsibilities and duties to ensure that any criticism towards you is actually unjustified.
- keep copies of all correspondence with the bully, including any information relating to your work ability and performance, and any memos that you wrote about an incident.
- try to find out whether you are the only "victim", or whether other colleagues are being treated similarly. It might be easier to deal with a collective complaint. Talk to your colleagues or someone in

authority in the organization and actively seek support. Seek help from your union. Bullies often pick on the individual who seems to be isolated at work.

- avoid being alone with the bully.
- seek help as soon as possible; do not delay in taking action but make sure you have written facts and details to present to your organization. Keep a record of events that follow once you have made a complaint.

Informally, the bully can be confidentially counseled, and advised that their behavior is contrary to organizational policy and must comply with the required standards. This means that they should be told about the impact of the bullying behavior and that it must stop. In addition, they are required to be advised of the consequences of failing to meet this demand, and that the situation will be monitored and reviewed. The ultimate sanction for the bully must be dismissal, although steps can be taken at an early stage to avoid this costly outcome.

A Canadian social worker took his case to the Human Rights Commission, complaining that he had been harassed and discriminated against because he was gay and perceived to have AIDS. Moffat kept his sexual orientation a secret, but it was the subject of speculation at work. He and his partner had recently provided a foster home for a 16-year-old boy. Returning to work following a period of illness, he discovered that rumors were rife about his sexual orientation, that he was stricken with AIDS and that the foster-child was subject to sexual abuse. He complained to his area director and the management team that he was a victim of gossip and slander, and that his human rights were violated. Management's response to this situation was that, without specific allegations tracing the rumors to a particular individual, it could, and would, do nothing. The Human Rights Commission Board of Inquiry agreed that Moffat had been subjected to harassment and discrimination. The employer was held liable for allowing a poisoned work environment to flourish. It had failed to undertake appropriate investigation and to address a workplace in which Moffat was targeted by discriminatory and derogatory comments. The fact that Moffat could not identify the source of the rumors did not relieve the employer's obligation to investigate the matter and curb the gossip. By failing to take his concern seriously, the employer was responsible for Moffat feeling isolated and vulnerable as a gay person.

The Commission argued that it is never appropriate for co-workers to refer directly or indirectly to the sexual orientation of another employee. In the UK, the trend has been towards more liberal views on sexuality (British Social Attitudes Survey, 2010). The campaigning group Stonewall compiles an annual index of UK employers, rating attitudes and behavior towards gay employees. The 2010 top award went to IBM UK and Ireland, with public and commercial organizations (such as the Home Office, Manchester City Council, Ernst & Young, and Goldman Sachs) represented in the top 20 (*The Guardian*, 2010b). Coverage was prominent for the five police forces that made the shortlist, following "very significant change in roles of police services as employers in the last five years", according to Ben Summerskill, Stonewall's chief executive (*The Guardian*, 2010b).

The high-profile publicity relating to the treatment of officers from black and minority ethnic backgrounds by the London Metropolitan Police, highlighted by the Mayor of London, suggests that there is considerable potential for progress on issues of equality and diversity (*Times Online*, 2009). Therefore, an organization should ensure that a harassment policy prohibits any form of derogatory remarks about employees relating to any prohibited ground such as race, color, gender, sexual orientation or creed. It is also necessary to monitor the workplace and address improper comments or rumors, and instigate a grievance procedure to identify potential problems. Action must be taken on all complaints about workplace gossip that could violate the Human Rights Code. Finally, if an employee comes forward with a complaint that he or she is the subject of rumors but cannot identify their source, the obligation to investigate is not reduced (Levitt, 1999). It is clear that there are consequences for the organization in failing to address these issues, but it is important to recognize that the suffering and shame experienced by the victims can last well beyond the period of bullying (Lewis, 2004).

Changes in the micro-environment

Rather than put the responsibility for stress management on the individual employee, well-being can be improved and exposure to stressful work conditions reduced by the redesign of work systems and practices (Sparks *et al.*, 2001). It is suggested that work redesign can improve worker morale, motivation and performance.

A number of popular models for analyzing the interface between the individual and their working environment have been proposed (Weinberg and Cooper, 2007). Of these, the one that has stimulated most research activity has been the Job Strain Model (Karasek, 1979; Karasek and Theorell, 1990), which indicates that attention is focused on job demands (volume of demand, pace of work, and so on) and job decision latitude (the ability to make decisions and the variety of skills used by workers on the job), and that the level of social support in the workplace can moderate the impact of these two factors. Warr's Vitamin Model (1989, 1999, 2007) has received less scrutiny from researchers; however, its size and scope make it a promising vehicle for assessing the role of a range of workplace variables in employee well-being. There are features common to both models – employee workload, levels of control, social support – as well as others, suggested by the research literature to share direct relationships with: psychological strain, for example, role clarity, variety of tasks, opportunity for skill use, status, pay and rewards (Warr, 1989); supervisory support (Warr, 1999); and equity and career progression (Warr, 2007). Thus, these areas have become the focus of attention in an attempt to reduce stress in the work environment. In this section on the micro-environment affecting individual employees' daily experiences, we discuss job design issues, the use of semi-autonomous work groups, flexible and family-friendly work arrangements, shift work, and reducing role stress. Following on from these, we consider ways of improving perceptions of job control.

Although many workers complain about having too much to do, or having to work at a pace that is too fast, they also complain that the job does not provide enough variety or challenge. This can lead to boredom, apathy and low motivation to work. Thus, job redesign interventions can be used to alleviate the problem of "rust out" in the workplace.

Job design

Prevention of stress associated with "rust out", due to boredom, and lack of stimulation in the workplace can be achieved by changing the "micro" work environment (Karasek, cited in ILO, 1993). This includes increasing workers' skills, their autonomy in the job, and providing more opportunities for decision making. Hackman and

Oldham's (1976) influential model explained how the core nature of a job influences one's attitudes and behavior, and how it affects both personal and work outcomes, such as motivation, job performance, job satisfaction and labor turnover. It is suggested that any job can be described according to five core dimensions and these influence certain critical psychological states. The first three core job characteristics help us to understand how meaningful we perceive our job to be:

1 **Skill variety**: This means the number of different activities, skills and talents the job requires. It is suggested that the more varied the skills we use, the more meaningful the job is seen to be.
2 **Task identity**: This means the degree to which a job requires completion of a whole, identifiable piece of work; doing a job from beginning to end with a visible result.
3 **Task significance**: This describes the job's impact on the lives or work of other people, whether within or outside the work environment.

The second psychological state that is known to influence both personal and work outcomes is our perception of the level of responsibility we have for the outcomes of the work. This is influenced by the amount of autonomy we have at work or in the job.

4 **Autonomy**: This is the degree of freedom, independence and discretion in scheduling the work and in determining procedures and practices.

Finally, knowledge of work results can have beneficial personal and work outcomes. This refers to the amount of feedback received from doing the job.

5 **Task feedback**: The degree to which carrying out the activities required results in direct and clear information about the effectiveness of performance.
   This includes:
   (a) *Feedback from other people* – receiving clear information about one's performance from supervisors and co-workers.
   (b) *Dealing with others* – the degree to which the job requires the employee to work closely with other people in carrying out work activities.

By redesigning or enriching the job to improve the amount of skill variety, task identity, task significance, autonomy and feedback, it is possible to improve both motivation and job performance, and reduce levels of stress. Decisions to carry out this type of change are usually made on the basis of a job analysis, and in workforce and job-holder discussions. For example, changes might be made that increase feelings of autonomy, job variety and levels of feedback:

- **Job rotation**: It might be desirable for workers to be able to rotate through a set of different but similar jobs, in order to provide more variety and reduce the boredom that might exist at work. Job rotation and job-share opportunities can also be provided so that no one is exposed to high stress levels for a long period of time.
- **Horizontal job enlargement**: This means that additional tasks are included within the scope of the job to increase the variety and diversity of the job. The relatively flat hierarchy of many organizations does not provide upward career progression. Therefore, job enlargement is a method of providing more variety and challenge in a job, especially for the older worker who realizes that he or she has reached a career plateau.
- **Vertical loading**: This entails assigning more important and challenging duties to the job – for example, additional decision making responsibilities. This has potential for increasing autonomy, variety and task identity. Some managers and supervisors are reluctant to delegate work to their subordinates, and so fail to achieve fully utilization of the potential of their staff. This leads to stress due to qualitative underload, or "rust out". Inability to delegate is often a problem for an individual newly appointed to management from the shop floor. This occurs because he or she does not receive the necessary supervisory or management skills training, and is often required to work within the same work group. This makes it difficult for the employee to adopt the new role. An intervention strategy to reduce role ambiguity and to improve role clarity should also be included in this type of job redesign.
- **Semi-autonomous work groups**: Job development opportunities can be improved when levels of responsibility are increased through horizontal job enlargement or by vertical loading. The use of semi-autonomous work groups is similar to the process of vertical loading, but is introduced at the level of the team, rather than the individual. A group of employees is empowered to make decisions that affect their work activities. Groups might also be established to work on specific

177

problems, including safety or quality improvement. Over ten years ago, multi-skilled groups were already operating in approximately two thirds of organizations and, at the time, 68 percent of managers believed that team working helped to reduce absence (CBI, 1997). In fact, the CBI found that organizations operating teamwork experienced 11 percent less absence than those organizations that did not. Consistent with this, significantly lower levels of psychological strain have been found among those working in teams in NHS settings where employee well-being is greater in better functioning teams, and is attributable to improved social support and more frequent opportunities to clarify roles carried out by team members (Borrill *et al.*, 1998).

Despite a substantial number of workers being involved in team-based work, with the possibility of rotating tasks with colleagues, many workers still describe the lack of opportunity and ability to use their skills. This is acknowledged as potentially detrimental to well-being, productivity and performance. As one electrician working in the offshore oil and gas industry said, "When you become bored you do not do a good job; you start getting stale, complacent and upset. The longer you continue like this, the more of a safety hazard you are, to everyone." Empowering employees to take on tasks that give them increased control over their work can have a range of beneficial effects, including improved job satisfaction and performance. For example, in autonomous work groups, improved psychological health is linked to group autonomy (van Mierlo *et al.*, 2001). Furthermore, this relationship is underpinned by individual experiences of control, task variety, workload and social support.

The stress prevention initiatives described above will help to alleviate the problems associated with boredom, job dissatisfaction and low work motivation. However, it is important to note that this type of job redesign rarely occurs in the absence of other changes, such as responsibility for decision making and remuneration (Leach *et al.*, 2003). There is also a need to remember that the effects of such change are not discrete and limited only to the job holder. For example, the nature of supervisory and managerial roles will be altered when the workforce is given more autonomy. Organizational change, therefore, is not simple. The process needs to be regarded in totality when changes are planned. Nevertheless, job enrichment intervention strategies can increase job satisfaction, improve production, and reduce job absence and turnover (Smith and Zehel, cited in ILO, 1992).

Flexible and family-friendly work arrangements

In order to meet challenges from consumers, governments and unions, and the internal pressures associated with the management of a more diverse workforce, organizations are now required to find ways of being flexible and responsive to rapidly changing economic and societal norms. However, the psychological impact of stressors at the boundaries between work and family life is well known (Brough and O'Driscoll, 2005). As the proportion of dual-earner families, single parent families and female-headed families has increased, it has become necessary for organizations to ensure a "family friendly" work environment in order to retain staff (Lewis and Cooper, 1995). The UK Employment Act (2002) provides many employees who have caring responsibilities (whether for children or other adults) with the right to request flexible working hours, stating that the organization should consider such requests seriously, declining them only if there are sound business reasons. Both in advance of and following this, policies and programs have been introduced to provide employees with flexibility in time and place of work, dependent care, financial aid and/or information on outside services (Lobel and Kosseck, 1996). Friedman (1991) suggests that this type of program is a critical component of strategies that improve a company's bottom line.

Alternative work arrangements that offer staff flexibility have been found to be popular with employees and beneficial to organizations. It helps to build employee commitment. Employees are more attached to organizations with family-friendly policies, regardless of the extent to which they might personally benefit, because offering assistance to employees in need symbolizes a concern for employees (Grover and Crooker, 1995).

Specific types of alternative work arrangements include part-time work; job share; leave of absence, telecommuting and other work-at-home arrangements; and flexitime. The provision of more flexible work patterns can eliminate the problems associated with travel to and from work during peak times, and facilitate coping with dependant care or parenting demands. Flexibility in working arrangements or hours provides employees with time during the normal working day to attend to domestic or family issues and crises. Therefore, the introduction of flexitime and flexible scheduling aims to meet the diverse needs of the modern workforce. Typically, the organization defines a "core time" and employees are permitted to arrive and leave

179

work between certain band hours outside of the core period. They are also required to work a minimum number of hours each week (or month) and are allowed take extra hours worked off with the approval of a supervisor.

Indeed, in our experience the greatest pressures reported by parents are the problems of childcare for older children, before and after school hours, and during school holidays. Flexitime would help to minimize the impact of this strain on working parents. Many companies also provide crèche facilities, after-school clubs, school holiday activity centers, or vouchers to contribute towards the costs of childcare in order to help employees cope with the demands of parenting. Together with flexible hours of working, such strategies help to reduce the strains of parenting, and enable the individual to gain greater control over their work and family lives. This, in turn, leads to lower levels of work–family conflict and high levels of job satisfaction (Thomas and Ganster, 1995).

As well as the positive individual effects of flexitime (such as job satisfaction, job control, increased autonomy and improved family relationships), research on the impact on profitability of the organization also suggests a number of advantages (Kinnunen *et al.*, 2005). Studies have indicated decreases in sickness absence, tardiness, overtime and turnover, and these can also have positive effects on an organization's profitability (Dalton and Mesch, 1990; Pierce *et al.*, 1989). In its 2001 survey of 300 organizations, the Industrial Society found that organizations operating policies of flexible annual leave, flexible working hours and arrangements whereby employees could work from the home occasionally, all had absence rates below the average experienced by the sample of respondents as a whole. In a German study, greater commitment to company aims, reduced absenteeism and improved quality of work have also been found (Kauffeld *et al.*, 2004). The benefits of flexitime need to be balanced against the extra organizational costs of administration and management.

The success of a more flexible approach to working hours can rest on two organizational factors: the level of support given by the line manager, and the extent to which the organization is perceived as valuing the personal and family lives of its staff (O'Driscoll *et al.*, 2003). For example, Powell and Mainiero (1999) observed that alternative work arrangements (AWAs) are unlikely to be successful unless they are supported by first-line managers. Their investigation found that the potential for work disruption was a major factor in the managers' decision making processes. Not surprisingly, they tended to focus on their own short-term self-interest. Thus, they were more likely to refuse requests for an AWA if it was perceived to be disruptive to work. First-line managers were most strongly against granting requests for unpaid leave, or requests from subordinates who were working on critical tasks and possessed critical skills. This approach and a focus on short-term, narrow perspectives are unlikely to foster commitment to the organization from the personnel that the strategy of AWAs was intended to achieve. While organizations are advised to offer AWAs to their key employees to ensure that they remain (Grover and Crooker, 1995), it would appear that first-line managers are resisting this innovative policy prescribed by senior management. They appear to be failing to recognize the long-term benefits for the organization in favor of their own immediate objectives. Powell and Mainiero (1999) suggest that organizations will not reap the benefits of AWAs until first-line managers are actively encouraged to support such company-sponsored programs.

Clearly, careful evaluation of the potential need and benefits is vital before embarking on this or other forms of stress management activity. However, it is important to remember that, in either private or public sector sectors, organizations that are viewed as unsupportive of employees will see more psychological distress amongst staff per se, as well as increased work–family conflict leading to such distress (Mauno et al., 2005). The experiences of the "Best Companies to Work For" (Sunday Times, 2009) strongly supports the organizational as well as individual value gained from operating in a more flexible and family-friendly manner. Again, this underlines the need for a stress audit that incorporates the attitudes and opinions of employees.

Reducing the stress of shift work

We have acknowledged that demands for efficiency and productivity, and the rapidly escalating pace of new technology can have a deleterious impact on the working population. The need to engage in shift work and to work long hours affects many people at work, and the spillover impact also causes negative consequences and costs for the individual, the family and for society. Most startlingly, this can include increased risk of heart disease and cancer for employees, owing (at least to some degree) to frequent desynchronization of natural circadian rhythms (Arendt, 2010). There are over 3.5 million shift workers in the UK (HSE, 2006), so it becomes a prudent part of a stress management strategy to minimize the impact of these potential sources of strain and distress that cannot be eliminated from the world of work – or, indeed, reconsider the adoption of shift working in jobs that are not essential for societal functioning – for example, 24-hour banking access (Doyle, 2004). "A 'tailor-made' shift system should be a compromise between the employers' goals, the wishes of the employees, and ergonomic recommendations for the design of shift systems" (Knauth, 1993: 159), with the emphasis on a participatory process of implementation, which is as important as the shift system itself. Options include the design of the shift arrangements, flexitime, selection and recruitment for shift working, stress management education, and physical interventions such as the use of light therapy.

Shift system design: It is possible to meet the needs of a 24-hour production or service schedule, and reduce the impact on the individual, by designing schedules that follow the principles of circadian rhythms. This will alleviate the biological problems associated with shift work. Essentially, this entails a shift system design that considers shift rotation, shift start times, and the number of days for recovery between work periods. Research evidence indicates circadian rhythm synchronization is best when the shift schedule is rotated in a forward manner (days, nights, evenings, days, and so on) rather than a backward rotation (nights, evenings, days, nights) (for a review, see Daus et al., 1998). The replacement of a continuous backward rotating shift system with very quickly forward rotating shifts, led to beneficial effects on employees' sleep, alertness and well-being – particularly among workers aged over-45 (Härmä et al., 2006). Although the new system meant longer working hours at night, it avoided consecutive night shifts and allowed for more time off between shifts. Following night work, employees benefited from more sleep, higher levels of alertness while working and during subsequent rest days, better psychomotor performance, and improved family and social life. All participants in the study voted for the continuation of the new system.

Speed of shift rotation is therefore a factor for consideration. However, there is divided opinion about this practice, since North America favors a slow rotating shift pattern as less disruptive, while Europeans regard rapidly rotating shifts as the least harmful. Rapidly rotating shifts are considered best, since temporary adjustment of the circadian rhythm is considered harmful. Therefore, no adaptation is viewed as better than partial adaptation. Thus, European employees work rapidly rotating shifts during a week, and work only a few (three or four) night shifts in succession, because this is the shift that requires the most physiological adjustment. In this way, circadian disruption is minimized and the problems associated with sleep debt are avoided (Knauth, 1993). Typically, workers in the US work a slow-rotation shift pattern – for example, three weeks of days, three weeks of evenings and three weeks of night shifts). While research evidence is available to suggest that this pattern of working is optimal for the employee, many of the changes to shift patterns include other alterations, such as time off and/or direction of shift rotation. This means that causality and effect are difficult to unravel. For example, the redesign of the shift work pattern for police officers included alterations to a forward shift rotation, the rate of rotation reduced from one week to three weeks, and the six-day week reduced to four or five work days in a row (Mitler, 1992). Nevertheless, after 11 months, a fourfold reduction in sleep problems was reported, a 25 percent reduction in sleep episodes on the night shift was observed. Also, these police officers reported a reduction in the use of sleeping pills and alcohol. Their families also appeared to be more satisfied with the new shift arrangements.

In some instances, employees prefer not to rotate their shift. However, permanent night shift workers report poorer health, lower job satisfaction and increased absenteeism than day workers, with poorer job performance and ill-health clearly linked in healthcare staff (Burch et al., 2009). A study of petroleum workers with up to 20 years experience of 12-hour rotating shifts has identified problems in relation to health, safety, reliability and management, as well as social and family life (Bourdouxhe et al., 1998). The decision to work a permanent night shift is usually the choice of the individual. Thus, the issue of self-selection into a unique work environment is a factor for consideration in the interpretation of these findings.

Shift start time is also a factor in optimizing performance for employees forced to work a shift pattern. Many organizations now start the 12-hour shift pattern at 07.00 rather than the traditional 06.00. In our experience, this slight change has tremendous psychological benefits and is viewed most favorably by the workforce. In fact, Knauth (1993) has found that an early-morning start appears to be associated with increased serious accident and error rates. Recovery time between shift changes is also a factor for consideration, since workers need time for adjustment. A day off after a period of night shift duties seems to be beneficial. Ultimately, a flexible work pattern to meet the needs of the individual and satisfy the demands of the workplace is desirable, but not always easy to put into practice.

Shift work – mandatory or self-selection: While it would seem to be practical to select individuals on the basis of their ability to work shifts, the current weakness of methods of selection (usually question-naires), and laws on discrimination on the grounds of disability, tend to preclude this as a stress management option. Theoretically, organi-zations should be able to reduce the impact of shift working by identi-fying those individuals most suited to shift work. This might include, for example, the selection of employees for their ability to stay awake (Mitler, 1992), for shift tolerance (Czeisler *et al.*, 1982), or stress resis-tance (Cervinka, 1993). However, companies usually report not being able to find enough employees to work the unsocial night shift and so cannot rely on a volunteer workforce. There is also considerable varia-tion between individuals, such as jet fighter pilots, in their cognitive functioning during sleep deprivation, which also differs from their perceptions of its effect on objectively assessed performance (Van Dongen, 2006). It would seem that, currently, the problems outweigh the benefits. Thus, a more useful strategy is to allow individuals to self-select for shift work, accepting that there will be differences in personal capacities to cope, and actively to identify limitations and preventa-tive measures. When people are able to choose their shift pattern, they can structure their work and family life to meet the needs of work and parenting demands with minimal disruption. While people vary according to their preferences on the time of day for working – some are "owls", others are "larks" – it makes sense to recognize the limita-tions of any individual. A failure to do so, combined with worsening job conditions, was blamed for the fatal passenger plane crash near Buffalo in 2009 (*The Guardian*, 2010c). Both pilot and co-pilot were overtired, having attempted to sleep in the busy crew lounge after long hours of travel to reach the airport from which they were to take off. In addition, the co-pilot was supplementing her pay by working in a coffee shop, thus lengthening her working week. In the cost-cutting by airlines following 9/11, falling pay, protracted commuting patterns and consequent fatigue have produced increasingly challeng-ing working conditions for US regional pilots.

Stress management and education: Understanding the nature of stress, individual vulnerability to potentially stressful situations, and the influence of time of day on behaviors are part of stress management education. It also includes the topics of relaxation training and cognitive restructuring. These are discussed in detail later (pp. 201–7). It is suggested that shift workers are also aware of the principles of sleep hygiene in order to minimize the impact of shift working (see Chapter 4).

Physical interventions: Two popular means of circadian rhythm adjustment are light therapy and chronobiotics; chronobiotics are "substances that adjust the timings of internal biological rhythms" (Touitou and Bogdan, 2007: 294). These are normally used by night shift workers, although the optimal doses and exposures have yet to be determined (Arendt and Skene, 2005). The purpose of these physical interventions is to readjust an individual's circadian rhythm. However, it must be remembered that the circadian rhythm will never completely adjust to a night schedule, mainly because the employee will usually revert to the normal societal 24-hour pattern during non-work time. In fact, Daniel (1990) suggests that it takes ten to 20 days of continuous night work to reverse the circadian rhythm, and that complete adaptation is practically impossible. If achieved, it would promote social isolation on days off and is not what most night shift workers would want.

Light therapy can be used to trick the body into believing it is daytime when it is actually night-time. This overcomes the disruption to the individual's circadian rhythm caused by the body being active in the absence of light. In normal conditions, the suprachiasmatic nucleus, reacting to the presence of light, assumes a period of activity. When the individual works at night, conflicting signals cause disruption to many bodily functions. The desynchronization of circadian rhythms can cause feelings of fatigue and general malaise, described by Mitler (1992) as "occupational jet lag". However, the use of four 15-minute bright light pulses during night shifts, wearing dark glasses outside, adhering to sleep schedules in dark bedrooms and exposure to light in the afternoons have all been shown to help the body reach a "compromise circadian phase position" that produces improved sleep and better work performance at night (Smith *et al.*, 2009). Research evidence suggests that light therapy can also reduce problems associated with sleep and alertness (Daus *et al.*, 1998).

Light therapy suppresses melatonin secretion and is often used in conjunction with the drug melatonin. The success of light therapy in readjusting circadian rhythms depends on "exposure to and avoidance of bright light at specific times of the 'biological night'" (Arendt, 2010). In its natural form, the hormone melatonin is produced mainly at night. Therefore, melatonin therapy involves the administration of low doses of exogenous melatonin, taken optimally at dawn or dusk, to bring forward or put back phases of sleep, body temperature and cortisol (Arendt and Skene, 2005). Its effects have been used successfully to combat sleep disorder as well as shift work. Although melatonin is a natural hormone, and travelers seem happy to use it to overcome the problems of jet lag, not everyone is happy taking pills on a daily basis to alter the body's time clock. However, the long-term effects of this type of intervention, and concerns about drug tolerance and dependence, are not well documented or understood.

The HSE guidance on shift working in the UK provides a simple five-step approach for use by employers; this highlights the importance of workload, type of work activity, the timing and duration of shifts, the direction of shift rotation and the number and length of breaks both within and between shifts.

Reducing role stress

The constructs of role ambiguity and role conflict are acknowledged as potent sources of stress in the work environment that are associated with a variety of negative attitudinal health and behavioral outcomes. Thus, role clarification interventions can be used as stress control strategies. For example, Quick (1979) used participative goal setting to reduce role stress amongst employees in an insurance company. During the 14-month period, 15 executive officers and their immediate staff took part in this field study. During a one-day training session, three dimensions of goal setting were emphasized: task goal properties (difficulty and clarity), supervisory goal behaviors (the quality and quantity of feedback), and subordinate goal behavior (participation). Measures were collected six months prior to formal training in goal setting and at the five- and eight-month post training points. Significant reductions in measures of role conflict and role ambiguity were observed. Considerable reductions in sickness absenteeism levels were recorded five months after training, but this effect was not observed at the eight-month point.

A responsibility charting approach was used by Schaubroeck *et al.* (1993) to reduce role ambiguity reported by personnel in the business services department of a university. After the management team had negotiated and clarified their own roles, they were assigned to either a "waterfall" condition (in which they were helped by consultants to negotiate and clarify roles with each of their subordinates), or a waiting control group. This intervention was clearly successful in reducing perceptions of role ambiguity, and also improved satisfaction with supervision. However, there were no measurable effects on subjective psychological strain, physical symptoms or lost time due to illness.

It is comparatively rare for a study to capture the narratives of employees participating in a stress management intervention. However, a hospital-based role stress reduction initiative (designed to ease the conflict between clinical and administrative duties) found that the nurses' perceptions of the organizational context, the processes involved in implementation, and the outcomes provided valuable insights into the success of organizational change that aims to benefit employees (Randall *et al.*, 2007). Following a series of "away days", in which nurses worked in groups to discuss the conflicting demands of office-based tasks and patient care needs, senior managers met with representatives from the senior nursing staff. It was decided to formally schedule staff office hours within the rota system, so as to protect the time nurses needed to complete administrative tasks; extra resources were agreed to provide cover on the ward as necessary. Alongside reductions in workload, the senior staff noticed that improvements in the time taken to complete paperwork had a positive knock-on effect on colleagues who had been awaiting its completion. Nurses' managerial performance improved, as they had more time to talk to their staff and carry out staff development functions, such as appraisals, as well as health and safety checks. This, in turn, helped to foster aspects of organizational culture, such as a sense of shared goals and closer working relationships. In addition, individual differences in experience of the work context and in the implementation of the intervention became apparent, which contributes to the debate over why the positive effects of change do not always match up to expectations (Randall *et al.*, 2007).

Role negotiation

Role negotiation as a way of reducing stress is a technique based on an idea described originally by Harrison (1972). It is a useful way of overcoming the problems that lead to ineffectiveness caused by behavior that an individual is unwilling to change because it would mean a loss of power or influence. Harrison believes that this method works because most people prefer a fair negotiated settlement to a state of unresolved conflict. Thus, they will be motivated to engage in some action themselves, and make concessions in order to achieve this aim. In role negotiation, the change effort is focused solely on the working relationships among the people involved. The matter of likes or dislikes for one another is avoided. It is important to acknowledge that issues concerning the personal feelings of the people involved are avoided. This technique has been used, for example, on hospital children's wards where the role of parents has become much more central to the child's care and has required renegotiation of mutual expectations, which can vary depending on the grade of staff involved (Callery and Smith, 1991).

During role negotiation, an imposed structure is created to allow a controlled negotiation to take place. Each person involved discusses and agrees in writing to change certain behaviors in return for changes in behavior by the other party. For example, each person asks for changes in the behavior of the other party that would permit them to do their own job more effectively. This is in exchange for changing some aspect of their own behavior that would serve to improve the effectiveness of the other party involved. Therefore, an accurate diagnosis of the problem is necessary. It is crucial to avoid generalities and to be specific. That is, you would ask the other person to: stop doing "x"; do more of "y"; or do less of "z". In turn, these are the type of actions that the other party might ask of you. A diagnosis should be carried out as the first step in role negotiation, as this helps to overcome the problems of generalized comments or resort to personalized attacks. All requests and agreements must be in writing, and each person must give something in order to get something. If one party reneges on their part of the bargain, the whole contract becomes invalid.

The technique can be used either within a group, to negotiate among work group members; or between a team leader or manager and his or her team. Often, use is made of an outside facilitator for optimal effectiveness. Some progress follow-up is required to determine whether the contracts are being honored, and to assess the effectiveness of negotiations. Those who recognize the similarity with the processes involved in political or peace agreements, or indeed industrial disputes, need not be surprised that role negotiation is taught on legal training programs. The relevance of this approach to tackling perceived violations of the psychological contract is also clear, by helping to clarify mutual expectations.

Improving perceptions of worker control

Lack of job control is acknowledged as a potent source of stress and perception of control seems to be important for job satisfaction, health and well-being. While the research evidence to support the interactive demand-control model proposed by Karasek (1979) has been inconsistent (de Lange *et al.*, 2003), there is sufficient evidence to suggest that a high level of work control has beneficial effects on levels of job satisfaction (Dwyer and Ganster, 1991), psychological well-being (Perrewe and Ganster, 1989), and indicators of cardiovascular disease (Karasek *et al.*, 1988). Warr *et al.* (1996) suggested that support for Karasek's model is found when a focused measure of work control is used (that is, the extent to which employees had control over specific items, and how and when they did the work related to these items – namely, method and timing control), rather than when a broad measure of control is assessed. Sargent and Terry, (1998) also report that "type of control" is an important factor in the demand-control model. Their study of administrative staff in a university found that job demands were buffered by "task control", but not the more peripheral aspects of work control such as decision and scheduling control. Task control also buffered the negative relationship between role ambiguity and job satisfaction, and between work overload and depressive symptoms. Another study of the rail transport industry investigated the impact of restoring control to managers for reporting and addressing faults with station equipment (Randall *et al.*, 2005). This had been previously withdrawn, and was reported to have had a negative impact on job satisfaction and employee well-being. The increase in the new level of responsibility was not uniformly applied, which permitted comparison between groups and the key finding that increased autonomy led to significantly improved well-being for those staff, while psychological strain increased for those excluded from the positive change initiative.

A variety of strategies exists to improve perceptions of worker control and increase the opportunities for decision making at work. These include building and developing semi-autonomous work groups, quality circles, safety improvement groups and health circles. Ultimately the aim is for the workforce to be empowered and involved in changes to any system or practice that induces stress at work. This is to create a better balance between the perceived levels of demand and worker control. The organizational benefits have been highlighted in a manufacturing setting where training employees how to rectify faults on the machines they were operating, resulted in an increase in production time of 6.3 percent and a gain in output estimated to be worth £125,000 (Leach *et al.*, 2001). In continuing research in a photographic paper manufacturing plant, Leach *et al.*, (2003) found that increasing employees' job-related knowledge led to significant reductions in psychological strain.

In a precursor to this line of research, the impact of training machine operators to fix faults in the production of computer circuit boards produced startling results (Jackson and Wall, 1991). Prior to the intervention, the amount of down time for the machines involved totaled 150 minutes per day, which dropped to 110 minutes after the training course, and still further to 26 minutes per day 40 days later! This demonstrates not only the organizational benefits, but also the psychological gains from empowering employees. Given the opportunity to control this aspect of their work, workers demonstrated implicit learning within their roles; this prevented the occurrence of faults, leading to direct savings for the production process. Wall and Clegg (1981) describe an intervention that aimed to increase worker autonomy among a group of employees with poor productivity, low morale and low motivation. This approach utilized the Hackman and Oldham Job Characteristics Model, and revealed low scores for "autonomy", "feedback" and "task identity". Job satisfaction and motivation levels were low, and high levels of emotional distress were recorded. Subsequent redesign of work increased group autonomy, group task identity and group feedback. Increases in group autonomy involved shifting responsibility and control from supervisors to the work teams. As part of this program, supervisors adopted a support role, and work teams took control over the pace of work, the organization of rest breaks, the allocation of tasks and overtime working. At the 18-month evaluation point, the observed increases in "autonomy" and "task identity" were sustained, but not for "group feedback". Emotional distress was also significantly reduced at the six-month and 18-month follow-up periods.

Warr's Vitamin Model, which predicts curvilinear relationships (for example, U-Shaped) between work characteristics and well-being, has been tested in a range of settings. A study of 1437 Dutch healthcare employees found that higher levels of emotional exhaustion – which are indicative of burnout – were linked to less than optimal levels of control, but that personal need for autonomy should be taken into account in future research (de Jonge and Schaufeli, 1998). The above studies demonstrate that employee well-being improves as worker control increases, conferring advantages for job and organizational performance. However, it is not necessarily the case that introducing these changes automatically improves the situation, as the implications and processes need careful attention. An essential part of this is to consult with, and incorporate the views of, the staff concerned; otherwise, the intervention might unintentionally appear to be a disempowering management-led ploy.

Increasing worker participation in decision making

Actual and perceived involvement in one's workplace, known as "employee voice", is increasingly acknowledged as an important predictor of well-being. In addition to the design of jobs, the extent to which employees are consulted and informed by the organization is significantly linked with job satisfaction, as well as with experiences on the continuum from contentment to anxiety (Wood, 2008). This finding is based on the Workplace Employee Relations Survey of 22,451 employees, and further illustrates the key role of management support in modulating the impact of workloads and control on workers. This is consistent with a wide-ranging review of the literature, which found that employee anxiety and depression is reduced when control is increased, although this might not protect employees from overall poor working conditions (Egan et al., 2007).

Lack of participation in decision making is a primary cause of role conflict and role ambiguity, mediated by one's perceived influence over the situation and the efficacy of communication in the organization. Feeling controlled rather than "in control" is associated with a state of stress; individuals who feel controlled are likely to perceive their job as a "strain", rather than a challenge and source of motivation. The use of small group discussions or focus groups is recommended, to examine how sources of stress might be reduced. Research has shown that increased participation in decision making has a beneficial affect by reducing role conflict and improving role clarity. Karasek's (1990) large scale assessment of 8504 Swedish white collar workers assessed the impact of change on a range of outcomes, comparing instances when employees were involved (and therefore had a sense of control) with results for non-participating individuals. The clear-cut findings show that, for workers who had been involved and able to participate in the change process, the rate of depression was half (27.8 percent versus 13.5 percent), as was coronary heart disease (3.4 percent versus

8.6 percent) and absenteeism (5.0 percent versus 10.7 percent). Far fewer incidences of participative change were found for women and older employees. Jackson (1983) described an intervention to reduce role stress by increasing participation in decision making amongst staff in an out patient facility within a university hospital. All nursing supervisors attended a two-day training workshop, and then employee participation was increased by requiring these supervisors to hold scheduled staff meetings at least twice a month. Measures taken after six months indicated that "participation" had a significant impact in reducing role conflict and role ambiguity. Positive effects were observed on perceived influence, emotional strain and job satisfaction. It was clear that the number of staff meetings held was a determinant of the level of both role conflict and role ambiguity in the work unit.

Health circles: The concept of scheduled staff meetings has been extended into the use of "health circles" (Aust and Ducki, 2004). Employees meet for active discussions on health problems and work-related stress, in an attempt to identify workplace stress and the strategies that could be used to reduce or eliminate stress. It is fundamental that the workers realize that they are the best placed people to do this task because they are directly involved and can benefit directly. However, to be effective they might need some initial help in understanding the process of stress. Aust and Ducki's (2004) review highlights that health circles "are an effective tool for the improvement of physical and psychosocial working conditions" and have noticeable positive effects on health, well-being and sickness absence. If the recommendations suggested are put into effect by the organization, positive effects on production are also observed (Kuhn, cited in ILO, 1993). The objectives of the health circle concept are:

- to expand knowledge and understanding about stress development
- to improve personal stress management by adopting sound health-promoting behaviors
- to create a work environment that is beneficial to health
- to recognize and modify work conditions that lead to stress.

This approach has been effectively used by crane operators working in the steel industry, but easily could be adopted into other work environments. Health circles usually require some expert help initially. This could include the occupational health doctor or nurse, safety officer, or other experts as required (for example, from design, engineering or maintenance departments). In "health circles", managers and workers join forces for the systematic consideration of work stress and health.

One of the main problems associated with an increase in worker participation in job design is the threat it poses to managers and supervisors. Foremen and shop stewards have reported that both competencies and functions are threatened. Thus, the issue of increased stress among these personnel should not be overlooked when this type of organizational change is introduced. Indeed, many of the individuals who take part in a health circle, a working party, or any small-group discussion in the workplace step outside their normal role. Therefore, they initially need help to overcome the stress associated with this situation, and to function as an effective member of the group.

Self-managed teams: Many organizations have introduced self-managed teams in response to the need for greater flexibility and improved speed of response to rapidly changing market competition and turbulent business circumstances. Peters and Waterman (1982) have suggested that the concept of "self-managed teams" is a basic building block through which to achieve goal competition advantage. However, potential "trip wires" for their success have been identified within bureaucratic systems (McHugh and Bennett, 1999), which is consistent with findings that the introduction of self-managed teams into small, service sector firms can have a mixed impact (Chaston, 1998). Chaston found that self-managed teams were successful at developing new products, executing new skill development programs, identifying new ways of enhancing employee productivity, using customer knowledge to define quality standards and utilizing computers to analyze key data. Conversely, the move towards self-managed teams did not impact on overall performance in terms of identifying specialist market niches, offering superior products, structuring the organization to optimize workforce effectiveness, increasing employee productivity, or measuring the customers' service quality expectations. This study did not report the impact of working in a self-managed team on the employees involved. While there are problems for employees, it is suggested that benefits exist in terms of job satisfaction, health and well-being. For example, membership of such a team has been related to a reduction in emotional exhaustion in manufacturing, as well as service sector settings (Elloy et al., 2001). In addition, one of the benefits of the self-managed team is in the improvement to the employee–customer interface (Griffen et al., 1994). The popularity of semi-autonomous work groups has been enhanced by the advent of, and rapid developments in, computer-based management and information systems. However, it must be kept in mind that the introduction of self-managing teams will not be the panacea for all the problems within an organization. This type of change can be rewarding, but is also time-consuming to execute and complex to manage.

SECONDARY LEVEL STRESS MANAGEMENT INTERVENTIONS

Although a growing body of evidence supports the view that organizational-level stress control and stress prevention interventions are more effective than individual-level coping strategies, because they have a more lasting effect (Giga *et al.*, 2003), it is clear from the previous discussion that the prevention of all sources of negative stress is not possible. Therefore, it is suggested that the effects of exposure to stress could be minimized by the use of techniques aimed at improving stress coping processes by the individual. Therefore, secondary prevention is concerned with the prompt detection and management of potentially deleterious conditions by increasing self-awareness and improving stress management skills. While these strategies are usually conceptualized as individual-level stress management options, they also embrace the view of individual employees working within a team or work group. Newman and Beehr (1979) grouped these strategies into four categories aimed at:

1 Psychological condition
 - planning ahead, managing one's life
 - self-awareness
 - realistic aspirations
2 Physiological or physical conditions
 - diet
 - sleep
 - exercise
 - relaxation and meditation
 - anger management
3 Changing behavior
 - taking time off for leisure and holidays
 - changing certain aspects of behavior that are stress inducing
 - building social support networks at home and work
 - being more assertive

4 Changing the environment
- changing to a less demanding job
- changing to a less demanding organization.

It is commonplace for organizations to help individuals either to minimize the effects of exposure to stress, or to learn techniques to cope more effectively with stress. We classify these under two separate headings: "skills training options" and "stress and healthy lifestyle education and management".

Skills training

The term "skills training options" refers to the fact that the stress management activity is in the provision of training per se. After training, individuals or work groups are required to put their new skills into practice by using them to deal with potentially stressful situations. Therefore, these stress management techniques tend to be classified as a "reactive" approach to stress management, in that they help the individual to cope effectively when exposed to a stressful situation. As we have stated, the objective is to improve or modify the individual's response to perceived strain to avoid a negative outcome. This includes a variety of skills training, including:

- interpersonal and social skills; leadership skills
- assertiveness
- cognitive coping techniques – for example, avoiding faulty thinking
- time management
- relaxation training, meditation, yoga, and biofeedback
- Type A behavior management
- anger management.

Before each of these is considered, the issue of training as an effective stress management strategy is discussed.

Training as method of stress reduction

Effective training is a method of reducing the adverse impact of stress at work. This type of program should be tailored by finding out what the employee already knows and expects, what they need to know and to do, and how the information should be presented and best received.

The transmission of information tends to be more effective if:

- The message is presented in more than one medium – that is, using both sight and sound. This explains why a poster campaign or news bulletins have only limited impact, and the recent success attributed to interactive video as an instruction technique.
- The receivers are active rather than passive during the communication of the message. A meeting that requires the workforce to be actively involved in small group, two-way discussions, rather than delivered during a briefing session or lecture, is likely to have a more positive impact.
- The message carrier has credibility with the audience. Information from an untrustworthy or unbelievable source will not be accepted.
- The audience is permitted to participate in the planning of a program or initiative, thus, they have ownership of the problem and the solution, and resistance to change will be reduced.

However, knowledge alone does not guarantee that it will be used when needed. In collaboration with the workforce, specific, observable and measurable behaviors need to be identified to enable a suitable training program to be designed. The skills and procedures necessary to handle a critical situation should be imprinted and memorized through training and rehearsal. Thereby, they become part of a routine that can be reproduced automatically when the individual is under stress. Realistic simulation exercises, drills and refresher training are vital for the maintenance of the skills and procedures necessary to maintain a safe environment and to deal with emergencies when they occur. In a recessionary climate, training budgets tend to be restricted, and this might limit access to training or the updating of training. This will exacerbate stress levels because the workforce realizes that they have not been allowed the opportunity to update their training, or might fear that the people around them will be not adequately trained. Unless the effectiveness of the training is evaluated, its true worth will not be recognized. Therefore, training departments are likely to continue to be regarded as being merely an organizational cost and "step-child", rather than as a cost–benefit strategy.

Research evidence suggests that older, experienced workers receive less formal training than their younger co-workers. This seems to be a short-sighted business strategy where we have an ageing population. Indeed, one of our challenges is to find ways of increasing the age at which people typically stop working, by ensuring the removal of barriers for them to remain in work (OECD, 2004). The Equalities and Human Rights Commission has gone as far as proposing the abolition of the compulsory UK retirement age, while political parties have pledged to increase it to 66, claiming this will benefit the economy by as much as £15 billion (*The Guardian*, 2010a). Since chronological age per se appears not to be a good predictor of job performance or health, training to meet job demands is one of the ways that we can extend the working life of employees. In rapidly changing jobs, lack of training could contribute to the under-performance of employees, particularly the older personnel who might be educated to a lower level than the younger co-workers. The stereotype of the older employee – held by managers as more reliable, conscientious, better at interpersonal skills and team working, but less effective in terms of ability to grasp new ideas, to adapt to change and to accept the introduction of new technology – builds barriers to the development of the older worker. Therefore, a continuous learning environment is important for personnel of all ages. Implementation of a training needs analysis, together with the use of training strategies that take account of the needs and anxieties of older employees, is critical. For example, exposure to computer training is more likely to provoke anxiety among those individuals who have never touched a keyboard before, compared with younger employees, who have been introduced to computer skills as part of a formal education program. It is possible that the older employee might also need more encouragement to retrain, not due to anxieties and a lack of confidence compared with younger workers, but also because of age bias. At least two thirds of jobs required information technology (IT) skills, yet only one fifth of employees aged 50–59 are likely to have received training recently (Age Concern, 2007). These are issues that are likely to be identified by the stress audit process. Also, it is suggested that older employees should help to develop their own training programs in order to overcome such problems.

Clearly, many of the sources of stress identified in a stress audit could be prevented by effective training initiatives. Is the training program targeted, developed with input from the potential trainees, and delivered in a mode that addresses the needs of employees, and then assessed for effectiveness?

Evaluation of training should include:

- A measure of trainees' reaction to the program. Kirkpatrick (1959) states that participants must rate a training session or course positively to obtain maximum benefits.
- A measure of the participants' learning. While participants might perceive a training program to be favorable or useful, we cannot assume that they have learned anything by attending the course. Therefore, it is important there is objective determination of the amount of learning, perhaps by the administration of a questionnaire.
- An "outcome" measure. This is a measure of the change in behavior as a result of attending the program. Have the training objectives been met, and is the employee able to behave in the manner specified by the job description?

In the following sections, we discuss interpersonal training skills and leadership, assertiveness, cognitive coping strategies, time management, relaxation and meditation, Type A behavior management, and anger control.

Interpersonal and social skills training

As Gazda (1973) says:

> As a result of a person's socialization, [s]he has already acquired some interpersonal skills. However, one's level of functioning in terms of these skills can be raised. Everyone has a vast capacity to being more understanding, respectful, warm, genuine, open, direct, and concrete in his [her] human relationships. With a sound body of theoretical knowledge, appropriate models, and numerous opportunities for personal experiencing, the process of becoming more fully human can be greatly accelerated.

This is the essence of interpersonal skills training. It covers a range of communication skills and the need to understand the barriers to good communication. Skills such as listening, assertiveness, conflict resolution and collaborative problem solving, are part of this type of skills program. Many of these skills are also embedded in leadership skills training programs. As has been mentioned earlier, workers exposed to a manager or supervisor who is excessively demanding and insensitive, or bullying (Hoel *et al.*, 2004) are likely to experience a high level of strain at work. Indeed, legal suits involving UK- and US-based high profile corporations have resulted in the extraction of damages on the charge that a supervisor in their employ was instrumental in the deterioration of a subordinate's health. Matt Driscoll, a sports reporter for the *News of the World* was awarded £792,736 following an employment tribunal ruling that his managers, of whom the most senior went on to become head of communications for the UK Conservative Party, had subjected him to bullying remarks and "a consistent pattern of bullying behaviour" (*The Guardian*, 2009a).

However, the impact of training courses designed to improve interpersonal skills is variable. Despite the increased emphasis on patient quality of care, an evaluation of communication training for general practitioners, with and without patient feedback, revealed little success (Cheraghi-Sohi and Bower, 2008). This might have been due to the absence of clear criteria and a theoretical basis, or, indeed, doctors' length of experience; however, there is also a question mark concerning the transferability of the training into the work setting (Clarke, 2001).

Heaney *et al.*, (1995) describe the effectiveness of the use of interpersonal skills training as part of a care giver support program. The goals of this field experiment were to teach employees about the helping potential of support systems, to build skills in mobilizing available support from others at work, to teach employees about participatory problem-solving approaches, and using these in work team meetings. As part of the program, participants, including managers, refined their interpersonal skills associated with exchanging social support with others, including clarifying misunderstandings, providing constructive feedback, and asking others for help. Six training sessions of approximately five hours each were held over a nine-week period. A total of 785 employees took part in the full program and responded to the post-test survey. Compared with a control group, program participants who had attended at least five of the six training sessions exhibited enhanced mental health and job satisfaction. Individual skill training and modifications in team decision making processes increased the amount of supportive feedback on the job, and strengthened participants' perceptions of their abilities to handle disagreements and overload at work. It also enhanced the work team climate in the group homes (Heaney *et al.*, 1995). Therefore, attendance on this program appears to have enhanced mental health and increased the coping resources of these care givers.

It is an important finding, because this occupational group is known to feel uncomfortable about seeking aid for themselves (Cherniss, 1980). In a more formal work context, the introduction of a communications strategy by Hinchingbrooke Healthcare NHS Trust at the instigation of the HSE emphasized management training workshops, monthly top-level managerial "walkabout" meetings, monthly two-way meetings for all managers with the staff for whom they are responsible, and the introduction of a policy of managers thanking their staff (HSE, 2005). Over a two-year period, staff absence dropped from 6 percent to 3.8 percent, and staff ratings of work pressure went from being among the highest 20 percent in the UK to being in the lowest 20 per cent (HSE, 2005).

However, the evidence on the efficacy of interpersonal skills training within organizations is variable, and dependent on the quality of the studies conduct to evaluate it. One of the more promising findings demonstrated the positive impact of an intervention designed to reduce burnout among mental health nurses in the UK (Ewers *et al.*, 2002). Participants were randomly allocated to either the training or the control group and, following the program, statistically significant decreases in emotional exhaustion and depersonalization were found among those in receipt of the training, with improvements in levels of personal accomplishment. Thus, training in interpersonal skills is usually a key issue in communication training. In addition to gaining an understanding of leadership roles and behavioral style, many such courses include various interpersonal skill modules, such as reflective listening; understanding body language; anger management; and recognition of the differences between assertiveness, aggression, and abrasive behaviors.

Assertiveness

The need to deal with other people as part of one's job can be one of the most stressful aspects of working life. It means that we can be exposed to difficult situations. For example:

- having to convey a decision that you know your staff will not like
- having to handle an irate customer without losing valuable business, or making promises that are difficult to keep
- being faced with unreasonable work demands or time deadlines; being asked to work extra time or at the weekend when you already have made other plans.

Assertiveness training helps us to deal with such demands without becoming angry or upset. When we are assertive, we are able to negotiate or say "No" to unreasonable demands without becoming aggressive or non-assertive. Thus, it is a useful stress management technique. A failure to handle difficult situations can make us feel angry, anxious, frustrated and "stressed". Assertiveness training teaches us to be able to speak up and be taken seriously without damaging the rights of other people. The aim of assertive behavior is to satisfy the needs and wants of both parties involved in a situation.

Typically, an assertiveness training course teaches the individual to:

- understand the differences between assertion, non-assertion and aggression
- recognize the verbal and non-verbal aspects of assertive, non-assertive and aggressive behaviors
- recognize and use different types of assertion, including empathy
- handle aggressive and non-assertive behaviors
- understand the concept of rights and responsibilities
- make and refuse requests
- give and receive praise; handle negative feelings and criticism; give bad news
- identify steps in reducing dependence on others (Back and Back, 1991; Fritchie and Melling, 1991; Hayes, 2002).

Cognitive coping strategies

Occupational stress is now viewed as a transactional process whereby employees appraise and react to a potential source of stress. Cognitive style influences our appraisal of a potentially stressful situation and the coping strategy subsequently used. Research evidence also suggests that the use of certain coping strategies, such as "avoidance coping" are associated with poor psychological well-being (Snow et al., 2003), while the use of problem-oriented coping is linked to positive mental health (Guppy and Weatherstone, 1997). Indeed, Beck (1987) suggests that individuals are instrumental in creating their own negative feelings by having irrational beliefs. These influence the individual's perception of an event, their ability to cope and the consequences of failure.

It is suggested (Beck *et al.*, 1991) that dysfunctional attitudes produce clinical symptomology. These include:

- vulnerability – "Whenever I take a chance or risk, I am only looking for trouble"; or, "People will reject you if they know your weaknesses".
- need for approval – "I need other people's approval for me to be happy".
- success–perfectionism – "My life is wasted unless I am a success", and "I must be a useful, productive or creative person or life has no meaning".
- imperatives – "I should be happy all the time", "I should always have complete control over my feelings", and "I should try to impress other people if I want them to like me".

The use of cognitive restructuring as a stress management technique aims to examine dysfunctional attitudes and irrational thoughts. By examining the potentially faulty thought processes that exist when the individual is confronted with a stressful event, the process aims to improve the balance between perceptions of a demand and our ability to cope. It involves thinking about stressful events to make them seem less threatening, and the challenging of irrational thoughts. Thus, reactions to a situation are changed by the way in which the circumstances are perceived. A variety of techniques are available to help in the cognitive reappraisal of stressful situations. In order to identify rational versus irrational beliefs, the individual is encouraged to examine beliefs, thoughts, feelings and actions, together with their consequences. To understand a coping strategy used in response to a potentially stressful situation, it is necessary to examine the rationality of a belief about the situation. A rational belief is one that sits comfortably with you and your outlook on life, while an irrational belief is one that causes discomfort or distress.

We tend to hold distorted or irrational beliefs in a variety of situations:

Jumping to conclusions, when there is no appropriate evidence or fact to justify a conclusion: This happens, for example, when we conclude that someone dislikes us because they fail to turn up for a meeting or an appointment. In reality, a number of other reasons could explain this action.

Ignoring important details: This is "minimization", and involves focusing on one detail taken out of its context and ignoring the more important aspects of a situation. An example would be feeling hopeless and a failure because you did not get a promotion, but ignoring the fact that ten other people on the promotion board were turned down also. In fact, only one person in 12 could have been promoted, and many others did not even reach the promotion board shortlist for consideration for the promotion.

Overgeneralizing: This means drawing conclusions from one or two isolated events and assuming that it can be applied to all situations. For example, assuming that you are hopeless at everything you do, and punishing yourself excessively and repeatedly because you found one mistake on a 50-page report.

Exaggerating the importance of things: This is known as "magnification", and occurs when we think that a situation is vital or very significant when, in reality, it is trivial. An example would be imagining that something awful is about to happen because your boss has asked to see you in his or her office.

Taking things personally: "Personalization" is the tendency to believe that events happening around us are somehow related to us in an important way, even when there is no evidence for this. For example, the boss asks everyone to take extra care in getting ready for a visit from an important customer. However, you assume that the boss is criticizing you alone, even though the request was presented to everyone at the morning staff meeting.

Thinking in terms of extremes: Often, we may see things only in terms of opposites, with no room for anything in between these points of view.

To avoid falling into such traps, it is necessary to examine our thoughts and feelings in order to detect and define the irrationalities. A five-step approach is recommended for refuting irrational ideas:

1 Write down the facts.
2 Write down your thoughts and feelings.
3 Focus on your emotional response.
4 Dispute and change the irrational thought or notion:
   - Is there any support for the idea?
   - What is the evidence for the falseness of the idea?
   - Does any evidence exist for the truth of the idea?
   - What is the worst thing that could happen?
   - What good things might occur if...?
5 Substitute alternative patterns of thought.

It is also suggested that we engage in a mental monologue and convert our destructive self-talk into constructive self-talk. Flexibility in thinking about a situation is necessary in order to manage stress effectively. By taking a problem-solving approach and reappraising the situation in a rational way, we avoid stress inducing situations.

Time management

As we have acknowledged, an ever-increasing volume of demand and pressure to do more and more, in less time, and with fewer resources are some of the "hot spot" sources of stress in contemporary organizations. However, a demand situation is only defined as stressful when the perception of that level of demand exceeds the perception of one's ability to meet the demand. Richards' (1987) review of interventions suggests that the concept of time management potentially gives employees a way of coping with demands. For example:

- grouping them into "key-result areas" so that they make sense
- concentrating on priorities so that attention is focused on fewer demands
- reducing demands through work scheduling.

However, this needs to be part of an overall strategy for the individual employee. In a study of university staff and students (Kearns and Gardiner, 2007), clear career direction proved to be the most important predictor of perceived work effectiveness, followed by planning and prioritizing. Thus, the goal of time management is, "Work smarter not harder" (Mackenzie, 1972). Time management is concerned with developing a personal sense of time, thinking about the future and setting goals; analyzing where, how and why you are spending your time; finding a proper balance between working life and leisure time; and achieving life goals by gaining control of time. Typically, individuals attending a time management course will be able to:

- put time management into perspective by understanding the nature of time
- recognize common time problems – such as, procrastination, lack of delegation, mismanaged meetings

- keep a time log
- make effective use of time by defining values, objectives, goals and priorities, and then spend as much time as possible engaged in priority activities; the ability to produce a list of tasks and identify each in terms of "priority" ("A" = must do; "B" = should do; "C" = can wait) is a key time management skill
- discover the time of day when one works best at certain tasks
- manage meetings more effectively
- delegate more effectively.

However, the ability to apply all of these strategies is not within the mandate of jobs that lack opportunities for autonomy and decision making, or for those confined to working a shift roster. Quite simply, much of time is not their own. Therefore, time management tends to be perceived as a stress management technique mainly for managers, white collar and administrative staff. Nevertheless, certain time management activities can be used to help shop-floor, blue collar employees to gain control over work demands. For example, the tendency to waste time or procrastinate can be identified by simply keeping a log or diary (Drucker, 2007). Also, the reorganization of jobs or tasks is a key factor in the elimination or reduction of stress at work. However, in our experience, certain employees are often exposed to a stressful situation because they are not allowed to take some time out to reorganize a system or practice that is stressful, inefficient or ineffective. They are like hamsters running in a wheel! When an opportunity to hold a focus group session is provided, in order to discuss better, safer or less stressful ways of working, ideas and suggestions usually flow. As Adair (2002) states, "To save time you must spend time: it is an investment that will pay rich dividends". Therefore, we are suggesting that organizations should give some time to employees in order to "make time" to reduce stress at work.

Relaxation and meditation

The purpose of relaxation training, meditation or yoga is to reduce the individual's arousal level when exposed to a source of stress. These techniques are also used to bring about a calmer state of affairs, both physiologically and psychologically. The effectiveness of meditation as an arousal reduction approach to stress management has been investigated and found to be effective. As a relaxation technique, it is easily taught and practiced. The psychological benefits of relaxation include a sense of personal control and mastery, a reduction in the level of tension and anxiety experienced, and an enhanced feeling of well-being. The physiological benefits of relaxation include:

- a decrease in blood pressure
- slower respiration and heart rate
- reduced muscle tension
- less stomach acid
- lower cholesterol in the blood
- alpha and theta brain waves to enhance creative and cognitive processes.

By learning and using controlled breathing techniques and relaxation, an individual can reduce tension at will, and develop the ability to adapt to stressful situations at work or home. Controlled breathing helps the individual to confront a source of stress, maintain self-control, and decrease the emotional impact of the stressor. The method acts at the mechanical, chemical and nervous levels. It helps the muscles to relax, which results in an immediate reduction of stress, and emotional and mental tension. Relaxation allows the individual to discharge emotional tension that has built up in the body. The technique helps one to recover quickly from accumulated psychological and physical fatigue. In time, the individual develops a capacity not only to cope with, but also to resist, stress. The techniques are easily learned and have a positive psychological and physical effect on the body when practiced regularly. One oil company in the UK has produced a "health passport" for each employee. This health passport includes basic information about weight, nutrition, caffeine, alcohol, smoking, exercise, blood pressure, and so on, in addition to coverage on stress, relaxation techniques and breathing exercises. Relaxation training exercises are provided with the aid of a cassette tape. This type of self-help information can provide a useful start for individuals wishing to embark on a stress management regime.

Relaxation techniques vary greatly and include meditation; progressive, deep muscle relaxation techniques; or a brief period of mental and physical relaxation while sitting comfortably in a chair at work or at home. A wide variety of audio tapes is available to help this process. Selection needs to be made carefully, because a voice or music that is perceived to be irritating is not likely to aid the process of relaxation.

Progressive muscle relaxation requires the individual to tense and relax groups of muscles in turn and in a set order. Each group of muscles should be tensed for ten seconds, and then relaxed for two minutes, using the following sequence:

1 clench fists and then relax;
2 bend arms to flex the biceps and then straighten; straighten arms tightly to flex triceps and then relax;
3 shrug shoulders up towards the ears and then drop them to relax;
4 press head back to tense the neck muscles and relax;
5 purse lips and relax; press tongue against back of teeth and relax; clench teeth to tense the jaw and relax;
6 squeeze eyes tightly shut, frown and then relax;
7 breath in deeply and hold to tense the chest, exhale deeply and relax;
8 tense stomach muscles as if preparing them for a blow and relax;
9 clench buttocks together tightly and relax;
10 keeping legs straight, point the toes downwards and then relax.

Progressive muscle relaxation should be practiced each day, because it becomes easier with time.

It is possible to purchase a variety of instruments that allow the individual to monitor the physiological reactions of the body to stress. This means it is possible to monitor the state of relaxation. For example, a commercially manufactured "stress dot" can by applied to a fleshy part of the hand between the base of the forefinger and thumb. This responds to skin temperature. When we are stressed or tense, blood supply is diverted away from the skin surface because it is needed to prepare the body for "fight or flight". As we relax, the blood supply will flow nearer to the skin surface for cooling purposes and the "dot" will change color to reflect this change. Therefore, this acts as a visual cue in the stress response. The process is known as "biofeedback". Other gadgets are available, including "watches" that monitor pulse or heart rate. It is recommended that this equipment is supplied and supervised by occupational health staff. It should be recognized that levels of sophistication, reliability and cost vary greatly, but such aids can assist in the process of understanding the physiological nature of stress.

Type A behavior management

We have already suggested that the Type A supervisor or manager might need to participate in an interpersonal skills training program in order to become a better leader or manager of other people. The objective of this strategy is to reduce the stress that their style of behavior causes other people around them in the workplace. In this section, we refer to the Type A behavior management programs that are available to modify the negative aspects of this style of behavior before these harm the health and well-being of the Type A prone individual.

In the late 1950s, cardiologists Friedman and Rosenman (1974), who were treating patients with heart disease, described a certain pattern of behavior among these heart attack survivors that they called "Type A behavior". After many years of research, it was acknowledged that the Type A Coronary Prone Style of Behavior (TAB) is a risk factor for heart disease, independent of heredity factors (that is, high blood pressure and levels of cholesterol), cigarette-smoking, alcohol consumption and obesity. However, more recent research findings have prompted a more critical appraisal of the concept and its role in impaired health (Espnes, 2002). This suggests that it is the hostility component of TAB that is likely to be the factor that increases the risk of a heart attack. TAB appears to be a type of response to a challenge in the environment, and has even been termed separately as "Type D behavior". By engaging in active coping in threat situations, the individual remains physiologically aroused, and this constant recurring sympathetic activity is associated with the process of atherosclerosis. While some researchers have tried to claim a heritability component to the Type A behavior style, it is more likely that it is learned. Indeed, it must be a way of coping that the Type A individual finds rewarding in some way in order for the behavior pattern to continue. While the TAB pattern is likely to be costly to an organization in the long term, the immediate outcome is one of gain from these workaholic individuals. Thus, Type As are usually tolerated and rewarded with promotion and privilege by their actions, and so their behavior pattern is reinforced. The Type A individual has been likened to Sisyphus, King of Corinth, who was condemned to push a huge marble block up a hill. When Sisyphus reached the top, the block rolled back down, and thus his task began again. This striving against real or imagined odds, irrespective of the outcome, together with an inability to enjoy the satisfaction of achievement or to relax, was the way in which Wolf (1960) perceived and described the coronary prone Type A person. Type A individuals tend to deny both physical and psychological responses to strain, and are often blind to the extent of their own behavior.

There are various ways in which Type A behaviors are displayed:

- **Devotion to work**: Type A individuals work long hours; feel guilty when they are relaxing, or not working; and tend to take work home.
- **Extreme urgency**: Type A individuals demonstrate a chronic sense of time urgency; they are always rushed and work under impossible deadline conditions.
- **A constant need to hurry**: This is reflected in their overt behavior, since they are likely to move, walk, and drive swiftly, and even eat rapidly – Type A behavior is known as "the hurry disease".
- **Use of emphatic gestures**: Banging a fist on a table, or clenching and waving a fist are typical Type A outbursts. This happens because they become frustrated with their own efforts, thwarted goals and ambitions, and with the efforts of those who work with them. Type A individuals often feel misunderstood by their boss.
- **Crowded schedules**: Type A individuals attempt to schedule more and more into less and less time, making few allowances for unforeseen events that might disrupt the work schedule.
- **Polyphasic activity**: Often, Type A individuals attempt to do two or more things at the same time. For example, it is the typical Type A individual who will want to read while eating, or continue to work on a document while talking on the telephone about a completely unrelated event.
- **Dislike of waiting**: Type A individuals experience an intense dislike of being kept waiting, particularly in queues. They are impatient with the rate at which most events take place. For example, they will prefer to rush up stairs three-at-a-time, rather than wait for the lift to arrive, even though they have pressed the lift call button. They also have the habit of finishing sentences for other people, and frequently urge them to the point by interspersing the dialogue with, "yes, yes", or repeating, "uh huh" over and over again. Frequent sighing during questioning is a typical Type A trait.
- **Speech patterns**: The speech pattern of the Type A individual reflects underlying aggression or hostility in their habit of explosively accentuating various keywords into ordinary speech without any real need. They usually have a strong voice, with clipped, rapid

and emphatic speech. The last few words of sentences are rushed out as if to quicken the delivery of what they want to say, thereby exhibiting impatience even with themselves!

- **Limited interests**: Type A individuals find it difficult to talk about anything other than work-related interests, and perhaps do not have any interests outside work to discuss with others. Type As rarely take all their holiday entitlement, and are likely to cut a holiday short. They really believe that the workplace cannot function without their presence!
- **Lack of awareness**: Type A individuals rarely notice things (or people) around them in the workplace that are not related to their job, or to the means of getting the job done.
- **Highly competitive nature**: Type A individuals are highly competitive with themselves and with everyone around them. They continually set themselves (and other people) goals that they try to better – for example, attempting to complete a regular car journey in a faster and faster time! Since Type A individuals constantly drive themselves (and others) to meet high, often unrealistic standards, it is not surprising that they feel angry when they make a mistake. They also experience frustration and irritation in the work situation, when they fail to achieve, or become dissatisfied with the efforts of their work colleagues and subordinates.
- **Need for control**: Type A individuals exhibit a strong need to be in control of events around them. A perceived lack of control over events will cause the Type A individual to become even more extreme in their time-urgent and hasty behaviors.

While the Type A individual is usually highly sociable, they are also regarded as a difficult colleague or boss because of their constant need to compete and win. They tend not to listen or to let you finish what you want to say, often because they believe they already have the perfect solution to the problem. Indeed, they think they are always right. As work colleagues, they are unlikely to be supportive of each other, and tend to be poor team-players. Subordinates of a Type A boss are likely to feel the strain of exposure to this difficult individual, because of their tendency to demand and maintain strict control over events. The Type A supervisor often finds it quicker to do a job him or herself rather than take the time to delegate the job to others. Thus, they often fail to develop the potential of their staff. This, of course, puts them under even more pressure, causing their levels of irritability and hostility to escalate. The employees of the Type A supervisor can experience the stress of qualitative work underload, because they feel underutilized or not trusted. Rarely is the Type A boss satisfied with the achievements of their staff. He or she constantly expects everyone around them to work to their demanding pace and schedule. The organization can also suffer the consequences of dysfunctional TAB. Sickness absence levels might increase as staff fail to report for duties in order to get away from the difficult Type A boss, who always attends work, however ill he or she feels!

Typically, training programs to reduce Type A behavior tendencies aim to encourage the individual to modify some of the potentially damaging aspects of their behavior. Obviously, the individual must acknowledge and accept the need to change. It is also important to encourage Type As to set realistic goals, since this is a manifest TAB problem. Sadly, many Type A behavior management programs have become part of cardiac rehabilitation programs because the individual has already become a victim of heart disease. Thus, it is necessary to ensure that this program is integrated into stress management activities before the individual and organization suffer the negative associated costs of this potentially deleterious style of behavior

Advice for Type A individuals might include:

- Type A individuals are not good listeners; they tend to speak for others, and even finish their sentences for them. Therefore, try to restrain yourself from being the centre of attention by constantly talking. Force yourself to listen to other people by remembering the axiom, "We have two ears, but only one mouth – use them in these proportions!"
- Thank your colleagues or subordinates when they have performed services for you.
- Control your obsessional, time-directed life. Type A individuals are not good at estimating the amount of time they need to complete tasks or make journeys. They need to identify how much time is needed, and add extra time (at least ten minutes). This will help to prevent them from driving in a "white-knuckle" manner from place to place. They must also ensure that they carry something to read, so if they arrive early for an appointment, they will not become impatient and feel they are wasting time. Ultimately, the goal should be to try to sit, relax, absorb the environment, unwind and mentally prepare yourself for the meeting. Initially, his strategy

can create too much stress for the Type A individual. Therefore, the advice is to gradually build up tolerance levels by deliberately exposing yourself to situations where this is likely to happen. Use the technique of "self-talk" to avoid becoming impatient or angry. Distract yourself by thinking about something pleasant that is going to happen soon. Make sure that you reward yourself for controlling your time-directed life.

- Do not try to do numerous tasks at the same time.
- The majority of work does not require immediate action and a slower, more deliberate pace might result in better quality decisions and judgment. When you feel under pressure, ask yourself, "Will this matter have any importance five years from now?", or, "Must I do this right now or do I have time to think about the best way to accomplish it?" Remember, only a "corpse" can be said to be finished.
- Reduce workaholic tendencies by engaging in social activities outside work. Do not engage in activities that create feelings of hostility, anger or irritation. Try to find interests that encourage a feeling of calm without triggering your natural Type A tendencies. The aim is to establish a more realistic balance between professional and personal life activities and achievements.
- Avoid setting unrealistic goals and deadlines for yourself and other people.
- Cease trying to be an idealist, because it is likely to end up in disappointment and hostility towards others.
- Do not bottle up emotions or anger; this is extremely damaging. Find ways to "vent steam". For example, engage in some vigorous physical activity that is not goal driven. Write an angry letter, but keep it somewhere safe until you calm down and can read it again. Then, choose the best course of action. Talk to trusted friends or colleagues about your thoughts, fears and anxieties.
- Learn to say "No" in order to protect your time. Stop trying to prove yourself!
- Avoid working for long periods of time without taking a break; this is not an effective work strategy. Leave the work area and engage in something that is not related to the task. Make sure you take work breaks and a lunch break, preferably in the company of colleagues. Type As mistakenly think that time spent in social interchange is time wasted.
- Monitor the number of times a week you are the first person to arrive and the last person to leave the place of work, and ask yourself

whether this behavior is really necessary. Try to resolve to arrive last and leave first at least twice during the week.

- Take all holiday entitlement and ensure that your staff follow your example.
- Take regular exercise.
- Learn and use some form of relaxation, meditation or yoga.
- Do not expect to achieve a complete change your TAB tendencies. This is an unrealistic and impossible goal. Trying to get a hare to move around just like a tortoise is evolutionary suicide; just ask the fox!

Next, we consider anger management. This is also a stress reduction technique used to control TAB tendencies. However, certain occupational groups have also found this to be an important skill in coping with unique and difficult work conditions faced on a daily basis.

Anger management

The inability to manage recurrent anger-provoking situations is associated with impulsive behaviors and cardiovascular disease (Williams *et al.*, 2000). Suppressed anger is viewed as maladaptive and it has been suggested that hostility is also linked to vulnerability to health problems following exposure to stressful events (Kivimaki *et al.*, 1998). Certain occupational groups, such as police, or nurses working with psychiatric or geriatric clients with severe learning difficulties, might be exposed to unique anger-provoking situations. While stress inoculation intervention could help to reduce the stress response when the individual is exposed to these difficult conditions, it seems that anger management courses can also help to avoid undesirable behavioral outcomes. High-profile occupational examples have included the development of bespoke anger management programs for US law enforcement officers (Abernethy, 1995; Brondolo *et al.*, 2003).

Anger is defined as an emotional state that includes feelings of irritation, annoyance and rage; aggression is a destructive behavioral response that is directed at others. Thus, anger can motivate aggression. Essentially, anger management programs comprise three components.

The first component, described as cognitive preparation, is needed to diagnose the anger-provoking situation. For example, the individual is asked:

- to think about the difficult person who is arousing their anger and to:
  - diagnose why that person is behaving as they are
  - consider whether the situation is exacerbating the problem
  - identify the trigger to the behaviour
  - consider whether they themselves are the cause of the other party's behaviour
  - consider their own reactions in this situation
  - identify whether this is a "one-off" event or a pattern of events with this person?

- to acknowledge their feelings:
  - why they feel angry
  - whether their feelings are justified?
  - whether they are being aggressive or difficult in their anger
  - whether they feel in control or overwhelmed
  - whether they are being realistic about the situation
  - whether they are jumping to conclusions.

In the second phase of training, the individual will learn and develop skills such as relaxation, communication techniques and cognitive control. This means that they should:

- stay in control; remember to keep calm
- use relaxation techniques. These are:
  - to take a few deep breaths; breathe from the diaphragm and force the stomach muscles out, to aid in slow and deep breathing; the breath should be held briefly before exhaling
  - to buy some thinking time while controlled breathing, help them to delay their first utterance, thus, controlling what is actually said.
- use assertion training to:
  - avoid becoming aggressive or non-assertive. This involves both verbal and non-verbal aspects of behavior. Ultimately, it means that the individual refuses to allow the other person to control their behaviour.
  - use empathetic assertion techniques. This is active listening towards the other person, to show that the individual has heard what they are saying, respects them, and takes them seriously.

In the third stage, the individual learns to:

- apply cognitive control by:
  o using silent self-talk to acknowledge how they are feeling
  o remembering that some people will try to provoke the individual to anger because they find this situation rewarding. Acknowledging this will help retain control of the situation.
  o thinking about what the individual will do next: – whether to ignore the situation or to respond. It is important to remember that we do not have either to defend or to prove ourselves.
  o the individual deciding what they want to get out of the situation
  o deciding whether they need more information before they can respond appropriately? If they are going to respond, they should say how they are feeling, avoiding the "yes, but" approach. The other person will usually dig in their heels and defend their own position in this situation. An argument will be the most likely outcome of this tactic
  o avoiding being confrontational: aggression breeds aggression.
  o practicing "self-talk", so they will be trained to deliver the right response and cope when anger is provoked
  o mastering and learning phrases to use in maintaining control when an individual feels they are becoming angry
  o using visual imagery to imagine themselves behaving in a controlled way when provoked.

Novaco (1980) reports a decrease in anger among probation officers following this type of training program. However, evaluation studies are rare. An example of a one-day anger management training program for police officers conducted by Abernethy (1995) included:

- an overview of stress
- barriers to acknowledging anger
- defining and recognizing anger
- managing anger; exercising choices
- relaxation and meditation
- dysfunctional styles of adaptation
- alcohol, nutrition and fitness
- defense mechanisms
- anger resolution process

- providing feedback
- anger-provoking scenarios.

While Abernethy reports some limited support for the effectiveness of this training module in anger management, it was suggested that a more extended program with opportunities for practice was needed. On the basis of the findings from this pilot program, the module was successfully extended. In our experience, follow-up sessions to monitor progress are vital. An opportunity to practice in a role-play situation is also helpful. Also, the use of closed circuit television to record and instantly analyze performance provides useful feedback on both verbal and non-verbal aspects of behavior.

In this section, we have described skills training as a stress management option. However, skills building can be acquired in a number of different ways, even in apparently "dead end" jobs. Managers can encourage the process by matching workers with people they can learn from, giving employees the chance to participate in cross-department task forces. This includes the concept of shadowing workers in other jobs, and promoting cross-functional training. A belief exists that people can best acquire new skills by being thrust into situations that stretch them beyond their comfort level. Although this can be a successful strategy, it must be used with some caution, and a "safety net" must be provided for employees who might experience stress and so fail to learn in this high-risk situation.

Also at the "secondary level" in the management of stress, options are available that aim to keep the individual fit to cope with the pressures of work and living. These options aim to improve employees' general health and include stress education and awareness programs; and on site healthy lifestyle options, such as wellness programs, smoking cessation, and exercise and fitness programs.

Stress education and raising awareness

This type of program, which forms the basis for many stress management activities, is designed to increase knowledge about psychosocial stress factors; to explain the physiological origins of stress; to increase awareness of links between stress, illness and personal behavior; and to improve personal stress coping skills. The premise of an educational approach is that promoting self-awareness helps an individual to take action to reduce their own stress levels. According to Kagan *et al.* (1995), stress reduction is due to "increased self-understanding and self-awareness of cognitive and affective reactions to interpersonal events". The aim is for the individual worker to enhance their ability to cope with occupational strain. For example, an employee learns the benefits of using adaptive coping strategies, rather than resorting to the maladaptive and damaging ways of coping with stress. However, educational programs are not generally used as stand-alone interventions, but they are commonly used to provide an introductory element to other stress management initiatives (Bunce, 1997). Also, a variety of stress coping skills are taught and practiced. Stress education and awareness raising modules are normally delivered to a group of employees at the work site, often during work hours. A combination of brief lectures, video presentations, group discussions and role play exercises might be included in the package, which includes:

Understanding what is meant by "stress": This involves clarifying the differences between the terms, "stress", "stressor", and "the stress response".

Awareness of how stress might affect us and others at work: This includes information on the physiological nature of stress, and how and why it affects us physically, emotionally and behaviorally.

Identifying stress and recognizing it in ourselves and others: This tends to require keeping a stress log or diary for one or two weeks prior to attending the session. (See the Appendix for an example of a stress log.) Also, group discussions and brainstorming techniques are used to identify the stressor barriers that exist and that adversely affect performance, job satisfaction and well-being at work. Standardized questionnaires can be used to produce stress profiles. This information can be fed back on an individual or group basis.

Options for stress management: This includes the use of adaptive versus maladaptive coping techniques.

Building a personal stress management action plan: This plan should identify the specific goals or target, the type of strategy to be used and the expected reward that the individual will receive for reaching the objective. Goals must be time-based, so that a follow-up session can monitor progress. It is useful for employees to identify a "buddy", preferably in the workplace, in order to meet regularly to discuss progress and problems. However, the most important function of the buddy system is to provide a supportive relationship while trying to achieve a change in one's behavior or lifestyle.

Stress management training initiatives: These iniatives – for example, relaxation, biofeedback, exercise and cognitive reappraisal – will vary according to the needs of the group and the length of time available for the program. Usually, employees are advised of these options and briefly counseled on the benefits, so they can use the information to develop their action plan. Further skills training takes place at a later date.

Organizations that offer this form of "awareness raising, assessment-focused" approach to stress management usually offer various action initiatives in the form of follow-up programs. Follow-up sessions might include interpersonal skills building, relaxation training, assertiveness training, keep fit exercise programs, and healthy life-style management assistance (that is, the management of substance abuse problems or weight control, and so on). Skills training targeted at the individual level is an appealing option, because it can be introduced within a short time-span and has almost immediate impact. Addressing and changing organizational stressors require longer-term initiatives that tend to take more time to produce any positive stress reduction benefits.

Therefore, this approach simply mirrors the Triple A approach already described: namely, Awareness: Analysis: Action. During stress management education, the individual receives information about the stress process, and takes part in some form of stress analysis. This might include psychological and physical health screening. On the basis of the results, a personal plan of action is written. We suggest that this action plan must always be produced in a written format and the document should:

- identify the individual's objective and goal
- identify how he or she intends to realize the set objective and goal – that is, describe the approach and method to be adopted
- provide a timeframe for the proposed activity, with a defined start and finish
- provide some mechanism of social support to improve the likelihood that the goal will be met. The "buddy system" structure enables employees to share their goals with another person. The purpose of this is to provide some form of monitoring and encouragement. Commitment to a goal and realization of the target are more likely to be achieved if other people are aware of the intentions of the plan.

Participation in stress management training initiatives has been linked to certain physiological changes connected with the activation of the stress response. A large-scale study of insurance workers in Sweden investigated the impact of a psychosocial training intervention for managers on the biochemical stress markers among their employees (Theorell *et al.*, 2001). Following the program, which included two hours training every fortnight for six months, very significant reductions in employees' levels of cortisol were found, although matching decreases in workers' perceptions of work strain were not found. This raises the possibility that physiological changes in individuals can occur without apparent corresponding alterations in psychological state. Similar research, which evaluated the effect of management training on psychological distress among employees in the Japanese brewing industry, found a significant positive impact on the well-being of younger men in white collar jobs (Takao *et al.*, 2006). As individual studies can vary in their aims, training methods and assessment of impact, a range of approaches should be considered by organizations that encompasses both physical and psychological health where appropriate.

The pharmaceutical company, AstraZeneca – formerly ICI, currently employing 10,000 staff in the UK – began an extensive in-house stress management program in 1988 that has gone from strength to strength. Winning a Unum Healthy Workplaces Award in 2007, 88 percent of its UK-based staff believed their organization to be committed to employee well-being, while 80 percent of those questioned during the award process felt they had sufficient flexibility to balance their home and work lives. Reduced staff absence costs – down by 8.5 percent – were of direct benefit to AstraZeneca's bottom line, with savings of £1.2m achieved in the period 2004–05. The organization's counselling and life management (CALM) program was noted for its service to improved employee well-being, as well as contributing to £80,000 in savings in its company health insurance spend. Receiving a similar award in 2005, London Underground, which employs 13,000 staff, was congratulated for providing its employees with a model of health intervention that enabled them to draw on a range of skills training including time management, relaxation, diet and exercise, work-life balance, relationships, personal responsibility and decision making.

In a review of stress management programs, Murphy (1996) confirms that well-designed programs can produce relatively short-term changes in measures of psychological distress, including anxiety, depression and irritation. Reductions in muscle tension, blood pressure, heart rate and stress hormones have also been observed. However, there is little evidence to suggest that these changes have long-term benefits unless periodic booster sessions are provided.

The main criticism of this approach is that it misattributes the responsibility for stress management (Giga *et al.*, 2003). Thus, the responsibility for managing stress is placed on the individual, who is expected to develop a better tolerance to potentially stressful work conditions. Organizations, such as those featured above, are becoming aware of the flaws inherent in using this approach. Unsurprisingly workplace stress management programs tend to be used in conjunction with other organizational change initiatives. Arroba and James (1990) suggest that indirect benefits could arise from this willingness of the organization to address the issue of work stress openly by offering stress management training. Employees can be reluctant to admit to strain or feelings of not coping, because of fears about job loss threat or barriers to further career development. The offer of stress management training can make a statement that the organization cares about the welfare of its employees. Therefore, stress management training remains popular as a means of protecting employees from the deleterious effects of unavoidable work site stressors. Clearly, there is a role for this type of intervention, which aims to help the individual employee or a task team cope with stress at work.

Healthy lifestyle options for the management of stress

It is estimated that more than half of the UK working population spends 60 percent of their waking time in the workplace (Peersman, 1998, cited in Bull *et al.*, 2008). It is also noted that only 28 percent of working UK adults take "sufficient physical activity for health" (Cavill *et al.*, 2006). As successive governments and organizations have come to acknowledge the growing importance of the health of the nation, it is no surprise that the number of initiatives aimed at encouraging positive lifestyle choices, particularly at work, has burgeoned. In addition to stress management training, many companies have adopted health promotion programs that attempt to keep employees healthy and to lower health risks. These include weight control and dietary advice, smoking and alcohol cessation programs, hypertension reduction, drug clinics and exercise programs. The generic term often used to describe these initiatives is "a wellness program". The change in the law banning smoking in workplaces and public places in England,

Scotland and Wales over the period 2006–07, has upheld the right to protect employees from the harmful effects and odors of cigarette smoke. This places the responsibility on work organizations to display appropriate notices and take reasonable steps to ensure the law is upheld. This has led to the migration of smokers at break times to the outside of their work buildings, leading many organizations to consider providing outside shelters for the staff members who smoke. Both sets of steps could be considered as acting in line with fulfilling employers' duty of care to all workers.

Wellness programs

Nestlé UK has prided itself on aiming to be at the forefront of healthy workplaces; its health screening and wellness programs are well supported by employees, although the effectiveness of such approaches has been less rigorously evaluated (Cooper and Williams, 1994). One third of Nestlé's staff participated in a Global Corporate Challenge in which employees were encouraged to "walk and talk" rather than have seated meetings, and walk a minimum of 10,000 steps per day, in line with World Health Organization guidelines (*London Evening Standard*, 2009). This has even extended to giving pedometers to staff in one regional office. Nestlé's head of employee wellness, Dr David Batman, said: "We are effectively paying people to walk and are legitimizing it. During the recession a lot of businesses are cutting back on these programmes and people are worried about leaving the office, but we need these schemes more than ever."

Funded by the British Heart Foundation, the "Well@Work" initiative established 11 projects across nine English regions, covering 10,000 employees in 32 organizations. The participants were drawn from the public, commercial and voluntary sectors (Bull *et al.*, 2008). The majority of the 546 schemes created under the auspices of this ambitious project were designed to raise awareness or to provide programs promoting well-being. Over half were one-offs aimed at getting employees involved. These were well-publicized within organizations, and participation rates ranged from 23 percent to 82 percent, averaging 65 percent overall (Bull *et al.*, 2008). Initiatives were categorized into physical activity, active travel (instead of relying on motorized transport), sport and recreation, nutrition, alcohol consumption, smoking cessation and health checks. Within these groupings, there were popular examples that were also evaluated. For instance, pedometer challenges pitted teams against each other and produced increases in the number of steps taken of between 32 percent and 48 percent over a 6–8 week period, when compared with baseline data collected for four weeks prior to the intervention.

The winning group of employees at Hindley Young Offenders Institution in north-west England clocked up 2000 miles, which was the equivalent of walking from New York to Dallas. Team-based weight loss programs resulted in percentage decreases that ranged from 0.8 kilograms to 4.7 kilograms, in line with previous worksite interventions. Participants' self-reports showed that 60 percent had gained self-confidence and 70 percent had increased energy levels, with high proportions valuing the competitive, team-supportive, weekly, voluntary and work-based nature of the scheme. Such a scheme at Provident Insurance in Yorkshire proved so popular with staff in desk-bound jobs that 25 percent took part. Meanwhile, at Heinz in Wigan, healthy eating options were promoted in the staff canteen (there is no mention of baked beans in the report!), and over 600 staff requested health checks. In addition, a bike purchase scheme was introduced and golf lessons were provided offsite. Stair-climbing initiatives utilized infrared beams and cameras to monitor stair use, recording a 28 percent increase, which was maintained six months after they began. Exeter City Council's scheme led to a 40 percent rise in stair use and, in a complementary initiative, it provided access to a gymnasium and to a bicycle pool, which was utilized by 15 percent of employees to travel to and from work: a 20 percent drop in absenteeism was recorded over the life of the project. The report's authors highlighted the need for recognized sponsors within the organization, acknowledging that it can take up to one year to establish a scheme, and that the shortage of physical space in some workplaces (for example, bicycle storage facilities) can provide a barrier to optimal outcomes. Bull *et al.* (2008) suggest that a five-year period is needed to fully realize the potential of any given initiative, although the continuation of 8 out of the 11 interventions beyond the envisaged lifetime of the project suggests that employee commitment is an essential ingredient for success.

A reduction in sickness absence is just one of the potential benefits to be gained from this type of initiative. From an organizational perspective, the provision of occupational health services is a key factor in reducing absence. Indeed, the conduct of risk assessment itself is associated with reduced costs to the organization in terms of employee well-being. DaimlerChrysler's (2000) award-winning initiative involving 38,318 staff found that completion of a health risk assessment led to decreased costs, which fell further when followed up by involvement in one of the organization's wellness activities. The mission of a wellness program, in an award-winning hospital-based project in the US, was described by Ballard (1988) as the creation of an environment that encourages employees to enhance their physical, emotional and spiritual well-being. This enabled staff to work productively, compassionately and with purpose, in support of the institution's commitment to quality patient care. While many organizations have adopted a form of wellness program, an example of excellence that has since burgeoned is provided by the Mount Sinai Medical Centers, New York. For example, the Center in Queens provides a range of medical health checks and educational workshops, as well as health fairs and community outreach. On-site wellness programs combine core health-promotion activities (such as breast screening and cardiovascular health) with courses, lectures, events and activities aimed at protecting the health of the whole person. Apart from primary healthcare, lifestyle enhancement activities cover prevention strategies (such as nutrition and stress management) as well as everyday challenges (from difficulties such as memory problems and interpreting food labels to dealing with major stressors including coping with sick dependants, as well as juggling home and work life).

From the above example, it can be seen that many programs extend beyond the original, and simple health screening concept of a wellness program. This includes the STAYWELL program, developed by the Control Data Corporation in 1979, where stress management training and education were combined with a physical health model. This program provided extensive evaluation data on the benefits of a wellness program combined with stress management training options. Covering 22,000 employees and their partners, dramatic economic savings and productivity benefits were reported, in addition to the improved well-being of employees. For example, health costs for employees who quit smoking were 20 percent less than for smokers, and those who engaged in exercise training had 30 percent fewer healthcare claims than the non-exercisers. Personnel who did not take part in this program were twice as likely to absent due to sickness, and were less productive than the program participants (Cooper, 1985). After ten years, the STAYWELL program gave birth to a spin-off company, StayWell Health Management, which has since become a market leader in worksite health interventions, providing services to 12 million people.

In the UK, the company Unipart has acknowledged that healthy employees can mean healthy profits. "The Orchard" is an onsite well-being center that includes nutrition advice, aromatherapy, reflexology, beauty treatments, a dance/aerobics studio and squash courts. Unipart has spent £1 million on its state-of-the-art fitness program, known as "Lean Machine", of which The Orchard is only a part. Their group chief executive, John Neill, has stated that the purpose of the Lean Machine is not solely to reduce absenteeism, but also acknowledges the pace of change and its likely toll on employees, which Unipart is keen to address by promoting health and avoiding preventable damage.

However, the investment in a wellness program need not be huge, as exemplified by the UK examples provided above. We would recommend that an organization begins by introducing a small scale pilot project that can be monitored and evaluated carefully before a large investment and commitment is made.

For example, the ruling in *Walton and Morse* v. *Dorrington* found that Dorrington (an employee who complained about the poor air quality at work) was entitled to resign and to complain of unfair dismissal. The firm failed to comply with its obligation to deal reasonably and promptly with Dorrington's grievance about her working conditions as a non-smoker. Changes at work resulted in her exposure to a smoky environment. The Health and Safety at Work Act (1974) (HSWA) implies that an employer will provide and monitor for the employee, so far as is reasonably practicable, a working environment that is reasonably suitable for the performance by the employee of his or her contractual duties. Even if sitting in a smoke-filled atmosphere could not be proven to be a risk to her health, it certainly affected her welfare at work. Thus, it was reasonably practicable for the firm to have provided a suitable working environment for her, by asking the smokers not to smoke.

Exercise and fitness programs

Employee exercise programs are probably the most popular and common form of stress management activity offered to employees in the workplace. Initiatives to improve the fitness of employees were originally introduced into the USA in an attempt by employers to stem escalating healthcare costs (see the description of the STAYWELL program on p. 223). Clearly, lack of fitness exacerbated the problems associated with exposure to stress and the stress response. For example, there is general agreement that a sedentary lifestyle is associated with increased coronary heart disease (CHD) risk. Estimates of increased risk through having a sedentary lifestyle vary; however, heart disease can occur almost twice as often in the inactive person as compared with the highly active person (Berlin and Colditz, 1990). In fact, a sedentary lifestyle counts as a risk factor for CHD alongside the well-known problems caused by high blood pressure, high levels of cholesterol and smoking (US Department of Health and Human Services, 1996). An increase risk of mortality of 25–59 percent is suggested, although it is acknowledged that changes in behavior can alter individual outcomes (Andersen, 2004). The projection by Australian economists of the uptake of 30 minutes walking for five to seven days each week, by those already able to do so, suggested direct savings to healthcare costs of AU$126.73 million in 2004 alone (Zheng *et al.*, 2009).

Although a number of European countries have government-subsidized healthcare services, exercise and fitness programs as a stress management strategy are offered to staff as a means of reducing the time lost due to sickness absence, and increasing work performance. Since 1994, employers in the UK have had an added incentive to help employees stay fit. The Statutory Sick Pay Act 1994 abolished the 80 percent reimbursement of employers' statutory sick pay costs, thereby making provision of sick pay a direct financial cost to employers.

As our understanding of the effects of work-related stress has increased, it has been acknowledged that our increasing sedentary lifestyle, both at work and at home, is a contributory factor to ill-health. A review of interventions aimed at increasing physical activity identified 14 well-designed studies from which reliable conclusions could be drawn (NICE 2006). Two of the most thorough found positive effects of varying degrees on activity (Dugdill *et al.*, 2008). Encouraging staff to use the stairs, through promotional posters and messages, did not yield the benefits expected, mainly due to the design of the studies, which revealed inconsistencies in counting methods, the length of efficacy of the intervention and the impact of overt observers. However, four out of seven studies chosen for inclusion in the review found stair use increased when posters advocated it (for example, Eves *et al.*, 2006). Interventions designed to encourage employees to walk found significant rises in the number of steps taken (measured with pedometers), which had positive as well as long-lasting benefits for health-related indicators, including behavior changes incorporating physical activity (Chan *et al.*, 2004; Thomas and Williams, 2006). Goal-setting, the use of diaries and walking routes helped to facilitate these improvements (Dugdill *et al.*, 2008). The success of some active travel or walk to work schemes has been noted, even doubling the numbers of employees walking to work, although this has not been the case with cycling. Numbers using their cars to reach work have dropped in response to this type of initiative (Wen *et al.*, 2005). Workplace counseling has had a beneficial impact on physical activity (Osteras and Hammer, 2006) although research in this area is often complicated by the use of more than one intervention. The lack of engagement of SMEs in this type of study limits generalization, although the defensiveness of managers in permitting access can be a stumbling block (Wright *et al.*, 2004).

Action to increase physical fitness and physical activity generally has been initiated at a national level, with organizations urged by governments to find ways of improving the health of their employees. In the UK, the response has been largely spearheaded by the 2004 Government White Paper, "Choosing health, making healthy choices easier". Workplace exercise programs are increasingly recommended as a means of protecting employees from the deleterious effects of unavoidable stress at work (Ivancevich *et al.*, 1990). Considerable research evidence exists to support the premise that the beneficial effects of regular exercise are mediated by cardiovascular fitness. Known as "aerobic fitness", this includes improvement in the vascular structure of the muscles and the heart; improved glucose tolerance and insulin sensitivity; reduced levels of blood pressure, cholesterol and triglycerides; increased fibrinolytic potential; weight loss, and changes in the balance of vagal-sympathetic cardiac drive, enhancing the electrical stability of the heart (Bouchard *et al.*, 1988). Research evidence also indicates that measured physical fitness (rather than physical activity per se) protects against CHD, but physical activity exerts its beneficial influence through changes in aerobic fitness. A 10-year follow-up study of the male population of Caerphilly in South Wales found that increasing levels of activity were linked to reduced risk of death from all causes, including cardiovascular disease (Yu *et al.*, 2003). Risk levels for those who engaged in intensive leisure-time physical activity were significantly lower than for others, while no relationship was found between physical activity as part of the job and risks to health.

The authors of the report recommend that habitual activities such as climbing stairs, jogging, swimming, badminton, tennis and heavy digging would provide the type of exercise most strongly linked with reduced risks of death from heart disease in middle-aged men with no pre-existing CHD. It is also suggested that over 40 percent of aerobic fitness is due to genetic endowment, although further studies on the impact of heritability on individual responses to training are ongoing (Rico-Sanz *et al.*, 2004).

Many studies have demonstrated the links between physical activity, blood pressure and cholesterol. These are acknowledged risk factors for CHD. While it is difficult to control for factors such as diet and body fat, evidence from research studies indicates that highly active individuals tend to exhibit a lower level of triglycerides and a higher level of high-density lipoprotein (the lipoprotein that reduces CHD). Several studies have shown that stress can raise levels of cholesterol (Friedman *et al.*, 1958), but sleep disturbance due to poorer psychological health has also been linked to increased cholesterol levels and increased health risks among half of those facing job loss (Mattiasson *et al.*, 1990), as well as to increased absenteeism (Westerlund *et al.*, 2008). The incidence of CHD itself seems directly related to the way people handle stress at work, with one third of the effect of job stress on CHD among 10,308 London-based civil servants being due to its effect on health behaviors and stress chemical pathways (Chandola *et al.*, 2008). This large-scale Whitehall study confirmed the link between work stress and Metabolic Syndrome, which is characterized by three of the following: elevated levels of blood pressure, high-density lipoprotein cholesterol, glucose after fasting, triglycerides and abdominal obesity. The findings were clear: those exposed to chronic work stress (on three or more occasions) had more than double the chances of developing Metabolic Syndrome than those who had not (Chandola *et al.*, 2006). Scrutiny of a cohort of 416 middle-aged, blue-collar workers in a six-year longitudinal study has also shown that status inconsistency, job insecurity, work pressure and the psychosocial characteristic of emotional immersion (that is, "need for control") independently predicted CHD, after adjusting for major risk factors (Siegrist *et al.*, 1990).

It is suggested that the adverse consequence of psychological stress on physical health is due to prolonged activation of the autonomic nervous system. Under normal conditions this response, known as "fight or flight" behavior, counters the effects of exposure to an imminent threat, thus protecting us from trauma, infection, or bleeding, and so on. However, the expression of these behaviors is inhibited at work, and strenuous physical activity is often denied due to the nature of work in contemporary employment. Therefore, continual disruption to bodily homeostasis might, in the long term, lead to disease – for example:

- unused energy sources released into the blood, such as free fatty acids, are converted to cholesterol (Dimsdale and Herd, 1982);
- increased, repeated cardiac output may result in the disregulation of blood pressure (Obrist, 1981), while at rest as well as during activity (Larson and Langer, 2001), or peripheral vascular resistance (Folkow, 1987), even among healthy individuals with borderline hypertension (Laine *et al.*, 1998);
- the circulation of unused adrenalin or nor-adrenalin can contribute to the development of atherosclerosis (Hauss *et al.*, 1990).

Stress causes the withdrawal of vagal cardiac activity in favor of sympathetic cardiac stimulation that may predispose the individual to heart rhythm disturbances (Verrier, 1989) and reshaping of the blood vessel wall (Manfrini *et al.*, 2008). It is also implicated in insulin metabolism (Helz and Templeton, 1990). It is possible that exaggerated cardiovascular reactivity to stress might be an independent risk indicator for future hypertension (Gianaros *et al.*, 2002) and CHD (Manuck and Krantz, 1984). Thus, it appears that physical exercise reduces reactivity to physical stress, such as a lowered pulse and mean arterial pressure, as noted after a 16-week intervention study with Texas fire-fighters (Throne *et al.*, 2000). In response to laboratory stressors, athletes show significantly less cortisol and a lower heart rate, as well as a lower state of anxiety, than untrained people (Rimmele *et al.*, 2009), while lower catecholamine secretion, heart rate acceleration, and rises in blood pressure have been noted among fit compared with unfit persons after carrying out demanding work (Åstrand and Rodahl, 1986).

Problems with research methodology (for example, the selective recruitment of subjects actively engaged in sport or exercise, compared with those who are not, controlling for baseline levels and circadian rhythm patterns among subjects) cause difficulties, both for researchers and in the interpretation of results from investigations into fitness, stress and reactivity. While these concerns are still not resolved, it seems from the evidence available that we can conclude that heart rate and blood pressure levels under stress seem to decline with increasing fitness.

Although rigorous evaluation studies have proved rare, proponents of exercise fitness as a stress management strategy believe that there are benefits for organizations participating in this type of program. Nevertheless, attempts to address the sparseness of evidence and the US-orientation (Proper *et al.*, 2003) of the majority of studies have been forthcoming in the UK in recent years (see pp. 225–6).

Kerr and Vos (1993) reported that, over a 12-month period at the ING Bank, both regular and irregular participants in a weekly one-hour physical exercise program showed a decrease in total absence frequency, compared with two control groups, where the absence frequency rates increased. It is noteworthy that one of the control groups in this study was composed of employees who claimed to exercise regularly, but not as part of the Employee Fitness Program (EFP). In this program, employees were assigned to the various groups on a random basis, drawn from a list of employees who expressed an interest in joining the program. Therefore, they were all potential EFP participants, and the groups were matched for age, gender and previous absence records. In a review of similar studies, Kerr and Vos (1993) concluded that participation in an EFP is effective in reducing rates of absenteeism, but the reason for this is not clear. It can not be assumed from these investigations that attendance at an EFP "caused" absence rates to decline. Rather, it is suggested that participation in this type of program might positively affect attendance motivation by improving employee satisfaction with the job situation (Cox *et al.*, 1981). A similarly positive impact on team-building has been noted in numerous settings, not least with the popularity of organizational events, which can range from "raft-building" to less strenuous group cooking exercises. The introduction of a twice weekly five-a-side football match by the chairman of APS, a leading food supplier, helped to break down communication barriers and build relationships at a site recently acquired from a competitor. Having used the same approach to help motivate employees at their packing warehouse in Middlewich, Phil Pearson found that the element of "fun" produced additional, yet valuable, spin-offs. Suddenly the workers, many of whom had moved to the UK to find work, found the universal language of football helped to overcome the challenges to communication created by a lack of English-speaking skills – not to mention the confidence to challenge their new manager on a literally level playing field! Indeed, a marked positive impact on the morale of all staff, playing and non-playing, was noted. While the psychological benefits of such initiatives are all too rarely investigated, they remain tangible to the participants and their organizations.

Recognizing that reducing stress precipitates a decrease in absenteeism, Cox *et al.* (1988) suggest that the contribution of exercise to the individual's health might be through improved physical fitness and cardiovascular health, as well as an improved sense of well-being. This might be reflected in greater self-confidence and higher perceived levels of physical fitness. Significant associations between self-reported psychological well-being and measures of perceived physical fitness and activity are also in evidence. Studies have shown that attendance on an EFP can reduce levels of anxiety and depression, and improve mood states (Biddle, 1995). Employees appear to feel "better" and report fewer symptoms of stress as a result of taking part in an EFP. As Long and Flood (1993) suggest, over time, exercise provides coping resources for stressed employees.

Whatmore *et al.* (1999) reported that a structured exercise program had positive effects on the health and well-being of the group; this program was tailored for those who previously were non-exercisers, was taught on-site in the workplace and practiced at home twice weekly for approximately 45 minutes. Comparison of measures taken pre-program and at the three-month point showed significant reductions in levels of anxiety and depression, and improvement to mental and physical health. Levels of job satisfaction and organizational commitment remained unchanged. Sickness absence rates were reduced from 3.59 percent for the year prior to the start of program to 0.78 percent at the six-month post intervention point. Sickness absence rates increased for the control group (non-volunteers) and the waiting-list control (who were volunteers to this program).

The social interaction that results from exercising in an EFP can explain some of these research findings. However, this finding was not fully supported by the investigation conducted by Whatmore *et al.* (1999). They found no significant differences between pre- and post-training session measures among volunteers on a cognitive restructuring program. This was part of a variety of stress management initiatives offered by the organization. The evaluation study controlled for opportunity for increased social interaction while attending the training program and follow-up sessions. Self-reported sickness absence rates also increased among this group, refuting the suggestion that participants are likely to perceive the organization as being interested in the health and welfare of their staff because they offer stress management training. This harks back to the potential impact of perceived organizational support (see Chapter 1). Research has shown that perceptions of the organization do improve when an EFP is provided. The image of the organization is changed, thereby influencing employees' perceptions of the job, motivation to attend work and their ability to cope with stress that cannot be eliminated (Cox and Gotts, 1988). Participation in exercise programs can also increase self-esteem, self-concept and self-efficacy as employees gain mastery and control.

Therefore, it is unsurprising that many organizations provide EFPs for their staff. These are usually provided as an "after work hours" perk, but can also be offered as free or concessionary rate access to local leisure or recreational facilities. Some companies provide an in-house gymnasium, fitness facilities, or the offer of attendance on a scheduled, tailored program during or after work duties. Nevertheless, Kerr and Vos (1993) suggest that an organization considering the implementation of an EFP should have a clear idea about the tangible and intangible benefits to be gained. They must calculate the return on the investment. This type of initiative must become part of a long-term organizational stress management strategy. Therefore, evaluation is vital to both the development and continuation of such an initiative.

One of the key problems with secondary-level interventions is the issue of who should attend. Many organizations simply offer stress management programs and stress management training, and wait for volunteers to sign up for the sessions. Some studies have shown that there were no differences between volunteer and non-volunteer employees (Whatmore *et al.*, 1999). Other studies have indicated that the volunteer subject might be one of the "worried well", or might even manifest "better" health and well-being than the non-volunteer (Conrad, 1987; Murphy, 1987; Sutherland, 1990). Conrad suggests that participants appear to be healthier and more concerned with fitness and health matters than non-participants. The perpetual nightmare for all practitioners who offer preventive medicine is that those who really need it do not come forward for help. It is would be difficult, and probably non-productive, to insist that an employee attends a stress management course by assigning him or her to a program. However, the use of a training needs analysis could be extended to identify certain weaknesses that could be addressed under the broad scope of stress management training options, such as time management or assertion training. Ultimately, the best approach is to develop a culture that recognizes stress, but does not label it in negative terms or as a weakness of the individual. This means that stress management training can be introduced as part of a package for everyone, just like an induction training package, because stress in the workplace is inevitable, but distress is not. Visible commitment to this policy must be endorsed by the active involvement and participation of personnel at the most senior levels within an organization. Ultimately, it is desirable that this type of training becomes just part of a portfolio of skills offered to optimize the health, well-being and performance of all employees.

TERTIARY LEVEL STRESS MANAGEMENT INTERVENTIONS

This type of intervention is directed at symptoms of exposure to stress. Thus, it is primarily a curative approach to stress management for individuals who are suffering from the effects of exposure to strain and pressure. It is concerned with the rehabilitation and recovery process of those individuals who have suffered, or are suffering, from ill-health as a result of stress. Many of the primary and secondary strategies described above take time to implement. It is likely that some form of tertiary initiative will be needed to "catch the people who fall through the net" and become victims of exposure to stress. These initiatives include the provision of counseling services, often as an employee assistance program (EAP), building social support networks, or offering a career sabbatical to stressed and burnt-out employees.

Counseling services

Counseling services typically help individual employees deal with a particular personal or work-related problem. Counseling is described by the British Association of Counselling as the task of giving a client an opportunity to explore, discover and clarify ways of living more resourcefully and towards a greater well-being: "Counselling takes place when a counsellor sees a client in a private and confidential setting to explore a difficulty the client is having, distress they may be experiencing or perhaps their dissatisfaction with life, or loss of a sense of direction and purpose. It is always at the request of the client as no one can properly be "sent" for counselling" (BACP, 2009).

The effectiveness of counseling programs in the workplace continues to be debated; however, the evidence leans towards the benefits to the individual employee (for example, McLeod, 2001), as well as the organization. Schemes such as those introduced by Kennecott in the US (Cooper, 1985) and the UK Post Office (Allinson *et al.*, 1989; Cooper and Sadri, 1991) resulted in reductions in absenteeism of approximately 66 percent over a one-year period, and a subsequent large-scale review of the counseling provision on offer to 30 percent of the Fortune 100 companies in the US has found improvements in job performance, attendance, relationships at work and levels of psychological strain (Masi and Jacobson, 2003). The earlier Post Office study in the UK stands out, as it was designed for the purposes of evaluation, involving pre- and post-counseling measures of employee mental health, job satisfaction, self-esteem, organizational commitment, and health behaviors. Comparisons were made with a control group, and counseling was found to result in a significant improvement in the mental health and self-esteem of the participating employees: there were 60 percent+ decreases in symptoms of depression and anxiety (Cooper and Sadri, 1991). However, neither job satisfaction nor organizational commitment showed significant pre-post changes. The decline in sickness absence of around 60 percent is a consistent finding from research into workplace counseling (McCleod, 2008).

Firth-Cozens and Hardy (1992) described the effects of psychotherapeutic counseling on the job attitudes of clinically depressed clients suffering from distress associated with their work. The 16-week intervention showed significant change in measures of mental health, job competence, the effect of work on home life, intrinsic job satisfaction and the perception of "opportunity for control". While this study did not include measures of work performance, it was observed that, as symptoms reduced, job perceptions became more positive. Guppy and Marsden (1997) reported positive changes among transportation workers with alcohol-related problems, assessed at the six-month point following (on average) eight counseling sessions. There were significant improvements in their mental health and levels of sickness absence, pre- and post-counseling. Also, based on both supervisor- and self-rating, improvement was recorded in work performance. However, neither job satisfaction nor job commitment levels had altered post-counseling. The perception of job stress also remained the same. The results from this study again support the view that counseling can have only a limited impact in dealing with the problems of stress in the workplace. Yet, there are distinct individual and organizational benefits to be gained from counseling employees who present with problems.

Certain problems are associated with "in-house" counseling services that need to be addressed. This includes the issues of confidentiality, the geographical location of the service within the company, and the process of access to the service. Employees may be sent for counseling on a referral basis only. In some organizations, they can "self-refer". Certain fears about counseling seem to be associated with the actual use of the service. Employees often perceive themselves to be "non-copers" because they need to attend counseling. They also fear the impact that this might have their subsequent career progression in the company, because the organization also perceives them to be a "non-coper". Nevertheless, there are some benefits of "in-house" versus "external specialist" stress counseling services. Internally provided services are already familiar with the organization. They are likely to be able to identify structures, policies and practices in the organization that might be changed to prevent stress, rather than limiting actions to the more restrictive, reactive and curative approach to stress management. Counseling that focuses on the problems existing within particular settings has met with "strikingly high success rates" (McCleod, 2008). However, external counseling services are also available. These EAPs claim to offer a preventive approach to stress management. It is suggested that a well-managed EAP will be able to work at a primary level, if the main sources of stress are reported to management in a confidential manner. Thus, sources of stress identified by the counselors can be tackled directly at an organizational level.

Employee assistance programs

An organization contracts an EAP provider to give employees (and sometimes their immediate families) access to an external, independent, confidential advice and short-counseling service. EAPs developed in the US during the late 1970s. The technique at the heart of an EAP is employee counseling for individuals with work-related problems, relationship difficulties, illness worries, redundancy or retirement concerns, substance abuse, or financial worries, and so on. This service can be defined as "the provision of brief psychological therapy for employees of an organization which is paid for by the employer" (McLeod and Henderson, 2003: 103). The prevalence of EAPs has increased rapidly, with a 40 percent rise in the five years up to the millennium alone, covering 1.75 million employees across 775 organizations (Arthur, 2000). Proportionally, this lagged behind the US, although there is a greater reliance on self-referral in the UK (Cuthell, 2004). The first telephone-based EAP to support UK doctors was established by the British Medical Association in 1996, following the example of Canada almost 10 years earlier: during its first year of operation, it received over 6000 calls, the majority related to experiences of anxiety, depression and psychological strain (*The Lancet*, 1998). Higher rates of anxiety than depression were highlighted in further studies of the use of EAPs, suggesting that employees with some psychological disorders will tend to remain in work more than others (Arthur, 2005). Either way, the levels of psychological distress among those self-referring for counseling through their workplace are likely to be extremely high – this was the case for 87 percent of respondents to one survey (Arthur, 2002). Over three-quarters of EAPs users in this study felt their problems were affecting job performance, while two thirds attributed their psychological strain to personal issues that would have obliged them to take time off work but for the existence of the EAP. Berridge and Cooper (1994) identified over 40 potential counseling issues to be dealt with by an EAP. Nevertheless, Highley and Cooper (1998) observed that only 22 percent of presenting problems were work-related. This compared with figures of 31 percent for emotional problems, 19 percent family or marital issues, and 18 percent financial or legal worries.

While counseling might not work for everyone who attends, the provision of an EAP by employers has come to serve a range of purposes. The UK House of Lords ruling in 2002 – that by offering counseling to employees, organizations were more likely to head off successful litigation – might have contributed to the expansion of EAPs. Likewise, there can be no doubting the positive impact on employees' perceptions of organizational support by providing an EAP. The lack of availability of evaluative studies of workplace counseling has been criticized (Henderson *et al.*, 2003); however, there are political and methodological reasons why an organization might be reluctant to assess the efficacy of its service, not least the need to offer an effective alternative in the event of poor service reviews. There is certainly a lack of EAP evaluation studies that incorporate a control group, yet it is easy to understand the ethical implications of withholding counseling to a section of those who need it. Also, the costs and benefits to organizations with differing priorities might differ and be complex to assess (Briner, 2000). One of the most promising evaluation studies was carried out for the US firm McDonnell Douglas by independent consultants who monitored the performance of the EAP over four years, utilizing a control group and collecting comparison data before and after its implementation – results yielded a US$4 return for each US$1 invested in the scheme (Alexander Consulting Group, 1989). Multinational healthcare organization Astrazeneca saved the equivalent of £600,000 over 10 years through using its EAP, while the Royal Mail made savings of £102,000 in just six months through reduced absenteeism (BACP, 2009).

Therefore, it can be appreciated that the content of such programs varies greatly and a standardized EAP does not exist. Typically, the function of an EAP is to assist in the identification of problems that lead to impaired job performance, and constructive confrontation of the issue. Once the individual has been referred (or self-refers), the EAP becomes the link between the problem employee and the management structure of the organization. Counseling in person through an EAP normally takes the form of "brief therapy", with most providers offering no more than six to eight sessions during one year (McLeod, 2001), five sessions being the average (McCleod, 2008). Some counselors are concerned that this limit is difficult to work within. They feel that they are only counseling the symptoms in the individual, rather than the causes in the organization that contributed to the problems.

Ultimately the outcome of the EAP is to improve job performance, in addition to:

- improving the changes of employee retention, with savings in recruitment, training costs and expertise protection
- reduced managerial workload resulting from problem employees shared with EAP
- disciplinary and dismissal issues treated more precisely, constructively and humanely
- improved financial control of labor costs
- enhanced employee morale. (Berridge and Cooper, 1994)

While some services offer the traditional form of face-to-face counseling on-site, it is usual practice for the first contact to be made over the telephone in order to discuss concerns. Meetings are then arranged at an agreed location off-site at professional consulting rooms; however, it is recognized that some clients do prefer the distance conferred by telephone/email counseling provision (McCleod, 2008). As has been noted, research evidence suggests that EAP counseling-based interventions seem to have a positive impact on employee groups presenting a range of problem types. Typically, levels of absence from the workplace decline, and there are significant improvements in 60–75 percent of those suffering with anxiety and depression (Mitchie, 1996; McLeod, 2001). Furthermore, a subsequent review of 34 counseling evaluation studies has detected improved job performance and attitudes towards work, as well as a decrease in the number of workplace accidents (McLeod, 2001):

> The provision of counselling services through an Employee Assistance Programme ensures that our staff always has somewhere to turn when life's pressures start to build up. Whether the primary source of stress lies within or outside the workplace, its early resolution will facilitate a rapid return to productivity by removing the distraction and worry caused by the unresolved problem. (Dr Marian Roden, Senior Medical Director, Corporate Health Management, GlaxoSmithKline, UK)

It is suggested that between 20–30 percent of the UK workforce now has access to a program, although take-up is actually around 10 percent (*Personnel Today*, 2008). Relationships constitute the most frequently reported issues, followed by stress, anxiety, bereavement and depression (BUPA Wellness, cited in *Personnel Today*, 2008). Given the likely focus of consultations, it is promising that the benefits of EAPs include:

- improved psychological health (less anxiety and depression), as well as high levels of satisfaction with the service
- improved self-esteem
- tendency to engage in more adaptive stress coping behaviors – such as yoga, exercise, and deep breathing – rather than the maladaptive behaviors noted prior to attendance at counseling
- decrease in absences due to sickness.

Almost all (99 percent) of service users say they would recommend the EAP to others; 98 percent would like their organization to retain this type of provision (BUPA Wellness, cited in *Personnel Today*, 2008).

In addition, Berridge and Cooper (1994) suggest that EAPs are seen by managers as a cost-effective way of handling stress at work, as well as the non-work stressors experienced by employees and imported by them into the job context. However, their survey of 30 EAP providers, 22 EAP counselors and 168 companies with external or internal counseling services, sponsored by the Health and Safety Executive (Highley and Cooper, 1998), confirmed that employers tended to introduce an EAP as a "sticking plaster" for work-related stress problems. Also, both employers and providers failed to monitor the EAP properly. This situation is likely to continue to be fraught with political considerations; however, it is interesting to note that between 2002 and 2007, the cost of providing an EAP dropped from an average of £28 per employee to £14 (*Personnel Today*, 2008). This might be, at least, partly attributed to the increased competition among EAP providers, but it is unlikely to be an atmosphere in which objective service evaluation can thrive.

Training supervisors and managers in basic counseling skills

Knowledge that a spouse or partner is unhappy can affect one's performance, safety or well-being. Management sometimes prefers to regard these issues as "none of our business". However, this view is unrealistic and shortsighted. An important part of the management process is ensuring that there is collaboration with employees in order to remove any barriers that exist that might adversely impact upon performance and productivity. Distressed employees who are anxious and depressed because of worries about home or the social aspects of their lives are likely to be ineffective, potentially unsafe, and often disruptive when they are at work. By helping the individual to resolve a home-related stress problem quickly and efficiently, the manager regains an effective worker and maximizes human resources potential.

Stress associated with the home and work interface can be prevented or reduced in a variety of ways, including the training of supervisors or managers in basic counseling skills. However, there is also a need to encourage employees to discuss concerns about home and family life that cause strain and pressure, providing this is done in a psychologically "safe" environment. Making stress a respectable topic for discussion in the workplace is the first step in this process, because a climate of trust and openness is necessary for the exchange of potentially sensitive information.

Therefore, team leaders, supervisors and managers will need training in counseling skills. These include: effective (active) listening, using empathy, and knowing when to refer a problem to more expert help. If they perceive that their actions will jeopardize future employment and career opportunities, personnel might resist these services or seeking help. In addition to basic counseling skills, the organization can find ways to develop and encourage a more supportive work climate as a means of reducing levels of stress.

SOCIAL SUPPORT AS A STRESS REDUCER

The value of emotional support in one's social network as a protection against adverse environmental forces or negative life events is well-documented (House, 1981; Losocco and Spitze, 1990; Haines *et al.*, 1991; Parkes *et al.*, 1994). House (1981) found that social support from one's fellow workers and supervisor moderated the effects of job stress more effectively than support from one's family and friends. While research evidence suggests that gender differences exist, and different sources of support appear to buffer the impact of different sources of stress, there is much evidence to suggest that social support can play a significant role in enhancing the level of employee well-being.

A more supportive climate could be developed or improved upon in the following ways. First, it is necessary to emphasize the importance of supportive relationships and networks during the selection process, in order to promote the desired climate and culture. The culture of an organization affects the quality of working relationships, and so this supportive image needs to be encouraged, reinforced and acknowledged as a criterion for selection and recruitment into the job. Since social support from a manager or supervisor seems to be a very important source of support in the perception of level of strain (Ulleberg and Rundmo, 1997), affecting both job satisfaction and health, it is necessary that managers and supervisors are selected and trained for their ability to understand this need, and that they reflect it in their style of supervision.

The development of structures to provide support includes access to occupational health and counseling services, provided either internally or externally. Also, social networks (work- and socially-orientated) and self-help groups (for example, "health circles", as already described) should be encouraged. Education about the importance of social support between work and home life is necessary, so that both the employee and his or her spouse or partner understand the value of social support, and the damaging consequences of lack of support.

The development of social support networks plays a significant part in enhancing the level of employee well-being, particularly social support from a boss. However, self-managed work teams or action groups all play a part in developing social support networks, particularly for employees who work in relative isolation. Social support helps to moderate the stress–strain relationship by creating in the individual a feeling of belonging and solidarity (Rook, 1995). This can have a positive effect on the person's mood. It is also suggested that a lack of strong bonding, compounded by feelings of isolation, leads people to engage in non-compliant behaviors. This includes absenteeism, tardiness, putting in less effort at work, engaging in idle gossip, and so on – particularly when job security is at stake (Hollinger, 1986; Lim, 1997).

CAREER SABBATICALS

The opportunities to take a career sabbatical can help an individual recover from the effects of exposure to stress. With so many people today working to the point of exhaustion, organizations should try to encourage staff to take sabbaticals to recharge themselves. Ideally, this strategy should be used before the individual becomes a casualty of exposure to stress. The prevention of stress-related problems is both desirable and more cost effective than waiting until a need exists to cure a victim of stress at work. However, a sabbatical can also be used to help the employee reflect on their next career steps, if they have come to a career crossroads. A sabbatical as short as two months can be beneficial, although some people need up to a year to recharge fully. Sabbaticals should not be tied to the level of job or length of service, but should reflect people's needs to adapt to a changing and demanding work environment. Given the high cost of replacing talent and experience, this can be a highly effective strategy for keeping people who might otherwise leave the organization.

SUMMARY OF AN INTEGRATED MODEL OF STRESS MANAGEMENT

It is desirable that organizations use proactive, preventive *and* curative approaches to the management of stress while simultaneously operating at more than one level of focus. Elkin and Rosch (1990) suggest that a multilevel approach to the management of stress might be introduced in three stages, such as:

- LEVEL ONE: Awareness
  This level comprises introductory workshops, health fairs, lunchtime speakers, questionnaires or stress scales;
- LEVEL TWO: Employee-directed strategies and programs
  This level comprises:
  - ○ employee needs assessment
  - ○ relaxation skills
  - ○ behavioral, cognitive coping skills
  - ○ work–life balance modification skills
  - ○ program maintenance skills
  - ○ assessment of program effectiveness
  - ○ introduction of reinforcement programs;
- LEVEL THREE: Organization-directed strategies and programs
  This level comprises:
  - ○ organization needs assessment
  - ○ identification of stress consequences
  - ○ identification of organizational stressors
  - ○ introduction of organizational change strategies
  - ○ assessment of program effectiveness.

As Elkin and Rosch (1990) remind us, the best approach is one that recognizes that changing lifelong patterns – those of the individual worker or those of the organization – take time and commitment. Therefore, it is suggested that certain issues are key to successful stress management in the workplace.

1 Have a clear idea about why you are becoming involved in a stress management program. A stress audit will highlight problem areas and the possible ways to overcome these problems. However, it is also important to identify clear objectives and goals. For example, is your objective to reduce sickness absence or accident levels? Do you want to improve supervisor–subordinate relationships? Do you want people to take more responsibility for quality performance? Make sure you identify a real goal and work towards it, rather than live in the hope that a program will work by "hitting" something!

2 Once you have clear and stated objectives, together with specific goals, you will be able to decide how you are going evaluate your initiative and measure the benefits. If there are benefits, share these rewards with employees to maintain and sustain a culture and climate that acknowledges the link between employee well-being and business effectiveness.

3 It is imperative that you take time to understand both staff and management attitudes to your stress management policy and strategy. Ask employees for their opinions. Ask what they need to be more effective, productive and healthy as employees. Ask them to describe the barriers that prevent them from optimizing their performance and well-being.

4 Define clearly who is to be involved in the initiative, both internally and externally. Define the project champions, and how the project will staffed. Identify who will be involved and what will you need from each employee. It is vital that a project is endorsed at the highest level to ensure that levels of commitment and support are strong.

5 Communicate your intentions in a clear manner using both verbal and visual messages; preferably, more than once.

6 Provide guarantees of confidentiality and ensure that the initiative does not breach any code of ethics or violate the rights of your employees.

7 Define how the feedback of any results of a stress audit or risk assessment will be treated and used. If a written report is to be prepared based on the results of an audit or subsequent evaluation studies, it is important that staff know what will happen to this information and who will have access to it. For example, you need to decide and communicate whether staff are to be allowed to see a full report or only a brief summary of key results. Staff will be unlikely to co-operate in an audit, if they perceive that information is being hidden from them. Also, plan how you intend to communicate this information. For example, do you intend to provide feedback sessions, a presentation, a team briefing, a personal feedback profile, group profiles, or a newsletter?

CONCLUSION

It is worth remembering that stress and pressure are an inevitable part of living and working, but distress is not! Our lives continue to become more complex. Like death and taxes, organization change will continue to be a feature of life in the twenty-first century and, thus, a potential source of stress. However, it is mismanaged stress that is damaging in its consequences. Both preventive and curative stress management strategies are essential in an organizational approach to stress control in the workplace, with education about psychological health, sound management skills and flexible working at their heart. Increasingly, evaluation studies indicate that prevention is more effective AND cheaper than trying to cure problems and victims of exposure to stress.

Undoubtedly, stress management in the workplace must be the joint responsibility of both the organization and the individual. Both parties have a duty of care, and need to exercise this obligation in order to remain healthy and free from harm. Ultimately, the effective management of potential sources of stress is about being in control of the pressures in one's life. While change will continue to exert a considerable force on our working lives, it must be acknowledged that some degree of pressure is inevitable and can be the spur to improved performance and motivation. Stress is a dynamic process, and this means that strategic stress management is not a one-off project. It must become an ongoing process within the organization based on awareness, analysis and action. To be successful, it must become part of day-to-day management and practice, and embedded within the culture of the organization. Ultimately, this is the only effective and cost-efficient strategy to avoid the unacceptable costs of distress in the workplace.

We need to understand the nature of stress at work before we can eliminate or moderate it. A stress control program can be effective, if resources are targeted to specific problems and aimed at the elimination of the source of stress. Those organizations that recognize the high costs of mismanaged stress in the workplace, and seek to achieve enhanced levels of effectiveness and the well-being of their workforce, will adopt this integrated approach to stress management. It embraces both individual coping and organizational change to combat the problems associated with stress at work. If we can successfully coordinate both levels, we might be able to enact the words of Gandhi and "Be the change you wish to see in the world."

APPENDIX

EXAMPLE OF A STRESS LOG

Stress log: stressors and strains

Strain can be identified or perceived as the result of a single, dramatic incident or an accumulation of less dramatic but related incidents. It might be interpreted as pressure or tension that creates anxiety, worry, anger or just mild irritation. This means that stress is in the eye of the beholder; thus, a situation or event is what you perceive as stressful.

In order to begin to identify and recognize stress, it is suggested that you keep this log.

1 At the end of each working day, try to identify your most stressful incident. It could be work- or home-related.
2 Complete the responses to stress and the coping strategies sections at the end of the week, when you have had some time to reflect on how you react to stress and cope with it.

   Do not cause yourself stress by trying to find something just to fill in the log. However, do try to be specific if possible about the source of stress and the people involved.
3 A diary is an important part of helping us to understand the pressures we face and how we cope with them. The information could be used for your own purposes, or even to generate discussion in small groups. However, the material remains your confidential property. It is entirely your decision to divulge any of the information in this log. The ultimate aim is to raise self-awareness and an understanding of stress, and the stress process among you and your colleagues. Only by correctly identifying a source of stress or pressure can we begin to manage the situation.

Thank you

	People involved What I did	No. of hours worked What I could have done

MONDAY
Incidents:
    Work-related
    Home-related		

TUESDAY
Incidents:
    Work-related
    Home-related		

WEDNESDAY
Incidents:
    Work-related
    Home-related		

THURSDAY
Incidents:
    Work-related
    Home-related		

FRIDAY
Incidents:
    Work-related
    Home-related		

SATURDAY
Incidents:
    Work-related
    Home-related		

SUNDAY
Incidents:
    Work-related
    Home-related		

Finally, please describe:

1 How you recognize your own reactions to stress: what symptoms do you experience?
2 How you cope with stress. Describe any techniques that you rely on and/or find helpful.

REFERENCES

Abdalla, I.A. and Al-Homoud, M.A. (2001) "Implicit Leadership Theory in the Arabian Gulf States", *Applied Psychology: An International Review*, 50: 506–31.

Abernethy, A.D. (1995) "The Development of an Anger Management Training Program for Law Enforcement Personnel", in L.R. Murphy, J.J. Hurrell Jr, S.L. Sauter and G.P. Keita (eds), *Job Stress Interventions*. Washington DC: American Psychological Association: 21–30.

ACAS (2006) "Workplace Bullying and Harassment: Building a Culture of Respect", Policy Discussion Papers, 4, June.

Adair, J. (2002) *Effective Time Management*. London: Pan Books.

Adams, J.S. (1965) "Inequity in Social Exchange", in L. Berkowitz (ed.), *Advances in Experimental Social Psychology, Volume 2*. New York: Academic Press.

Adkins, J.A., Quick, J.C. and Moe, K.O. (2000) "Building World Class Performance in Changing Times", in L.R. Murphy and C.L. Cooper (eds), *Healthy and Productive Work: An International Perspective*. Philadelphia, PA: Taylor & Francis: 107–32.

Age Concern (2007) "Older People Missing Out on IT Skills Training for the Workplace", 30 April. Accessed on DATE from http://www.ageconcern.org. uk/AgeConcern/D14A62D40F7846A78898EF10F72879FE.asp

Aida, R.I.R.Z., Azlina, A.B. and Balqis, M.N.S. (2007) "Technostress: A Study among Academic and Non Academic Staff", *Economic and Health Aspects of Work with Computers*. Berlin: Springer-Verlag.

Aiello, J.R. (1993) "Computer-Based Work Monitoring: Electronic Surveillance and its Effects", *Journal of Applied Social Psychology*, 23 (7): 499–507.

Akerstedt, T. (1997) "Invasion of the Sleep-Wakefulness Pattern: Effects on Circadian Variation in Psychophysiological Activation", *Ergonomics*, 20: 459–74.

Akerstedt, T. (1988) "Sleepiness as a Consequence of Shift Work", *Sleep*, 11: 17–34.

Alder, G.S. (2001) "Employee Reactions to Electronic Performance Monitoring: A Consequence of Organizational Culture", *Journal of High Technology Management Research*, 12 (2): 323–42.

Alexander, S. and Ruderman, M. (1987) "The Role of Procedural and Distributive Justice in Organisational Behaviour", *Social Justice Research*, 1: 177–98.

Alexander Consulting Group (1989) *Employee Assistance Program Financial Offset Study*. Westport, CT: Alexander & Alexander.

Allinson, T., Cooper, C.L. and Reynolds, P. (1989) "Stress Counselling in the Workplace – The Post Office Experience", *The Psychologist*: 384–8.

Andersen, L.B. (2004) "Relative Risk of Mortality in the Physically Inactive is Underestimated because of Real Changes in Exposure Level during Follow-Up", *American Journal of Epidemiology*, 160: 189–95.

Ansoff, H.I. (ed.) (1969) *Business Strategy*. London: Penguin.

Antoniou, A.-S.G. (2005) "Emotional Intelligence and Transformational Leadership", in A.-S. Antoniou and C.L. Cooper (eds), *Research Companion to Organizational Health Psychology*. Cheltenham: Edward Elgar: 633–55.

Antoniou, A.-S.G. and Dalla, M. (2009) "Immigration, Unemployment and Career Counselling: A Multicultural Perspective", in A.-S.G. Antoniou, C.L. Cooper, G.P. Chrousos, C.D. Spielberger and M.W. Eysenck, *Handbook of Managerial Behaviour and Occupational Health*. Cheltenham: Edward Elgar: 311–27.

Arendt, J. (2010) "Shift Work: Coping with the Biological Clock", *Occupational Medicine*, 60 (1): 10–20.

Arendt, J. and Skene, D.J. (2005) "Melatonin as a Chronobiotic", *Sleep Medicine Review*, 9: 29–39.

Arroba, T. and James, K. (1990) "Reducing the Costs of Stress: An Organisational Model", *Personnel Review*, 19 (1): 21–7.

Arthur, A. (2005) "When Stress is Mental Illness: A Study of Anxiety and Depression in Employees Who Use Occupational Stress Counselling Schemes", *Stress and Health*, 21(4): 273–80.

Arthur, A.R. (2002) "Mental Health Problems and British Workers: A Survey of Mental Health Problems in Employees who receive Counselling from Employee Assistance Programmes", *Stress and Health*, 18: 69–74.

Arthur, A.R. (2000) "Employee Assistance Programmes: The Emperor's New Clothes of Stress Management", *British Journal of Guidance and Counselling*, 28: 549–59.

Arulampalam, W., Booth, A.L. and Bryan, M.L. (2005/06) "Is There a Glass Ceiling over Europe? Exploring the Gender Pay Gap across the Wages Distribution", Institute of Social and Economic Research Working Paper, University of Essex: ISER

Ashford, S.J. (1988) "Individual Strategies for Coping with Stress during Organisational Transitions", *Journal of Applied Behavioural Science*, 24(1): 19–36.

Åstrand, P.-O. and Rodahl, K. (1986) *Textbook of Physiology: Physiological Bases of Exercise*, 3rd edn. Copenhagen: McGraw-Hill.

Aust, B. and Ducki, A. (2004) "Comprehensive Health Promotion Interventions at the Workplace: Experiences with Health Circles in Germany", *Journal of Occupational Health Psychology*, 9: 258–70.

Austin Knight (1995) *The Family Friendly Workplace*. London: Austin Knight.

Back, K. and Back, K. (1991) *Assertiveness at Work: A Practical Guide to Handling Difficult Situations*. London: McGraw-Hill.

BACP (British Association for Counselling and Psychotherapy) (2009) "Guidelines for Counselling in the Workplace: A Free Resource for Employers". Accessed on 19 February 2010 from http://aiponline.org.uk/media/what_we_dophp?newsId...

BACP (British Association for Counselling and Psychotherapy) (no date) "What is Counselling?" Accessed on 19 February 2010 from bacp.co.uk/education/whatiscounselling.html

Bainbridge, L. (1983) "Ironies of Automation", *Automatica*, 19: 775–79.

Baldwin T.T. and Ford J.K. (1988) "Transfer of TRAINING: A REVIEW and Directions for Future Research", *Personnel Psychology*, 41: 63–105.

Ballard, J. (1998) "Keeping the Wellness Ball Rolling", *Occupational Health Review*, May/June, 73: 10–13.

Barling, J. (1996) "The Prediction, Experience, and Consequences of Workplace Violence", in G.R. Vandenbos and E.Q. Bulatao (eds), *Violence on the Job*. Washington, DC: American Psychological Association.

Barton, J. (1994) "Choosing to Work at Night: A Moderating Influence on Individual Tolerance to Shift Work", *Journal of Applied Psychology*, 79 (3): 449–54.

Barton, J. and Folkard, S. (1991) "The Response of Day and Night Nurses to Their Work Schedules", *Journal of Occupational Psychology*, 65: 207–18.

Bauch, H.J. and Hauss, W.H. (1989) "The Significance of Plasma Catecholamine Levels in the Pathogenesis of Arteriosclerosis", *Chromatographia*, 28: 69–77.

BBC News (2006) "Workers Turning to 'Second Jobs'". Accessed on 20 February 2010 from http://news.bbc.co.uk/1/hi/business/4729550.stm

Beatson, M. (1995) "Labour Market Flexibility", *Employment Department Research Series*, 48.

Beck, A.T. (1987) "Cognitive Models of Depression", *Journal of Cognitive Psychotherapy*, 1: 5–37.

Beck, A.T., Brown, G., Steer, F. and Weissman, A.N. (1991) "Factor Analysis of the Dysfunctional Attitude Scale in a Clinical Population", *Psychological Assessment*, 3: 478–83.

Beehr, T.A. and Newman, J.E. (1978) "Job Stress, Employee Health and Organisational Effectiveness: A Facet Analysis Model and Literature Review", *Personnel Psychology*, 31: 665–99.

Belojevi, G., Jakovljevi, B. and Alesky, O. (1997) "Subjective Reactions to Traffic Noise with regard to Some Personality Traits", *Environment International*, 23 (2): 221–6.

Benyon, H. and Blackburn, R.M. (1972) *Perceptions of Work: Variations within a Factory*. Cambridge: University Press.

Berlin, J.A. and Colditz, G.A. (1990) "A Meta-Analysis of Physical Activity in the Prevention of Coronary Heart Disease", *American Journal of Epidemiology*, 132 (4): 612–28.

Bernin, P., Theorell, T., Cooper, C.L., Sparks, K., Spector, P.E., Radhadkrishnan, P. and Russinova, V. (2003) "Coping Strategies among Swedish Female and Male Managers in an International Context", *International Journal of Stress Management*, 10: 376–91.

Berridge, J.R. and Cooper, C.L. (1994) "The Employee Assistance Programme", *Personnel Review*, 23 (7): 4–20.

Bhagat, R.S. (1983) "Effects of Stressful Life Events upon Individual Performance Effectiveness and Work Adjustment Processes within Organizational Settings: A Research Model", *Academy of Management Review*, 8 (4): 660–71.

Biddle, S.J.H. (1995) "Exercise and Psychosocial Health", *Research Quarterly for Exercise and Sport*, 66 (4): 292–7.

Birdi, K.S., Gardner, C.R. and Warr, P.B. (1998) "Correlates and Perceived Outcomes of Four Types of Employee Development Activity", *Journal of Applied Psychology*, 82: 845–57.

Black Report (2008) "Working for a Healthier Tomorrow". London: TSO. Accessed on 19 November 2009 from www.workingforhealth.gov.uk/documents/working-for-a-healthier-tomorrow-tagged.pdf

Blake, R.R. and Mouton, J.S. (1984) *Solving Costly Organizational Conflicts*. San Francisco: Jossey-Bass.

Blinsky, G. (1991) "The New Attack on Killer Diseases: There's Fresh Hope for Ailments from Cancer to Alzheimer's", *Fortune*, 22 April, 123: 181.

Bond, F.W. and Bunce, D. (2000) "Mediators of Change in Emotion-Focused and Problem-Focused Worksite Stress Management Interventions", *Journal of Occupational Health Psychology*, 5: 156–63.

Bonnet, M.H. (1990) "Dealing with Shift Work: Physical Fitness, Temperature, and Napping", *Work and Stress*, 4 (3): 261–74.

Bordia, P., Restubog, S., Lloyd, D. and Tang, R.L. (2008) "When Employees Strike Back: Investigating Mediating Mechanisms between Psychological Contract Breach and Workplace Deviance", *Journal of Applied Psychology*, 93: 1104–17.

Borrill, C.S., Wall, T.D., West, M.A., Hardy, G.E., Shapiro, D.A., Haynes, C.E., Stride, C.B., Woods, D. and Carter, A.J. (1998) "Stress among Staff in NHS Trusts: Final Report", Institute of Work Psychology, University of Sheffield and Psychological Therapies Research Centre, University of Leeds.

Bortner, R.W. and Rosenman, R.H. (1967) "The Measurement of Pattern A Behaviour", *Journal of Chronic Disorders*, 20: 525–33.

Bouchard, C., Shepard, R.J., Stephens, T., Sutton, J.R. and McPherson, B.D. (1988) *Exercise, Fitness and Health: A Consensus of Current Knowledge*. Champaign, IL: Human Kinetic Books.

Bourdouxhe, M., Queinnec, Y., Granger, D., Baril, R., Guertin, S. and Massicotte, P. (1998) "Effects of Rotating 12-Hour Shiftwork on the Health and Safety of Petroleum Refinery Operators – Phase 1: Survey, Assessment and Shiftwork Design Considerations (Effets de l'horaire rotatif de 12 heures sur la santé et la sécurité des opérateurs d'une raffinerie de produits pétroliers – Phase 1: Enquête. Diagnostics, pistes de réflexion pour des aménagements), Etudes and Recherches/Résumé RR-170. Montréal: IRSST.

Boyatzis, R. (2005) "Developing Leadership through Emotional Intelligence", in A.-S. Antoniou and C.L. Cooper (eds), *Research Companion to Organizational Health Psychology*. Cheltenham: Edward Elgar: 599–622.

Bradley, J. and Sutherland, V. (1995) "Occupational Stress in Social Services: A Comparison of Social Workers and Home Help Staff", *British Journal of Social Work*, 25: 313–31.

Breaugh, J.A. (1981) "Predicting Absenteeism from Prior Absenteeism and Work Attitudes", *Journal of Applied Psychology*, 36: 1–18.

Breslow, L and Buell, P. (1960) "Mortality from Coronary Heart Disease And Physical Activity of Work in California", *Journal of Chronic Diseases*, 11: 615–26.

Briner, R. (2000) "Do EAPs Work? A Complex Answer to a Simple Question", *Counselling at Work*, 29: 1–3.

Briner, R. and Hockey, G.R. (1988) "Operator Stress and Computer-Based Work", in C.L. Cooper and R. Payne (eds), *Causes, Coping and Consequences of Stress at Work*. Chichester: Wiley: 115–40.

British Institute of Management (1986) "The Management of Acquisitions and Mergers", Discussion Paper 8, Economics Department, September.

British Retail Consortium (1997) *Retail Crime Survey*. London: BRC.

British Social Attitudes Survey (2010) 26th Report. London: National Centre for Social Research.

Britt, T.W., Thomas, J.L. and Dawson, C.R. (2006) "Self-Engagement Magnifies the Relationship between Qualitative Overload and Performance in a Training Setting", *Journal of Applied Psychology*, 36 (9): 2100–14.

Broadbent, D.E. and Little, F.A. (1960) "Effects of noise reduction in a work situation", *Occupational Psychology*, 34: 133–40.

Brockner, J.M., O'Malley, T., Reed T. and Glynn, M. (1993) "Threat of Future Layoffs, Self-Esteem and Survivors' Reactions: Evidence from the Laboratory and the Field", *Strategic Management Journal*, 14, special issue: 153–66.

Brodsky, C.M. (1987) "Long-Term Work Stress", *Psychosomatics*, 25 (5): 361–8.

Brodbeck, F.C., Frese, M, Akerblom, S. *et al.* (2000) "Cultural Variation of leadership Prototypes across 22 European Countries". Journal of Occupational and Organizational Psychology, 73, 1: 1–29

Brondolo, E., Eichler, B.F. and Taravella, J. (2003) "A Tailored Anger Management Program for Reducing Citizen Complaints against Traffic Agents", *Journal of Police and Criminal Psychology*, 18 (2):1–11.

Brotheridge, C.M. and Lee, R.T. (2003) "Development and Validation of the Emotional Labour Scale", *Journal of Occupational and Organizational Psychology*, 76: 365–79.

Brough, P. and O'Driscoll, M. (2005) "Work–Family Conflict and Stress", in A.-S. Antoniou and C.L. Cooper (eds), *Research Companion to Organizational Health Psychology*. Cheltenham: Edward Elgar: 346–65.

Brown, S.P., Westbrook, R.A. and Challagalla, G. (2005) "Good Cope, Bad Cope: Adaptive and Maladaptive Coping Strategies following a Negative Critical Negative Work Event", *Journal of Applied Psychology*, 90: 792–8.

Buchan, A. (1997) "Workplace Stress – The Legal View", in *The A–Z of Occupational Diseases*. Conference Proceedings, London: IBC UK Conferences, February: 15.

Buck, V. (1972) *Working under Pressure*. London: Staples.

Buckingham, L. (1994) "A Headache That Just Won't Go", *The Guardian*, 31 October.

Bulatao, E.Q. and VandenBos, G.R. (1996) "Workplace Issues: Its Scope and the Issues", in G.R. Vandenbos and E.Q. Bulatao (eds), *Violence on the Job*. Washington, DC: American Psychological Association.

Bull, F.C., Adams, E.J., Hooper, P.L. and Jones, C.A. (2008) *Well@Work: A Summary Report and Calls to Action*. London: British Heart Foundation.

Bunce, D. (1997) "What Factors are Associated with the Outcome of Individual-Focused Worksite Stress Management Interventions?", *Journal of Occupational and Organisational Psychology*, 70 (1): 1–17.

Burch, J.B., Jasmine, T., Zhai, Y., Criswell, L., Leo, E. and Ogoussan, K. (2009) "Shiftwork Impacts and Adaptation among Health Care Workers", *Occupational Medicine*, 59 (3): 159–66.

Bureau of Labor Statistics (1997) "Workers are on the Job More Hours over the Course of a Year", *Issues in Labor Statistics*, Summary, 97-3. Washington, DC: US Department of Labor.

Burke, R. (1993) "Organisational-Level Interventions to Reduce Occupational Stressors", *Work and Stress*, 7 (1): 77–87.

Burke, R.J. (1987) "Issues and Implications for Healthcare Delivery Systems", in J.C. Quick, R.S. Bhagat, J.E. Dalton and J.D. Quick (eds), *Work Stress: Health Care Systems in the Workplace*. New York: Praeger: 27–49.

Burns, J.M. (1978) *Leadership*. New York: Harper & Row.

Bylinsky, G. (1993) "How Companies Spy on Employees", *Fortune*, November: 131–40.

Callan, V.J. (1993) "Individual and Organisation Strategies for Coping with Organisational Change", *Work and Stress*, 7 (1): 63–75.

Callery, P. and Smith, L. (1991) "A Study of Role Negotiation between Nurses and the Parents of Hospitalized Children", *Journal of Advanced Nursing*, 16: 772–81.

Cameron, K.S., Kim, M.U.and Whetten, D.A. (1987) "Organisational Effects of Decline and Turbulence", *Administrative Science Quarterly*, 32: 222–40.

Campbell C.P. and Cheek G.D. (1978) "Putting Training to Work", *Journal of European Industrial Training*, 13 (4): 32–6.

Cannon, W.B. (1935) "Stresses and Strains of Homeostasis", *American Journal of the Medical Sciences*, 189 (1): 1–14.

Carayon, P. (1994) "Effects of Electronic Performance Monitoring on Job Design and Worker Stress: Results of Two Studies", *International Journal of Human–Computer Interaction*, 6: 177–90.

Carayon, P. (1993) "Effect of Electronic Performance Monitoring on Job Design and Worker Stress: Review of the Literature and Conceptual Model", *Human Factors*, 35 (3): 385–95.

Carroll, M. (1996) *Workplace Counselling*. London: Sage.

Cartwright, S and Cooper, C.L. (1996) *Managing Mergers, Acquisitions and Joint Ventures*. Oxford: Butterworth Heinemann.

Cartwright, S. and Cooper, C.L. (1993) "The Psychological Impact of Merger and Acquisition on the Individual: A Study of Building Society Managers", *Human Relations*, 3: 327–47.

Cartwright, S. and Cooper, C.L. (1992) *Mergers and Acquisitions: The Human Factor*. Oxford: Butterworth Heinemann.

Cascio, W.F. (1998) "On Managing a Virtual Workplace", *Occupational Psychologist*, 35, August: 5–11.

Cascio, W.F. and McEnvoy, G.M. (1989) "Cumulative Evidence of the Relationship between Employee Age and Job Performance", *Journal of Applied Psychology*, 74: 11–17.

Casey, D. (1993) *Managing Learning in Organizations*. Buckingham: Open University Press: 5.

Casey, D. (1984) "Transfer of Learning – There are Two Separate Problems", in J. Beck and C. Cox (eds), *Management Development: Advances in Practice and Theory*. UK: Wiley.

Cavill, N., Kahlmeier, S. and Racioppi, F. (2006) *Physical Activity and Health in Europe: Evidence for Action*. Copenhagen, WHO Europe.

CBI (Confederation of British Industry) (1997) *Managing Absence: In Sickness and In Health*, April. London: CBI.

CCH Unscheduled Absence Survey (2007) Accessed on 30 November 2009 from http://hr.cch.com/press/releases/20071010h.asp

Cervinka, R. (1993) "Night Shift Dose and Stress at Work", *Ergonomics*, 361 (1–3): 152–60.

Chalykoff, J.and Kochan, T.A. (1989) "Computer-Aided Monitoring: Its Influence on Employee Satisfaction and Turnover", *Personnel Psychology*, 40: 807–34.

Chan, C.B., Ryan, D.A. and Tudor-Locke, C. (2004) "Health Benefits of a Pedometer-Based Physical Activity Intervention in Sedentary Workers", *Preventive Medicine*, 39: 1215–22.

Chandola, T., Britton, A., Brunner, E., Hemmingway, H., Malik, M., Kumari, M., Badrick, E., Kivimaki, M. and Marmot, M.G. (2008) "Work Stress and Coronary Heart Disease: What are the Mechanisms?", *European Heart Journal*, 29: 640–8.

Chandola, T., Brunner, E. and Marmot, M. (2006) "Chronic Stress at Work and the Metabolic Syndrome: Prospective Study", *BMJ*, Clinical Research edn, 332: 521–5.

Chang, E. and Hancock, K. (2003) "Role Stress and Role Ambiguity in New Nursing Graduates in Australia", *Nursing and Health Sciences*, 5 (2): 15–63.

Chaston, T. (1998) "Self-Managed Teams: Assessing the Benefits for Small Service Sector Firms", *British Journal of Management*, 9: 1–12.

Chater, R.E.J. and Chater, C.V. (1992) "Positive Actions: Towards a Strategic Approach, *Women in Management Review*, 7 (4): 3–14.

Cheraghi-Sohi, S. and Bower, P. (2008) "Can the Feedback of Patient Assessments, Brief Training, or their Combination, Improve the Interpersonal Skills Of Primary Care Physicians? A Systematic Review", *BMC Health Services Research*, 179 (8).

Cherniss, C. (1980) *Staff Burnout: Job Stress in the Human Services*. Beverly Hills, CA: Sage.

Christian, P. and Lolas, F. (1985) "The Stress Concept as Problem for Theoretical Pathology, *Social Science and Medicine*, 21 (2), 1363–5.

CIPD (Chartered Institute of Personnel and Development) (2010) "The Psychological Construct". Accessed on 7 June 2010 from http://www.cipd. co.uk/subjects/empretlns/psycntrct.htm

CIPD (Chartered Institute of Personnel and Development) (2009a) "Employee Engagement". Accessed on 9 November 2009 from http://www.cipd.co.uk/ subjects/empreltns/general/empengmt.htm

CIPD (Chartered Institute of Personnel and Development) (2009b) "Working Hours in the UK". Accessed on 9 November 2009 from http://www.cipd. co.uk/subjects/hrpract/hoursandholidys/ukworkhrs

CIPD (Chartered Institute of Personnel and Development) (2009c) "Employee Turnover and Retention". Accessed on 7 June 2008 from http://www.cipd. co.uk/subjects/hrpact/turover/empturnretent.htm

CIPD (Chartered Institute of Personnel and Development) (2007) "Recruitment, Retention and Turnover". London: Chartered Institute of Personnel and Development.

CIPD (Chartered Institute of Personnel and Development) (2006) "Working Life: Employee Attitudes and Engagement", December. Accessed on DATE from http://www.cipd.co.uk/publicpolicy/_mntlcptl.htm

Clarke, N. (2001) "The Impact of In-Service Training within Social Services", *British Journal of Social Work*, 31: 757–74.

Clarke, S. (1994) "Presentees: New slaves of the Office who Run in Fear", *Sunday Times*, 16 October.

Coats, D. and Max, C. (2005) *Healthy Work: Productive Workplaces*. London: London Health Commission.

Cobb, S. and Rose, R.H. (1973) "Hypertension, Peptic Ulcer and Diabetes in Air Traffic Controllers", *Journal of the Australian Medical Association*, 224: 489–92.

Cohen, A. (1976) "The Influence of a Company Hearing Conservation Program on Extra-Auditory Problems in Workers", *Journal of Safety Research*, 8: 146–62.

Cohen, A. (1974) "Industrial Noise, Medical Absence and Accident Record Data on Exposed Workers", Proceedings of the International Congress on Noise as a Public Health Problem, W.D. Ward (ed.). Washington: US Environmental Protection Agency.

Cohen, B.G.F. (1984) "Organisational Factors Affecting Stress in the Clerical Worker", in B.G.F. Cohen (ed.), *Human Aspects in Office Automation*. Amsterdam: Elsevier.

Commission on Social Determinants of Health (2008) "Closing the Gap in a Generation". Geneva: World Health Organization.

CBI/AXA (2007) "Attending to Absence: Absence and Labour Turnover Survey 2007". London: Confederation of British Industry.

CBI/AXA (2006) "Cost of UK Workplace Absence Tops £13bn – New CBI Survey". Accessed on 15 May 2006 from http//:www.cbi.org.uk/ndbs/press.nsf

Conrad, P. (1987) "Who Comes to Worksite Wellness Programs? A Preliminary Review", *Journal of Occupational Medicine,* 29 (4): 317–20.

Conway, N., Briner, R.B. and Wylie, R. (1999) "A Daily Diary of Psychological Contracts", Annual Conference of the Division of Occupational Psychology. Leicester: British Psychological Society.

Cooper, C.L. (1998) "The Psychological Implications of the Changing Patterns of Work", *RSA Journal*, 1 (4): 74–8.

Cooper, C.L. (1996) "Hot under the Collar", *Times Higher Education Supplement*, 21 June: 15.

Cooper, C.L. (1985) "The Road to Health in American Firms", *New Society*: 35–6.

Cooper, C.L. (1981) *The Stress Check*. Englewood Cliffs, NJ: Prentice-Hall.

Cooper, C.L. and Bramwell, R. (1992) "Predictive Validity of the Strain Components of the Occupational Stress Indicator", *Stress Medicine*, 8: 57–60.

Cooper, C.L., Cooper, R.D. and Eaker, L.H. (1988) *Living with Stress*. Harmondsworth: Penguin.

Cooper, C.L., Davidson, M.D. and Robinson, P. (1982) "Stress in the Police Service", *Journal of Occupational Medicine*, 24: 30–6.

Cooper, C.L. and Dewe, P. (2008) "Well-Being – Absenteeism, Presenteeism, Costs and Challenges", *Occupational Medicine*, 58 (8): 522–4.

Cooper, C.L., Faragher, B. and Rout, U. (1989) "Mental Health, Job Satisfaction and Job Stress among General Practitioners", *BMJ*, 289: 366–70.

Cooper, C.L. and Jackson, S. (1997) *Creating Tomorrow's Organisations: A Handbook for Future Research in Organizational Behaviour*. Chichester and New York: Wiley.

Cooper, C.L. and Kelly, M. (1984) "Stress among Crane Operators", *Journal of Occupational Medicine*, 26 (8), 575–8.

Cooper, C.L. and Marshall, J. (1978) *Understanding Executive Stress*. London: Macmillan.

Cooper, C.L. and Payne, R. (1988) *Causes, Coping and Consequences of Stress at Work*. Chichester and New York: Wiley.

Cooper, C.L. and Roden, J. (1985) "Mental Health and Satisfaction among Tax Officers", *Social Science and Medicine*, 21 (7): 747–51.

Cooper, C.L. and Sadri, G. (1991) "The Impact of Stress Counselling at Work", in P.L. Perrewe (ed.), *Handbook on Job Stress, Journal of Social Behaviour and Personality*. 6 (7), special issue: 411–23.

Cooper, C.L., Sloan, S.J. and Williams, S. (1988) *Occupational Stress Indicator Management Guide*. Windsor, England: ASE a Division of NFER-Nelson.

Cooper, C.L. and Sutherland, V.J. (1991) "The Stress of the Executive Lifestyle: Trends in the 1990s". *Employee Relations,* 13 (4): 3–7.

Cooper, C.L. and Williams, S. (eds) (1994) *Creating Healthy Work Organisations*. Chichester: Wiley.

Cox, C.J. and Makin, P.J. (1994) "Overcoming Dependency with Contingency Contracting", *Leadership and Organizational Development Journal*, 15 (5): 21–6.

Cox, M., Shephard, R. and Corey, P. (1981) "Influence of An Employee Fitness Programme upon Fitness, Productivity and Absenteeism", *Ergonomics*, 24 (10): 795–806.

Cox, T. (1993) "Stress Research and Stress Management – Putting Theory to Work", Contract Research Report 61/93. Sudbury: HSE Books.

Cox, T. (1985) *Stress*. London: Macmillan.

Cox, T. and Gotts, G. (1988) *Manual for the Development of Well-Being Questionnaire*. Nottingham, Centre for Organisational Health and Development: University of Nottingham.

Cox, T., Gotts, G., Boot, N. and Kerr, J.H. (1988) "Physical Exercise, Employee Fitness and the Management of Health at Work", *Work and Stress*, 1 (2): 71–7.

Cox, T. and Leather, P. (1994) "The Prevention of Violence at Work: Application of a Cognitive Behaviour Therapy", in C.L. Cooper and I.T. Robertson (eds),

International Review of Industrial and Organisational Psychology, 9: 213–45. Chichester: Wiley.

Coyle-Shapiro, J.A.-M. and Conway, N. (2005) "Exchange Relationships: Examining Psychological Contracts and Perceived Organizational Support", *Journal of Applied Psychology*, 90: 774–81.

Crawford, J.O., Laiou, E., Spurgeon, A., McMillan, G. and Ieromnimon, A. (2005) "The Prevention of Musculoskeletal Disorders within the Telecommunications Sector: A Systematic Review of the Literature. Accessed on 19 July 2006 from http//www.msdonline.org/docs/pdf/The_Prevention_ of_MuSculoskeletal_Disorders_pdf

Crown, S. and Crisp, A.H. (1979) *Manual of the Crown Crisp Experiential Index*. London: Hodder & Stoughton.

Crump, J.H., Cooper, C.L. and Smith, M. (1980) "Investigating Occupational Stress: A Methodological Approach", *Journal of Occupational Behaviour*, 1 (3): 191–204.

Cuthell, T. (2004) "De-Stressing the Workforce", *Occupational Health*, 56: 14–17.

Czeisler, C.A., Moore-Ede, M.C. and Coleman, R.C. (1982) "Rotating Shift Work Schedules that Disrupt Sleep are Improved by Applying Circadian Principles", *Science*, 217 (30): 460–2.

Daily Telegraph (2010) "Older Workers Hit Hardest by Unemployment Crisis", 11 January.

Dalgard, O.S., Sørensen, T., Sandanger, I., Nygård, J.F., Svensson, E. and Reas, D.L. (2009) "Job Demands, Job Control, and Mental Health in an 11-year Follow-Up Study: Normal and Reversed Relationships", *Work and Stress*, 23 (3): 284–96

Dalton, D.R. and Mesch, D.J. (1990) "The Impact of Flexible Scheduling on Employee Attendance and Turnover", *Administrative Science Quarterly*, 35: 370–87.

Daniel, J. (1990) "Circadian Patterns of Changes in Psychophysiological Indicators of Adaptation to Shift Work", *Studia Psychologica*, 32: 173–7.

Daniels, J. (1995) *The Long Hours Campaign in Workplace Culture – Long Hours, High Stress*. London: Women's National Commission Parents at Work.

Daus, C.S., Sanders, D.N. and Campbell, D.P. (1998) "Consequences of Alternate Work Schedules", in C.L. Cooper and I.T. Robertson (eds), *International Review of Industrial and Organisational Psychology*, 13: 185–223.

Daus, D. (1991) "Technology and the Organisation of Work", in A. Howard (ed.), *The Changing Nature of Work*. San Francisco: Jossey Bass.

Davidson, M.J. (1989) "Restructuring Women's Employment in British Petroleum", in R. Pearson and D. Elias (eds), *Women's Employment and Multinationals in Europe*. London: Macmillan: 206–21.

Davidson, M.J. and Cooper, C.L. (1992) *Shattering the Glass Ceiling: The Woman Manager*. London: Paul Chapman.

Davidson, M.J. and Cooper, C.L. (1981) "Occupational Stress in Female Managers – A Review of the Literature", *Journal of Enterprise Management*, 3: 115–38.

Davidson, M.J. and Veno, A. (1980) "Stress and the Policeman", in C.L. Cooper and J. Marshall (eds), *White Collar and Professional Stress*. London: Wiley.

Davies, A. (2009) "Stress", in Workplace Law Network (eds), *Workplace Law Handbook: Essential Guidance for Workplace Managers on Law, Regulation, Policy and Practice*. Cambridge: Workplace Law Group: 671–6.

Davies, N. and Teasdale, P. (1994) *The Costs to the British Economy of Work-Related Accidents and Work-Related Ill Health*. Sudbury: HSE Books.

Dayal, I. and Thomas, J.M. (1968) "Operation KPE: Developing a New Organisation", *Journal of Behavioural Science*, 4: 473–506.

De Croon, E., Sluiter, J., Kuijer, P.P. and Frings-Dresen, M. (2005) "The Effect of Office Concepts on Worker Health and Performance: A Systematic Review of the Literature", *Ergonomics*, 48 (2): 119–34.

De Jonge, J. and Schaufeli, W.B. (1998) "Job Characteristics and Employee Well-Being: A Test of Warr's Vitamin Model in Health-Care Workers using Structural Equation Modelling", *Journal of Organizational Behavior*, 19: 387–407.

De Lange, A.H., Taris, T.W., Kompier, M.A.J., Houtman, I.L.D. and Bongers, P.M. (2003) "The Very Best of the Millennium: Longitudinal Research and the Demand–Control– (Support) Model", *Journal of Occupational and Organizational Psychology*, 8: 282–305.

Dean, J.A. and Wilson, K. (2009) "'Education? It is irrelevant to my job now. It makes me very depressed ...' Exploring the Impacts of Under/ Unemployment among Highly Skilled Recent Immigrants in Canada", *Ethnicity and Health*, 14 (2): 185–204.

DeFrank, R.S. and Cooper, C.L. (1987) "Worksite Stress Management Interventions. Their Effectiveness and Conceptualisation", *Journal of Managerial Psychology*, 2 (1): 4–10.

Deming, W.E. (1982) *Quality, Productivity and Competitive Position*. Boston: MIT Press.

Department of Trade and Industry (2005) "Practical Ways to Reduce Long Hours and Reform Working Practices", Accessed on 26 February 2010 from http://www.berr.gov.uk/files.file14239.pdf

DeTienne, K.B. (1994) "Big Brother is Watching: Computer Monitoring and Communication", *Transactions on Personal Communication*, 37 (1), March: 5–10.

Dewe, P.J. and Guest, D.E. (1990) "Methods of Coping with Stress at Work: A Conceptual Analysis and Empirical Study of Measurement Issues", *Journal of Organisational Behaviour*, 11: 135–50.

Dibb Lupton Alsop (1999) "Handling Stress at Work", 11 February. London: DLA Business and Law Training.

Dickson, R., Leather, P., Beale, D. and Cox, T. (1994) "Intervention Strategies to Manage Workplace Violence", *Occupational Health Review*, 50: 15–18.

Dimsdale, J.E. and Herd, J.A. (1982) "Variability of Plasma Lipids in Response to Emotional Arousal", *Psychosomatic Medicine*, 44: 413–27.

Douglas, D. (1996) "Healing the Impact of Bullying", *Counselling at Work*, winter: 7–8.

Dowall, J., Bolter, C., Flett, R. and Kammann, R. (1988) "Psychological Well-Being and its Relationship to Fitness and Activity Levels", *Journal of Human Movement Studies*, 14: 39–45.

Doyle, C.E. (2004) *Work and Organizational Psychology: An Introduction with Attitude*. Hove: Taylor & Francis.

Drucker, P.F. (2007) *The Effective Executive*. Oxford: Elsevier.

DSS (Department of Social Security) (1993) *Social Security Statistics*. London: HMSO.

Duchon, I.C. and Smith, T.J. (1992) "Extended Work Days and Safety", *International Journal of Industrial Ergonomics*, 11: 37–49.

Duffy, C.A. and McGoldrick, A.E. (1990) "Stress and the Bus Driver in the UK Transport Industry", *Work and Stress*, 4: 17–27.

Dugdill, L., Brettle, A., Hulme, C., McCluskey, S. and Long, A.F. (2008) "Workplace Physical Activity Interventions: A Systematic Review", *International Journal of Workplace Health Management*, 1 (1): 20–40.

Dwyer, D.J. and Ganster, D.C. (1991) "The Effects of Job Demands and Control on Employee Attendance and Satisfaction", *Journal of Organizational Behavior*, 12: 595–608.

Earley, C.P. (1988) "Computer-Generated Performance Feedback in the Magazine-Subscription Industry", *Organizational Behaviour and Human Decision Processes*, 41: 50–64.

Earnshaw, J. and Cooper, C.L. (1994) "Employee Stress Litigation", *Work and Stress*, 8 (4): 287–95.

Economist, The (2009) "Female Power", 30 December.

Edmans, A. (2008) "Does the Stock Market Fully Value Intangibles? Employee Satisfaction and Equity Prices", SSRN (Social Science Research Network). Accessed on 30 November 2009 from http://ssrn.com/abstract = 985735.

Egan, M., Bambra, C., Thomas, S., Petticrew, M., Whitehead, M. and Thomson, H. (2007) "The Psychosocial and Health Effects of Workplace Reorganisation. A Systematic Review of Organisational-Level Interventions that Aim to Increase Employee Control", *Journal of Epidemiology and Community Health*, 61: 945–54.

Einarsen, S. and Mikkelsen, E.G. (2003) "Individual Effects of Exposure to Bullying at Work", in S. Einarsen, H. Hoel, D. Zapf and C.L. Cooper (eds), *Bullying and Emotional Abuse in the Workplace: International Perspectives in Research and Practice*. London: Taylor & Francis.

Eisenberger, R., Huntington, R., Hutchison, S. and Sowa, D. (1986) "Perceived Organizational Support", *Journal of Applied Psychology*, 71: 500–7.

Eisenman, E.J. (1986) "Employee Perceptions and Supervisory Behaviours in Clerical VDT Work Performed on Systems that Allow Electronic Monitoring". Report prepared for the OTA assessment", *The Electronic Supervisor: New Technology, New Tensions*, OTA-CIT-333. Washington, DC: US Government Printing Office.

Elkin, A.J. and Rosch, P.J. (1990) "Promoting Mental Health at the Workplace: The Prevention Side of Stress Management", *Occupational Medicine: State of the Art Review*, 5, 4: 739–54.

Elloy, D.F., Terpening, W. and Kohls, J. (2001) "A Causal Model of Burnout among Self-Managed Work Team Members", *Journal of Psychology: Interdisciplinary and Applied*, 135: 321–34.

Erera, I.P. (1992) "Social Support under Conditions of Ambiguity", *Human Relations*, 45: 247–61.

Espnes, G.A. (2002) "The Type A Behavior Pattern and Coronary Heart Disease: A Critical and Personal Look at the Type A Behavior Pattern at the Turn of the Century", International Congress Series, 1241, September: 99–104.

Eurofound European Working Conditions Observatory (2008) "Gender Pay Differential". Accessed on30 November 2009 from http://www.eurofound.europa.eu/ewco/2008/05/BG0805049I.htm

Eurofound (2005a) "Nature of Work", Fourth European Working Conditions Surveys. Accessed on 30 November 2009 from http://www.eurofound.europa.eu/ewco/surveys/ewcs2005/ewcs2005individualchapters.htm

Eurofound (2005b) "Violence, Harassment and Discrimination in the Workplace", Fourth European Working Conditions Surveys. Accessed on 12 February 2010 from http://www.eurofound.europa.eu/ewco/surveys/ewcs2005/ewcs2005individualchapters.htm

Eurofound (1997a) "Preventing Absenteeism in the Workplace". Luxembourg: Office for Official Publications of the European Communities.

Eurofound (1997b) "Second European Survey on Working Conditions". Dublin, Ireland: European Foundation Office for Official Publications.

Eurofound (1997c) "Combating Age Barriers in Employment: Research Summary'. Luxembourg: Office for Official Publications of the European Communities.

European Working Conditions Survey (2005) "Impact of Work on Health". European Working Conditions Observatory. Accessed on 7 June from http://www.eurofound.europa.eu/ewco/surveys/ewcs2005individualchapters.htm

Eves, F.F., Webb, O.J. and Mitre, N. (2006) "A Workplace Intervention to Promote Stair Climbing: Greater Effects in the Overweight", *Obesity*, 14: 2210–6.

Ewers, P., Bradshaw, T., McGovern, J., Ewers, B., Ewers, P., Bradshaw, T., McGovern, J. and Ewers, B. (2002) "Does Training in Psychosocial Interventions Reduce Burnout Rates in Forensic Nurses?", *Journal of Advanced Nursing*, 37: 470–6.

Eysenck, H.J., Eysenck, S.B.G. (1987) *Manual of Eysenck Personality Inventory*, 5th edn. UK: Hodder & Stoughton.

Falkenberg, L.E. (1987) "Employee Fitness Programs: Their Impact on the Employee and the Organization", *Academy of Management Review*, 12 (3): 511–22.

Faragher, B.E., Cooper, C.L. and Cartwright, S. (2004) ASSET – A Shortened Stress Evaluation Tool, *Stress and Health*, 20 (4): 189–201.

Federation of European Employers (2005a) "The History of Working Time Regulation 1784–2002". Accessed on DATE from www.fedee.com/histwt.html

Federation of European Employers (2005b) "Untangling the Myths of Working Time". Accessed on DATE from www.fedee.com/workinghours.shtml

Feldman, D. (2002) "Managers' Propensity to Work Longer Hours: A Multilevel Analysis", *Human Resource Management Review*, 12: 339–57.

Ferrie, J. (1997) "Labour Market Status, Insecurity and Health", *Journal of Health Psychology*, 2 (3).

Firns, I., Travaglione, A. and O'Neill, G. (2006) "Absenteeism in Times of Rapid Organizational Change", *Strategic Change*, 15: 113–28.

Firth-Cozens, J. and Hardy, G.E. (1992) "Occupational Stress, Clinical Treatments and Changes in Job Perceptions", *Journal of Occupational and Organizational Psychology*, 65: 81–8.

Flanagan, J. (1954) "The Critical Incident Technique", *Psychological Bulletin*, 51: 327–58.

Flannery, R.B. (1996) "Violence in the Workplace, 1970–1995: A Review of the Literature". *Aggression and Violent Behaviour*, 1: 57–68.

Flin, R. (2009) "Enhancing Occupational Safety: Non-Technical Skills", in A.-S.G. Antoniou, C.L. Cooper, G.P. Chrousos, C.D. Spielberger and M.W.Eysenck, *Handbook of Managerial Behaviour and Occupational Health*. Cheltenham: Edward Elgar: 130–42.

Flin, R., O'Connor, P. and Crichton, M. (2008) *Safety at the Sharp End: A Guide to Non-Technical Skills*. Aldershot: Ashgate.

Folkow, B. (1987) "Psychosocial and Central Nervous Influences in Primary Hypertension", *Circulation*, 76 (1): 119–20.

Foresight Project (2008) "Mental Capital and Wellbeing". Accessed on 19 November 2009 from www.foresight.gov.uk/Ourwork/ActiveProjects/Mental%20Capital/Welcome.asp

Foresight Project(2009) "Mental Capital and Wellbeing Project". Strategy Unit seminar, 5 May. Accessed on 19 November from http://www.slideshare.net/whatidiscover/mental-capital-and-wellbeing-project

Fox, S. and Stallworth, L.E. (2005) "Racial/Ethnic Bullying: Exploring Links between Bullying and Racism in the US Workforce", *Journal of Vocational Behaviour*, 66: 438–56.

Foxon, M. (1978) "Transfer of Training – A Practical Application", *Journal of European Industrial Training*, 11 (3): 17–20.

Frankenhauser, M. and Johansson, G. (1986) "Stress at Work: Psychobiological and Psychosocial Aspects", *International Review of Applied Psychology*, 25: 287–99.

French, J.R.P. (1973) "Person-Role Fit", *Occupational Mental Health*, 3 (1).

French, J.R.P. and Caplan, R.D. (1973) "Organisational Stress and Individual Strain", in A.J. Marrow (ed.), *The Failure of Success*. New York: Amacon: 30–66.

French, J.R.P. and Caplan, R.D. (1970) "Psychosocial Factors in Coronary Heart Disease", *Industrial Medicine*, 39: 383–97.

Friedman, D. (1991) "Linking Work – Family Issues to the Bottom Line", Conference Board Report 962. New York: Conference Board.

Friedman, M.D. and Rosenman, R.H. (1974) *Type A Behaviour and Your Heart*. New York: Knopf.

Friedman, M.D., Rosenman, R.H. and Carroll, V. (1958) "Changes in Serum Cholesterol and Blood Clotting Time in Men Subjected to Cyclic Variation of Occupational Stress", *Circulation*, 17: 852–61.

Fritchie, R. and Melling, M. (1991) *The Business of Assertiveness*. London: BBC Books.

Frone, M.R. (2003) "Work–Family Balance", in J.C. Quick and L.E. Tetrick (eds), *Handbook of Occupational Health Psychology*. Washington, DC: American Psychological Association: 143–62.

Fulmer, R. (1986) "Meeting the Merger Integration Challenge with Management Development", *Journal of Management Development*, 5 (4): 7–16.

Gakovic, A. and Tetrick, L.E. (2003) "Psychological Contract Breach as a Source of Strain for Employees", *Journal of Business and Psychology*, 18: 235.

Ganster, D.C., Mayes, B.T., Sime, W.E. and Tharp, G.D. (1982) "Managing Occupational Stress: A Field Experiment", *Journal of Applied Psychology*, 67: 533–42.

Gardner, L. and Stough, C. (2002) "Examining the Relationship between Leadership and Emotional Intelligence in Senior Level Managers", *Leadership and Organization Development Journal*, 23: 68–78.

Gazda, G. (1973) *Human Relations Development: A Manual for Educators*. Boston: Allyn & Bacon: 34.

Gianaros, P.J., Bleil, M.E., Muldoon, M.F., Jennings, J.R., Sutton-Tyrrell, K., McCaffery, J.M. and Manuck, S.B. (2002) "Is Cardiovascular Reactivity associated with Atherosclerosis among Hypertensives?", *Hypertension*, 40: 742–7.

Giga, S.I. and Cooper, C.L. (2003) "Psychological Contracts within the NHS", *Human Givens Journal*, 10 (2): 38–40.

Giga, S.I., Cooper, C.L. and Faragher, B. (2003) "The Development of a Framework for a Comprehensive Approach to Stress Management Interventions at Work". *International Journal of Stress Management*, 10(4): 280–96.

Gilbreath, B. and Benson, P.G. (2004) "The Contribution of Supervisor Behaviour to Employee Psychological Well-Being", *Work and Stress*, 18: 255–67.

Gillespie, N.A., Walsh, M., Winefield, A.H. and Stough, C. (2001) "Occupational Stress in Universities: Staff Perceptions of the Causes, Consequences and Moderators of Stress", *Work and Stress*, 15: 53–72.

Gillow, E., Hopkins, M. and Williams, A. (2003) *Harassment at Work*, 2nd edn. Bristol: Jordans.

GLA (Gangmasters Legislative Authority) (2009) Annual Review 2008 – Executive Summary. Nottingham: Gangmasters Licensing Authority.

Glozier, N. (2002) "Mental Ill Health and Fitness for Work", *Journal of Occupational and Environmental Medicine*, 59: 14–720.

Glozier, N., Hough, C., Henderson, M. and Holland-Elliott, K. (2006) "Attitudes of Nursing Staff towards Co-Workers returning from Psychiatric and Physical Illnesses", *International Journal of Social Psychiatry*, 52: 525–34.

Goetzel, R., Long, S., Ozminkowski, R., Hawkins, K., Wang, S. and Lynch, W. (2004) "Health, Absence, Disability and Presenteeism Cost Estimates of Certain Physical and Mental Health Conditions Affecting U.S. Employers", *Journal of Occupational and Environmental Medicine*, 46: 398–412.

Goldberg, D.P. and Hillier, V.F. (1979) "A Scaled Version of the General Health Questionnaire", *Psychological Medicine*, 9: 139–45.

Goldberg, D.P. and Williams, D. (1988) General Health Questionnaire. Windsor: NFER-Nelson.

Goldstein, R.Z., Hurwitz, B.E., Llabre, M.M., Schneiderman, N., Gutt, M., Skyler, J.S., Prineas, R.J. and Donahue, R.P. (2001) "Modeling Preclinical Cardiovascular Risk for Use in Epidemiologic Studies: Miami Community Health Study", *American Journal of Epidemiology*, 154 (8): 765–76.

Goodell, H., Wolf, S. and Rogers, F.B. (1986) "Historical Perspective, Chapter 2", in S. Wolf and A.J. Finestone (eds), *Occupational Stress. Health and Performance at Work*. Littleton, MA: PSG Inc.

Grant, Adam M. and Sumanth, John J. (2009) "Mission Possible? The Performance of Prosocially Motivated Employees Depends on Manager Trustworthiness", *Journal of Applied Psychology*, 94 (4): 927–44.

Grant, R.A., Higgins, C.A. and Irving, R.H. (1988) "Computerised Performance Monitoring: Are They Costing You Customers?", *Sloan Management Review*, spring, 29: 39–45.

Graves, D. (1981) "Individual Reaction to a Merger of Two Small Firms of Brokers in the Reinsurance Industry – A Total Population Study", *Journal of Management Studies*, 18 (1): 89–113.

Grebner, S., Semmer, N.K., Lo Faso, L., Gut, S., Kalin, W. and Elfering, A. (2003) "Working Conditions, Well-Being, and Job-Related Attitudes among Call Centre Agents", *European Journal of Work and Organizational Psychology*, 12: 341–65.

Griffen, R.K., Baldwin, D. and Sumichrast, R.T. (1994) "Self-Management Information", *Journal of Management Information Systems*, spring, 10 (4): 111–33.

Griffith, T. (1993) "Teaching Big Brother to be a Team Player: Computer Monitoring and Quality", *Executive*, 7: 73–80.

Griffiths, A. (1997) "Ageing, Health and Productivity: A Challenge for the New Millennium", *Work and Stress*, 11 (3): 197–214.

Grover, S.L. and Crooker, K.J. (1995) "Who Appreciates Family-Responsive Human Resource Policies: The Impact of Family-Friendly Policies on the Organisational Attachment of Parents and Non-Parents", *Personnel Psychology*, 48: 271–88.

Grover, S.L. and Hui, C. (1994) "The Influence of Role Conflict and Self-Interest on Lying in Organizations", *Journal of Business Ethics*, 13 (4): 295–303.

Guardian, The (2010a) "Scrap Forced Retirement – Its Ageist, Says Watchdog", 25 January.

Guardian, The (2010b) "Five Police Forces Are Among the Best Employers for Gay Workers", 13 January.

Guardian, The (2010c) "A Pilot's Life: Farewell to Romance, Hello to Exhausting Hours for Meagre Wages", 11 January.

Guardian, The (2009a) "News of the World Faces £800,000 Payout in Bullying Case", 23 November.

Guardian, The (2009b) "France Telecom Halts Shake-Up after Suicides", 21 October.

Guardian, The (2005a) "Suicide Blights China's Young Adults", 26 July.

Guardian, The (2005b) "Women in Private Sector Paid 45% Less than Men, Says Equality Watchdog", 20 December.

Guest, D., Conway, N., Briner, R. and Dickman, M. (1996) *The State of the Psychological Contract in Employment*. London: Institute of Personnel and Development.

Guppy, A. and Marsden, J. (1997) "Assisting Employees with Drinking Problems: Changes in Mental Health, Job Perceptions and Work Performance", *Work and Stress*, 11 (4): 341–50.

Guppy, A. and Weatherstone, L. (1997) "Coping Strategies, Dysfunctional Attitudes and Psychological Well-Being in White Collar Public Sector Employees", *Work and Stress*, 11 (1): 58–67.

Hackman J.R and Oldham, G.R. (1976) "Motivation through the Design Of Work: Test of a Theory", *Organisational Behaviour and Human Performance*, 16: 250–79.

Haines, V.A., Hurler, J.S. and Zimmer, C. (1991) "Occupational Stress, Social Support and the Buffer Hypothesis", *Work and Occupations*, 18: 212–35.

Hall, D.T. (1976) *Careers in Organisations*. Santa Monica: Goodyear.

Hall, P.D. and Norburn, D. (1987) "The Management Factor in Acquisition Performance", *Leadership and Organizational Development Journal*, 8 (3): 23–30.

Halpern, S. (1992) "Big Boss Is Watching You", *Details*, May: 18–23.

Handy, C. (1994) *The Age of Paradox*. Boston, MA: Harvard Business School Press.

Handy, C. (1985) *Understanding Organizations*. New York: Penguin.

Härmä, M., Hakola, T., Kandolin, I., Sallinen, M., Virkkala, J., Bonnefond, A. and Mutanen, P. (2006) "A Controlled Intervention Study on the Effects of A Very Rapidly Forward Rotating Shift System on Sleep–Wakefulness and Well-Being among Young and Elderly Shift Workers", *International Journal of Physophysiology*, 59: 70–9.

Harrison, R. (1972) "When Power Conflicts Trigger Team Spirit", *European Business*, spring: 27–65.

Hart, K.E. (1987) "Managing Stress in Organisational Settings: A Selective Review of Current Theory and Research", *Journal of Managerial Psychology*, 2 (1): 11–17.

Hartley, J. (1995) "Challenge and Change in Employment Relations: Issues for Psychology, Trade Unions and Managers", in L.E. Tetrick and J. Barling (eds), *Changing Employment Relations: Behavioural and Social Perspectives*. Washington, DC: AMA.

Harz, N. (1985) "Aptitude Testing – Is "Big-Brother" Watching?", *Data Management*, July: 21–2.

Hasle, P. and Jensen, P.L. (2006) "Changing the Internal Health and Safety Organisation through Organisational Learning and Change Management", *Human Factors and Ergonomics in Manufacturing*, 16(3): 269–85.

Hauge, L.J., Skogstad, A. and Einarsen, S. (2007) "Relationships between Stressful Work Environments and Bullying: Results from a Large Representative Study". *Work and Stress*, 21: 220–42.

Hauss, W.H., Bauch, H.J. and Schulte, H. (1990) "Adrenaline and Noradrenaline as Possible Chemical Mediators in the Pathogenesis of Arteriosclerosis", *Annals of New York Academy of Science*, 598: 91–101.

Hayes, J. (2002) *Interpersonal Skills at Work*, 2nd edn. Hove: Routledge.

Haynes, S.G., Eaker, E.D. and Feinleib, M. (1984) "The Effects of Unemployment, Family and Job Stress on Coronary Heart Disease Patterns in Women", in E.B. Gold (ed.), *The Changing Risk of Disease in Women: An Epidemiological Approach*. Lexington, MA: Heath: 37–48.

Haynes, S.G., Feinleib, M. and Kannel, W.B. (1980) "The Relationship of Psychosocial Factors to Coronary Heart Disease in the Framingham Study III. Eight-year Incidence of Coronary Heart Disease", *American Journal of Epidemiology*, 111: 34–58.

Head, J., Martikainen, P., Kumari, M., Kuper, H. and Marmot, M. (2002) *Work Environment, Alcohol Consumption and Ill-Health: The Whitehall II Study*. London: HSE.

Health Strategy Unit (1998) *Our Healthier Nation: A Contract for Health*, CM 3852, April. London: HMSO.

Heaney, C.A., Price, R.H. and Rafferty, J. (1995) "The Caregiver Support Program: An Intervention to Increase Employee Coping and Enhance Mental Health", in L.R. Murphy, J.J. Hurrell Jr, S.L. Sauter and G.P. Keita (eds), *Job Stress Interventions*. Washington, DC: American Psychological Association: 93–108.

Hecker, H.L. and Lunde, D.T. (1985) "On the Diagnosis and Treatment of Chronically Hostile Individuals, in M.A.", in M.A. Chesney and R.H. Rosenman (eds), *Anger and Hostility in Cardiovascular and Behavioural Disorders*. Washington, DC: Taylor & Francis: 227–40.

Hellesøy, Odd H. (1985) *Work Environment Statfjord Field*. Bergen: Universitestsforlaget.

Hellgren, J. and Sverke, M. (2003) "Does Job Insecurity Lead to Impaired Well-Being or Vice Versa? Estimation of Cross-Lagged Effects using Latent Variable Modeling", *Journal of Organizational Behavior*, 24: 215–36.

Helz, J.W. and Templeton, B. (1990) "Evidence of the Role of Psychosocial Factors in Diabetes Mellitus: A Review", *American Journal of Psychiatry*, 147 (10): 1275–82.

Henderson, M., Hotopf, M. and Wessely, S. (2003) "Workplace Counselling. An Appeal for Evidence", *Journal of Occupational and Environmental Medicine*, 60: 899–900.

Herriot, P. and Pemberton, C. (1995) *New Deals*. Chichester: Wiley.

Higgs, M. (2005) Cited in "Leading from the Front", *Sunday Times*, 6 February.

Highley, J.C. and Cooper, C.L. (1998) "An Assessment of Employee Assistance and Workplace Programmes in British Organisations", Research Report, 167. Sudbury: HSE Books.

Hilton, M.F., Sheridan, J., Cleary, C.M. and Whiteford, H.A. (2009) "Employee Absenteeism Measures Reflecting Current Work Practices may be Instrumental in a Re-Evaluation of the Relationship between Psychological Distress/Mental Health and Absenteeism", *International Journal of Methods in Psychiatric Research*, 18 (1): 37–47.

Hinkle, L.E. (1973) "The Concept of Stress in the Biological and Social Sciences", *Science, Medicine and Man*, 1: 31–48.

Hirsch, P. (1989) *Pack Your Own Parachute*. Reading, MA: Addison-Wesley.

Hitt, H., Harrison, J., Ireland, R.D. and Best, A. (1998) "Attributes of Successful and Unsuccessful Acquisitions of US Firms", *British Journal of Management*, 19: 91–114.

Hiyama, T. and Yoshihara, M. (2008) "New Occupational Threats to Japanese Physicians: Karoshi (Death due to Overwork) and karojisatsu (Suicide due to Overwork)", *Occupational Environmental Medicine*, 65: 428–9.

Hockey, G.R. (1972) "Effect of Loud Noise on Attentional Selectivity", *Quarterly Journal of Occupational Medicine*, 24: 445–51.

Hoel, H. and Cooper, C.L. (2000) "Workplace Bullying in Britain", *Employee Health Bulletin*, April.

Hoel, H., Cooper, C.L. and Faragher, B. (2001) "The Experience of Bullying in the UK: The Impact of Organizational Status", *European Journal of Work and Organizational Psychology*, 10: 443–65.

Hoel, H., Faragher, B. and Cooper, C.L. (2004) "Bullying is Detrimental to Health, But All Bullying Behaviours Are Not Necessarily Equally Damaging", *British Journal of Guidance and Counselling*, 32: 367–87.

Hofstede, G. (2001) *Culture's Consequences*, 2nd edn. London: Sage.

Hofstede, G. (1980) *Culture's Consequences: International Differences in Work-Related Values*. London: Sage.

Hollinger, R.C. (1986) "Acts against the Workplace: Social Bondinh and Employee Deviance". *Deviant Behavior*, 7: 53–75.

Holman, D.J. (2002) "Employee Well-Being in Call Centres", *Human Resource Management Journal*, 12 (4): 35–50.

Holman, D.J. and Wall, T.D. (2002) "Work Characteristics, Learning Outcomes and Strain: A Test of Competing Direct Effects, Mediated and Moderated Models", *Journal of Occupational Health Psychology*, 7: 283–301.

Hongisto, V., Haapakangas, A. and Haka, M. (2008) "Task Performance and Speech Intelligibility – A Model to Promote Noise Control in Open Offices", 9th International Congress on Noise as a Public Health Problem.

House, J.S. (1981) *Work Stress and Social Support*. Reading, MA: Addison-Wesley.

Houtman, I.L.D. and Kompier, M.A.J. (1995) "Courses on Work Stress: A Growing Market, But What About Their Quality?", in L.R. Murphy, J.J. Hurrell, S.L. Sauter and G.P. Keita (eds), *Job Stress Interventions*. Washington DC: American Psychological Association: 337–49.

HSE (Health and Safety Executive) (2010a) "Vibration at Work". Accessed on 26 February 2010 from http://www.hse.gov.uk/vibration/index/htm

HSE (Health and Safety Executive) (2010b) "What is Stress?". Accessed on 20 February from http://www.hse.gov.uk/stress/furtheradvice/whatis stress.htm

HSE (Health and Safety Executive) (2009a) "Management Standards Indicator Tool". Accessed on 17 February 2010 from http://docs.google.com/viewer? a=v&q=cache:Wj_lAy1sg-UJ:www.hse.gov.uk/stress/standards/pdfs/ indicatortool.pdf+hse+stress+indicator+tool&hl=en&gl=uk&sig= AHIEtbTZpOIeYZe3ttqhyrcBr055CdVOKg

HSE (Health and Safety Executive) (2009b) "Stress at Work: Causes, Signs and Symptoms". Accessed on 8 February 2010 from: http://news.hse.gov. uk/2009/11/18/stress-at-work-causes-signs-and-symptoms/

HSE (Health and Safety Executive) (2009c) "Stress-Related and Psychological Disorders: Summary". Accessed on 12 February 2010 from www.hse.gov.uk/statistics/causdis/stress/index.htm

HSE (Health and Safety Executive) (2007) *Managing the Causes of Work-Related Stress: A Step-by-Step Approach using the Management Standards*, 2nd edn. London: HSE.

HSE (Health and Safety Executive) (2006) "Managing Shift Work: Health and Safety Guidance, HSG 256". Accessed on 19 Febryary 2010 from http://www.hse.gov.uk/pubns/books/hsg256.htm

HSE (Health and Safety Executive) (2005) "Work Related Stress: Case Studies". Accessed on 19 February 2010from www.tuc.org.uk/extras/Casestudies

HSE (Health and Safety Executive) (2004a) "Operational Circular OC 202/1, Health and Safety (Display Screen Equipment) Regulations 1992, As Amended By The Health And Safety (Miscellaneous Amendments) Regulations 2002".

HSE (Health and Safety Executive) (2004b) "What are the Management Standards?". Accessed on 12 February 2010 from http://www.hse.gov.uk/stress/standards/

HSE (Health and Safety Executive) (1998a) Health and Safety News Bulletin, April, 286: 7–9. HSE

HSE (Health and Safety Executive) (1998b) "Mental Health Trust Settles Widow's Stress Suicide Claim", *Health and Safety Bulletin,* April, 268: 7. HSE.

HSE (Health and Safety Executive) (1997) "1990 Survey of Self-Reported Work-Related Illness in England and Wales", August: 1–2. Health and Safety Commission.

HSE (Health and Safety Executive) (1995a) "Casenotes – Employer Liable for Stress-Related Illness", Health, Safety and Environment Bulletin, 229, January: 15–16.

HSE (Health and Safety Executive) (1995b) *Stress at Work – A Guide for Employers*, HS(G)116. Sudbury: HSE Books.

Hunt, J. (1998) "Managing the Successful Acquisition, A People Question", *London Business School Journal*, summer: 2–15.

Hurrell, J.J. and McLaney, A.M. (1988) "Exposure to Job Stress: A New Instrument." *Scandinavian Journal of Work Environment and Health*, 14 (supplement 1): 27–8.

Huxley, P., Evans, S., Gately, C., Webber, M., Mears, A., Pajak, S., Kendall, T., Medina, J. and Katona, C. (2005) "Stress and Pressures in Mental Health Social Work: The Worker Speaks", *British Journal of Social Work*, 35: 1063–79.

IDS (Income Data Services) (2007) "Bullying and Harassment at Work", Employment Law Supplement 15 (Series 2). London: IDS.

IHSM Consultants (1994) *"Creative Career Paths in the NHS". Report Number 1 – Top Managers*, Study conducted for the NHS Women's Unit. London: NHS Executive.

ILO (2007) Europe's Working Hours". Accessed on 30 April 2007 from http//:ilo.org/public/english/employment/strat/kilm/download/kilm06.pdf

ILO (1993) "Safety and Related Issues Pertaining to Work on Offshore Petroleum Installations", Tripartite Meeting, Geneva: ILO.

ILO (1992) *Conditions of Work Digest – Preventing Stress at Work*, 11 (2). Geneva: ILO.

ILO (1986) "Manpower Planning and Development in the Petroleum Industry. Report No. III", ILO Petroleum Committee, 10th Session. Geneva: ILO.

ILO (1984) "Psychosocial Factors at Work: Recognition and Control", Report of the Joint ILO/WHO Committee on Occupational Health, 9th Session. Geneva: ILO.

Income data Services (IDS) (2007) *Bullying and Harassment at Work*. Employment Law Supplement 15 (Series 2). London: IDS.

Industrial Society (2001) "Managing Best Practice", *Flexible Work Patterns*, 85, Industrial Society.

Industrial Society (1997a) "Maximising Attendance", Industrial Society.

Industrial Society (1997b) "Sick Notes: Main Causes of Absence", cited in *Personnel Today*, 27 March, 1997, "Yardstick".

Institute for Social Research (1995) "Employee Satisfaction: Tracking European Trends". London: ISR.

Institute of Employment (2009) "Organizational Responses to the HSE Management Standards for Work-Related Stress", Research Report RR-693, Health and Safety Executive, March.

Institute of Employment Studies (1997) "Stress Big Issue, But What Are The Problems?", IES Report 331. London: IES.

Institute of Management Studies (1996) *Are Managers Under Stress? A Survey of Management Morale*. Corby: IMS.

Irving, R. H., Higgins, C.A. and Safayeni, F.R. (1986) "Computerised Performance Monitoring Systems: Use and Abuse", *Communications of the ACM*, 29: 794–801.

Ivancevich, J.M. and Matteson, M.T. (1980) *Stress at Work*. Glenview, IL: Foresman, Scott.

Ivancevich, J.M., Matteson, M.T., Freedman, S.M. and Phillips, J.S. (1990) "Worksite Stress Management Interventions", *American Psychologist*, 45: 252–61.

Jackson, P.R. and Wall, T.D. (1991) "How Does Operator Control Enhance Performance of Advanced Manufacturing Technology?", *Ergonomics*, 34: 1301–11.

Jackson, S.E. (1983) "Participation in Decision Making as a Strategy for Reducing Job-Related Strain", *Journal of Applied Psychology*, 68: 3–19.

Jacobson, D.A. (1987) "A Personological Study of the Job Insecurity Experience, *Social Behaviour*, 2: 143–55.

Jamal, M. and Baba, V.V. (1992) "Shiftwork and Department-Type Related to Job Stress, Work Attitudes and Behavioural Intentions: A Study of Nurses" *Journal of Organizational Behavior*, 13: 449–64.

Jamdar, S. and Byford, J. (2003) *Workplace Stress: Law and Practice*. London: Law Society.

Jenkins, P. (2007) *Counselling, Psychotherapy and the Law*, 2nd edn. London: Sage.

Jenkins, P. (2008) "Organisational Duty of Care: Workplace Counselling as a Shield against Litigation?", in A. Kinder, R. Hughes, and C.L. Cooper (eds), *Employee Well-Being Support: A Workplace Resource*. Chichester: Wiley: 99–109.

Jick, T. (1985) "As the Axe Falls: Budget Cuts and the Experience of Stress in Organizations", in T.A. Beehr and R.S. Bagat (eds) *Human Stress and Cognition in Organizations: An Integrated Perspective*. New York: Wiley: 83–114.

Johnstone, H. (1999) "Woman is Awarded £67,000 for Stress", *The Times*, 6 July: 4.

Jones, D.M. (1983) "Noise", in R. Hockey (ed.), *Stress and Fatigue in Human Performance*. Chichester: Wiley.

Jones, F. and Bright, J. (2001) *Stress: Myth, Theory and Research*. Harlow: Pearson Education.

Judge, T.A. and Bono, J.E. (2000) "Five-Factor Model of Personality and Transformational Leadership", *Journal of Applied Psychology*, 85: 751–65.

Kagan, A. and Levi, L. (1971) "Adaptations of the Psychosocial Environment to Mans' Abilities and Needs", in L. Levi (ed.), *Society, Stress and Disease, Volume 1*. Oxford: Oxford University Press.

Kagan, N. I., Kagan, H. and Watson, M.G. (1995) "Stress Reduction in the Workplace: The Effectiveness of Psychoeducational Programs", *Journal of Counseling Psychology*, 42 (1): 71–8.

Kahn, R.L., Wolfe, D.M., Quinn, R.P., Snoek, J.D. and Rosenthal R.A. (1964) *Organisational Stress: Studies in Role Conflict and Ambiguity*. Chichester: Wiley: 41.

Kaliterna, L., Vidacek, S., Prizmic, Z. and Radosevic-Vidacek, B. (1995) "Is Tolerance to Shiftwork Predictable from Individual Difference Measures?", *Work and Stress*, 9 (2/3): 140–7.

Kanter, R.M. (1991) "Transcending Business Boundaries: 12,000 World Managers View Change", *Harvard Business Review*, May–June: 151–66.

Karasek, R. (1990) "Lower Health Risk with Increased Job Control among White Collar Workers", *Journal of Organizational Behavior*, 11 (3), May: 171–85.

Karasek, R. (1979) "Job Demands, Job Decision Latitude, and Mental Strain: Implications for Job Redesign", *Administrative Science Quarterly*, 24: 285–308.

Karasek, R. and Theorell, T. (1990) *Healthy Work: Stress, Productivity and The Reconstruction of Working Life*. New York: Basic.

Karasek, R., Theorell, T., Schwartz, J.E., Schnall, P.L., Pieper, C.F. and Michele, J.L. (1988) "Job Characteristics in relation to the Prevalence of Myocardial Infarction in the US Health Examination Survey (HES) and the Health and Nutrition Examination Survey (HANES)", *American Journal of Public Health*, 78: 910–18.

Kauffeld, S., Jonas, E.and Frey, D. (2004) "Effects of a Flexible Work-Time Design on Employee and Company-Related Aims", *European Journal of Work and Organizational Psychology*, 13: 17–100.

Kaye, A. and Sutton, M. (1985) "Productivity and Quality of Working Life for Office Principals and the Implications for Office Automation", *Office: Technology and People*, 2 (4): 267–86.

Kearns, H. and Gardiner, M. (2007) "Is It Time Well Spent? The Relationship between Time Management Behaviours, Perceived Effectiveness and Work-Related Morale and Distress in a University Context", *Higher Education Research & Development*, 1469-8366, 26(2): 235–247

Keenan, V. and Kerr, W. (1951) "Psychological Climate and Accidents in an Automotive Plant", *Journal of Applied Psychology*, 35 (2): 108–11.

Kelly, M. and Cooper, C.L. (1981) "Stress among Blue-Collar Workers. A Case Study of the Steel Industry", *Employee Relations*, 3 (2): 6–9.

Kemery, E.R. (2006) "Clergy Role Stress and Satisfaction: Role Ambiguity Isn't Always Bad", *Pastoral Psychology*, 54 (6): 561–70.

Kenexa Research Institute (2009) "Mergers and Acquisitions Typically Disengage Employees, But Kenexa Research Institute Finds that Effective Leadership Can Help Ensure Employee Retention". Accessed on 1 February 2010 from http:// www.kenexa.com/MediaRoom/Press Releases/2007/Mergers-and-Acquisitions-Typically-Disengage-Emplo

Kerr, J.H. and Vos, M.C.H. (1993) "Employee Fitness and General Well-Being", *Work and Stress*, 7 (2): 179–90.

Kerr, W.A. (1950) "Accident Proneness of Factory Departments", *Journal of Applied Psychology*, 34: 167–70.

Kessler, R.C. and Frank, R.G. (1997) "The Impact of Psychiatric Disorders on Work Loss Days", *Psychological Medicine*, 27: 179–90.

Kessler, R.C., Greenberg, P.E., Mickelson, K.D., Meneades, L.M. and Wang, P.S. (2001) "The Effects of Chronic Medical Conditions on Work Loss and Work Cutback", *Journal of Occupational and Environmental Medicine*, 43 (3): 218–25.

Keyes, J.B. (1995) "Stress Inoculation Training for Staff Working with Persons with Mental Retardation: A Model Program", in L.R. Murphy, J.J. Hurrell Jr, S.L. Sauter and G.P. Keita (eds), *Job Stress Interventions*. Washington, DC: American Psychological Association: 45–56.

Kidwell, R.E. Jr and Bennett, N. (1994) "Employee Reactions to Electronic Control Systems: The Role of Procedural Fairness", *Group and Organization Management*, 19 (2): 203–18.

Kinman, G. and Jones, F. (2004) *Working to the Limit*. London: AUT.

Kinnunen, U., Mauno, S., Geurts, S. and Dikkers, J. (2005) "Work–Family Culture: Theoretical and Empirical Approaches", in S. Poelmans (ed.), *Work and Family: An International Research Perspective*. Mahwah, NJ: Lawrence Erlbaum Associates: 87–120.

Kirkpatrick, D.T. (1959) "Techniques for Evaluating Training Programs", *American Society of Training Directors Journal*, 13: 3–9.

Kivimaki, M., Vahtera, J., Koskenvuo, M., Uutela, A. and Pentti, J. (1998) "Response of Hostile Individuals to Stressful Change in their Working Lives. Test of a Psychosocial Vulnerability Model", *Psychological Medicine*, 28: 903–13.

Kizer, W.M. (1987) *The Healthy Workplace: A Blueprint for Corporate Action*. New York: Wiley.

Knauth, P. (1993) "The Design of Shift System", *Ergonomics*, 36: 15–28.

Knauth, R. and Rutenfranz, J. (1982) "Development of Criteria for the Design of Shiftwork Systems", *Journal of Human Ergology*, 11, Supplement: 337–67.

Kobasa, S. (1979) "Stressful Life Events, Personality and Health: An Enquiry into Hardiness", *Journal of Personality and Social Psychology*, 37 (1): 1–11.

Koep, S. (1986) "The Boss That Never Blinks", *Time*, 28 July: 46–7.

Kogut, B. (1988) "A Study of the Life Cycle of Joint Ventures", *Management International Review*, special edition, April.

Kolbell, R.M. (1995) "When Relaxation Is Not Enough", in L.R. Murphy, J.J. Hurrell Jr, S.L. Sauter and G.P. Keita (eds), *Job Stress Interventions*. Washington, DC: American Psychological Association: 31–44.

Kornhauser, S.V. (1965) *Mental Health of the Industrial Worker*. New York: Wiley.

Kundi, M., Koller, M., Stefan, H., Lehner, L., Kaindlsdorfer, S. and Rottenbücher. S. (1995) "Attitude of Nurses towards 8-hour and 12-hours Systems", *Work and Stress*, 9 (2/3): 134–9.

Labour Force Survey (1994) London: HMSO.

Laine, H., Raitakari, O.T., Niinikoski, H., Pitkanen, O.-P., Iida, H., Viikari, J., Nuutila, P. and Knuuti, J. (1998) "Early Impairment of Coronary Flow Reserve in Young Men with Borderline Hypertension", *Journal of the American College of Cardiology*, 32: 147–53.

Lamond, D., Daniels, K. and Standen, P. (2003) "Teleworking and Virtual Organizations: The Human Impact", in D. Holman, T.D. Wall, C.W. Clegg, P. Sparrow and A. Howard (eds), *The New Workplace*. Chichester: Wiley.

Lancet, The (1998) "Prevention and Treatment of Occupational Mental Disorders: Editorial", 352, 26 September: 999.

Langan-Fox, J. (2005) "New Technology, the Global Economy and Organizational Environments: Effects on Employee Stress, Health and Well-Being", in A.-S. Antoniou and C.L. Cooper (eds), *Research Companion to Organizational Health Psychology*. Cheltenham: Edward Elgar: 413–29.

Lapper, R. (1994) "Insurers Fear Stress Claims Will Increase", *Financial Times*, 10 February.

Larson, M.R. and Langer, A.W. (2001) "Systemic Overperfusion and Resting Blood Pressure", *Psychophysiology*, 38: 678–84.

Lavie, P., Kremerman, S. and Wiel, M. (1982) "Sleep Disorders and Safety at Work in Industrial Workers", *Accident Analysis and Prevention*, 14 (4): 311–14.

Lazarus, R.S. (1966) *Psychological Stress and the Coping Process*. New York: McGraw-Hill.

Leach, D.J., Jackson, P.R. and Wall, T.D. (2001) "Realising the Potential of Empowerment: The Impact of a Feedback Intervention on the Performance of a Complex Technology". *Ergonomics*, 44:, 870–86.

Leach, D.J., Wall, T.D. and Jackson, P.R. (2003) "The Effect of Empower-ment on Job Knowledge: An Empirical Test involving Operators of Complex Technology", *Journal of Occupational and Organizational Psychology*, 76: 27–52.

Leather, P., Beale, D., Lawrence, C. and Dickson, R. (1997) "Effects of Exposure to Occupational Violence and the Mediating Impact of Fear", *Work and Stress*, 11 (4): 329–40.

Lee, S., Colditz, G., Berkman, L. and Kawachi, I. (2003) "Caregiving to Children and Grandchildren and Risk of Coronary Heart Disease in Women", *American Journal of Public Health*, 93: 1939–44.

Leka, S., Griffiths, A. and Cox, T. (2007) "Work, Organisation and Stress", *Protecting Workers' Health Series*, 3. Nottingham: Institute of Work, Health and Organisations.

Levi, L. (1998) "Preface: Stress in Organizations – Theoretical and Empirical Approaches", in C.L. Cooper (ed.), *Theories of Organizational Stress*. New York: Oxford University Press.

Levi, L. (1987) "Definitions and the Conceptual Aspects of Health in Relation to Work", in R. Kalimo, M.A. El-Batawi and C.L. Cooper (eds), *Psychosocial Factors at Work and Their Relation to Health*. Geneva: WHO.

Levine, D.I. (1990) "Participation, Productivity and the Firm's Environment", *California Management Review*, 32 (4): 86–100.

Levinson, H. (1978) "The Abrasive Personality", *Harvard Business Review*, 56, May–June: 86–94.

Levinson, H. (1965) "Reciprocation: The Relationship between Man and Organization", *Administrative Science Quarterly*, 9: 370–90.

Levitt, H.A. (1999) "Employers Need to Halt Idle Gossip among the Workers", *National Post*, 30 August: D8.

Lewis, D. (2004) "Bullying at Work: The Impact of Shame among University and College Lecturers", *British Journal of Guidance and Counselling*, 32 (3): 281–99.

Lewis, S. and Cooper, C.L. (1995) "Balancing the Home–Work Interface: A European perspective", *Human Resource Management*, 5: 289–305.

Lim, V.K. (1997) "Moderating Effects of Work-Based Support on the Relationship between Job Security and Its Consequences", *Work and Stress*, 11 (3): 251–66.

Lim, V.K. (1996) "Job Insecurity and Its Outcomes: Moderating effects of work-based and nonwork-based social support", *Human Relations*, 49 (2): 171–94.

Lin, Y.-H., Chen, C.-Y.and Lu, S.-Y. (2009) "Physical Discomfort and Psychosocial Job Stress among Male and Female Operators at Telecommunication Call Centers in Taiwan", *Applied Ergonomics*, 40: 561–8.

Lind, E.A. and Tyler, T.R. (1988) *The Social Psychology of Procedural Justice*. New York: Plenum.

Lipin, S. (1997) "Corporations' Dreams Converge on One Idea: It's Time to do a Deal", *Wall Street Journal*, 26 February: A1, A12.

Livy, B. and Vant, J. (1979) "Formula for Selecting Roughnecks and Roustabouts", *Personnel Management*, February.

Lobel, S.A. and Kossek, E.E. (1996) "Human Resource Strategies to Support Diversity in Work and Personal Lifestyles: Beyond the 'Family-Friendly' Organisation", in E.E. Kossek and S.A. Lobel (eds), *Managing Diversity: Human Resource Strategies for Transforming the Workplace*. Oxford: Blackwell: 221–44.

Locke, E.A. (1976) "The Nature and Causes of Job Satisfaction", in M.D. Dunnette (ed.), *Handbook of Industrial and Organizational Psychology*. Chicago: Rand McNally: 1297–349.

Locke, E.A., Feren, B.B., McCaleb, V.M., Shaw, K.N. and Denny, A.J. (1980) "The Relative Effectiveness of Four Methods of Motivating Employee Performance", in K. Duncan, M. Greenberg and D. Wallis (eds), *Changes in Working Life*. Chichester: Wiley: 363–88.

London Evening Standard (2009) "Nestlé Staff Walk and Talk to be the World's Fittest Firm", 1 June.

Long, B.C. and Flood, K.R. (1993) "Coping with Work Stress: Psychological Benefits of Exercise", *Work and Stress*, 7 (2): 109–19.

Long, R.J. (1984) "The Application of Microelectronics to the Office: Organisational and Human Implications", in N. Piercy, (ed.), *The Management Implications of New Information Technology*. London: Croom Helm.

Losocco, K.A. and Spitze, G. (1990) "Working Conditions, Social Support, and the Wellbeing of Female and Male Factory Workers", *Journal of Health and Social Behaviour*, 31: 313–27.

Love, P.E.D., Irani, A., Standing, C. and Themistocleous, M. (2007) "Influence of Job Demands, Job Control and Social Support on Information System Professionals' Psychological Well-Being", *International Journal of Manpower*, 28 (6): 513–28.

Macik-Frey, M., Quick, J., Cambell Quick, J. and Nelson, D.L. (2009) "Occupational Health Psychology: From Preventative Medicine to Psychologically Healthy Workplaces", in A.-S.G. Antoniou, C.L. Cooper, G.P. Chrousos, C.D. Spielberger and M.W. Eysenck (eds), *Handbook of Managerial Behaviour and Occupational Health*. Cheltenham: Edward Elgar.

Mackenzie, R.A. (1972) *The Time Trap*. New York: Amazon.

Maclach, C. and Jackson, S. (1986) *The Maslach Burnout Inventory*. Palo Alto: Consulting Psychologists Press.

MacLeod, D. and Clarke, N. (2009) *Engaging for Success: Enhancing Performance through Employee Engagement*. Kew: Office of Public Sector Information.

Majchrzak, A. and Borys, B. (1998) "Computer-Aided Technology and Work: Moving the Field Forward", in C.L. Cooper and I.T. Robertson (eds), *International Review of Industrial and Organisational Psychology*, 13: 305–54. Chichester: Wiley.

Manfrini, O., Pizzi, C., Viecca, M. and Bugiardini, R. (2008) "Abnormalities of Cardiac Autonomous Nervous Activity Correlate with expansive Coronary Artery Remodelling", *Atherosclerosis*, 197: 183–9.

Mankin, D., Bikson, T. and Gutek, B. (1984) "Factors in Successful Implementation of Computer-Based Office Information Systems: A Review of the Literature and Suggestions for OBM Research", *Journal of Organisational Behaviour Management*, 6 (3/4): 1–20.

Manuck, S.B. and Krantz, D.S. (1984) "Psychophysiologic Reactivity in Coronary Heart Disease", *Behavioral Medicine Update*, 6: 11–15.

Margolis, B., Kroes, W. and Quinn, R. (1974) "Job Stress, An Unlisted Occupational Hazard", *Journal of Occupational Medicine*, 1(16): 659–61.

Marks M.L. (1998) "The Merger Syndrome: The Human Side of Corporate Combinations", *Journal of Buyouts and Acquisitions*, January–February: 18–23.

Marmot, A.F., Eley, J., Stafford, M., Stansfeld, S.A., Warwick, E. and Marmot, M.G. (2006) "Building Health: An Epidemiological Study of 'Sick Building Syndrome' in the Whitehall II Study", *Occupational Environmental Medicine*, 63: 283–9.

Maruyama, S., Kohno, K. and Morimoto, K. (1995) "A Study of Preventive Medicine in relation to Mental Health among Middle-Management Employees (Part 2) – Effects of Long Working Hours on Lifestyles,

Perceived Stress and Working-Life Satisfaction among White-Collar Middle-Management Employees", *Japanese Journal of Hygiene*, 50: 849–60.

Masi, D.A. and Jacobson, J.M. (2003) "Outcome Measurements of an Integrated Employee Assistance and Work-Life Program", *Research on Social Work Practice*, 13: 451–67.

Maslow, A.H. (1970) *Motivation and Personality*, 2nd edn. New York: Harper & Row.

Mattiasson, I., Lindärde, R., Hilsson, J.A. and Theorell, T. (1990) "Threat of Unemployment and Cardiovascular Risk Factors: Longitudinal Study of Quality of Sleep and Serum Cholesterol Concentrations in Men Threatened with Redundancy", *British Medical Journal*, 310: 461–6.

Mauno, S., Kinnunen, U. and Pyykko, M. (2005) "Does Work–Family Conflict Mediate the Relationship between Work–Family Culture and Self-Reported Distress? Evidence from Five Finnish Organizations", *Journal of Occupational and Organizational Psychology*, 78: 509–31.

Mayer, J.D., Caruso, D. and Salovey, P. (1999) "Emotional Intelligence Meets Traditional Standards for an Intelligence", *Intelligence*, 27: 267–98.

McCall, T.M. (1988) "The Impact of Long Working Hours on Resident Physicians", *New England Journal of Medicine*, 319: 775–8.

McCloy, E. (1995) "Stress – A Clinical Perspective for Managers", *Occupational Stress – Causes and Victims*, Conference proceedings, Civil Service Occupational Health and Safety Agency, June.

McGrath, J.E. (1976) "Stress and Behavior in Organisations", in M.D. Dunette (ed.), *Handbook of Industrial and Organizational Psychology*. Chicago: Rand McNally.

McGrath, R. Jr (1994) "Organisationally Induced Helplessness: The Antithesis of Empowerment", *Quality Progress*, 27 (4): 89–92.

McHugh, M. and Bennett, H. (1999) "Introducing Teamwork within a Bureaucratic Maze", *Leadership and Organization Development Journal*, 20 (2): 81–93.

McKenna, E. (1994) *Business Psychology and Organisational Behaviour: A Students Handbook*. Hillsdale, USA and Hove, UK: Lawrence Erlbaum.

McLean, A.A. (1979) *Mind, Self and Society*. Chicago: University of Chicago Press.

McLeod, J. (2008) *Counselling in the Workplace: A Comprehensive Review of the Research Evidence*, 2nd edn. Lutterworth: BACP.

McLeod, J. (2001) *Counselling in the Workplace: The Facts. A Systematic Study of the Research Evidence*. Warwickshire: British Association for Counselling and Psychotherapy.

McLeod, J. and Henderson, M. (2003) "Does Workplace Counselling Work?", *British Journal of Psychiatry*, 182: 103–4.

McNamee, R.I., Carder, M., Money, A. and Agius, R. (2007) "Time Trends in the Incidence of Work-Related Disease in the UK, 1996–2006: Estimation from ODIN/THOR Surveillance Data". HSE.

McNeely, B.L. and Megliano, B.M. (1994) "The Role of Dispositional and Situational Antecedents in Prosocial Organizational Behaviour: An Examination of the Intended Beneficiaries of Prosocial Behaviour", *Journal of Applied Psychology*, 79: 836–44.

Melcrum (2005) *Employee Engagement: How to Build a High Performance Workforce*. Chicago: Melcrum.

Michie, S. and Cockcroft, A. (1996) "Overwork Can Kill?", *British Medical Journal*, 312: 921–2.

Michie, S. and Williams, S. (2003) "Reducing Work-Related Psychological Ill Health and Sickness Absence, A Systematic Literature Review", *Occupational Environmental Medicine*, 60: 3–9.

Miguel-Tobal, J.J. and Gonzalez-Ordi, H. (2005) "The Role of Emotions in Cardiovascular Disorders", in A.-S. Antoniou and C.L. Cooper (eds), *Research Companion to Organizational Health Psychology*. Cheltenham: Edward Elgar: 455–77.

Miles, H.H.W., Waldfogel, S. and Cobb, S. (1954) "Psychosomatic Study of 46 Young Men with Coronary Artery Disease", *Psychosomatic Medicine*, 16: 455–77.

Miles, R.H. and Perreault, W.D. (1976) "Organisational Role Conflicts: Its Antecedents and Consequences", *Organisational Behaviour and Human Performance*, 17: 19–44.

Miller, D.M. (1994) "Gaining Control over the Work Environment", in C.L. Cooper and S. Williams (eds), *Creating Healthy Work Organisations*. Chichester: Wiley.

Miller–Keane Encyclopedia (2005) *The Encyclopedia and Dictionary of Medicine, Nursing and Allied Health*. Rev.7th edn. London: Elsevier.

Mitchie, S. (1996) "Reducing Absenteeism by Stress Management: Valuation of a Stress Counselling Service", *Work and Stress*, 10: 367–72.

Mitler, M.M. (1992) "The Realpolitik of Narcolepsy and Other Disorders with Impaired Alertness", *Psycholosocial Aspects of Narcolepsy*. New York: Haworth Press.

Mohr, A.T. and Puck, J.F. (2007) "Role Conflict, General Manager Satisfaction and Stress and the Performance of IJVs", *European Management Journal*, 25 (1): 25–35.

Monk, T. and Folkard, S. (1983) "Circadian Rhythms and Shiftwork", in R. Hockey (ed.), *Stress and Fatigue in Human Performance*. Chichester and New York: Wiley.

Monk, T. and Tepas, D. (1985) "Shift Work", in C.L. Cooper and M.J. Smith (eds), *Job Stress and the Blue-Collar Workers*. Chichester and New York: Wiley.

Moore-Ede, M. (1993) *The Twenty-Four Society*. Reading, MA Addison-Wesley.

Morrell, D.C., Evans, M.E. and Roland, M.O. (1989) "The "Five Minute" Consultation: Effect of Time Constraint on Clinical Content and Patient Satisfaction", *BMJ*, 292: 870–3.

Moyle, P. (1998) "Longitudinal Influences of Managerial Support on Employee Wellbeing", *Work and Stress*, 12 (1): 29–49.

MSF (1995a) *Bullying at Work: How to Tackle It. A Guide for MSF Representatives and Members*. Bishop Stortford, UK: College Hill Press.

MSF (1995b) *Preventing Stress at Work: An MSF Guide*, MSF Health and Safety Information 40: 9–10. Bishop Stortford, UK: College Hill Press.

Mullarkey, S., Wall, T.D., Warr, P.B., Clegg, C.W. and Stride, C.B. (eds) (1999) *Measures of Job Satisfaction, Mental Health and Job-Related*

Well-Being: A Bench-Marking Manual. Sheffield University: Institute of Work Psychology.

Munsterberg, H. (1913) *Psychology and Industrial Efficiency.* New York: Houghton & Mifflin.

Murchinsky, P.M. (1993) *Psychology Applied to Work. An Introduction to Industrial and Organisational Psychology.* Pacific Grove, CA: Brooks/Cole.

Murphy, L.R. (1996) "Stress Management Techniques: Secondary Prevention of Stress". In M.J. Schabracq, J.A.M. Winnubst and C.L. Cooper (eds), *Handbook of Work and Health Psychology.* Chichester: John Wiley: 427–41.

Murphy, L.R. (1988) "Workplace Interventions for Stress Reduction and Prevention", in C.L. Cooper and R. Payne, *Causes, Coping and Consequences of Stress at Work.* New York: Wiley: 301–39.

Murphy, L.R. (1987) "A Review of Organizational Stress Management Research: Methodological Considerations", in J.M. Ivancevich and D.C. Ganster (eds), *Job Stress: From Theory To Suggestion.* New York: Haworth.

Myerson, S. (1991) "Doctors' Methods of dealing with 'Ongoing' Stress in General Practice", *Medical Science Research,* 19: 267–9.

Nasar, J.L. and Jones, K.M. (1997) "Landscapes of Fear and Stress", *Environment and Behaviour,* 29: 291–323.

Nebeker, D.M. and Tatum, B.C. (1993) "The Effects of Computer Monitoring, Standards, and Rewards on Work Performance, Job Satisfaction, and Stress", *Journal of Applied Social Psychology,* 23 (7): 508–36.

Nelson, A. and Cooper, C.L. (1995) "Uncertainty Amidst Change: The Impact of Privatization on Employee Satisfaction and Well Being", *Journal of Occupational and Organizational Psychology,* 68: 57–71.

Nemek, J. and Granjean, E. (1973) "Noise in Landscaped Offices", *Applied Ergonomics,* 4: 19–22.

Netterstrom, B. and Juel, K. (1988) "Impact of Work-Related and Psychosocial Factors on the Development of Ischaemic Heart Disease among Urban Bus Drivers in Denmark", *Scandinavian Journal of Work and Environmental Health,* 14: 231–8.

Newell, H. and Dopson, S. (1996) "Muddle in the Middle: Organisational Restructuring and Middle Management Careers", *Personnel Review,* 25 (4).

Newman, J.D. and Beehr, T. (1979) "Personal and Organisational Strategies for Handling Job Stress: A Review of Research and Opinion", *Personnel Psychology,* 32: 1–43.

NICE (National Institute for Clinical Excellence) (2009) "Promoting Mental Wellbeing through Productive and Healthy Working Conditions: Guidance for Employers", Public Health Guidance 22. London: NICE.

NICE (National Institute for Clinical Excellence) (2006) *Public Health Guidance Development Process and Methods.* London: NICE.

Nicholson, A.N. and Marks, J. (1983) *Insomnia: A Guide for Practitioners.* London: MTP Press.

NIOSH (2008) 'NIOSH Generic Job Stress Questionnaire'. Accessed on 17 February 2010 from http://www.cdc.gov/niosh/topics/workorg/tools/niosh-job-stress-questionnaire.html

Noor, N.M. (2002) "The Moderating Effect of Spouse Support on the relationship between Work Variables and Women's Work–Family Conflict", *Psychologia: An International Journal of Psychology in the Orient*, 45: 12–23.

Norgate, S.H. (2006) *Beyond the 9 to 5: Your Life in Time*. London: Weidenfeld & Nicolson.

Novaco, R.W. (1980) "Training of Probation Counsellors for Anger Problems", *Journal of Counselling Psychology*, 27: 385–90.

O'Driscoll, M.P. and Cooper, C.L. (1994) "Coping with Work-Related Stress: A Critique of Existing Measures and Proposal for an Alternative Methodology", *Journal of Occupational and Organizational Psychology*, 67: 343–54.

O'Driscoll, M.P., Poelmans, S., Spector, P.E., Kalliath, T., Allen, T.D., Cooper, C.L. and Sanchez, J.I. (2003) "Family-Responsive Interventions, Perceived Organizational and Supervisor Support, Work–Family Conflict, and Psychological Strain", *International Journal of Stress Management*, 10: 326–44.

Oborne, D.J. (1994) *Ergonomics at Work*, 3rd edn. Chichester: Wiley.

Obrist, P.A. (1981) *Cardiovascular Psychophysiology: A Perspective*. New York: Plenum.

OECD (2004) *Ageing and Employment Policies*: UK. Paris: OECD.

ONS (Office of National Statistics) (2007) Accessed on 19 February 2010 from http://www.statistics.gov.uk/pdfdir/pproj1007.pdf)

ONS (Office of National Statistics) (no date) "Economic Structure of the UK Population". Accessed on 29 November 2009 from www.statistics.gov.uk/cci/nugget.asp?id=1838

Osipow, S.H. and Spokane, A.R. (1983) *A Manual for Measures of Occupational Stress: Strain and Coping*. Odessa, FL: PAR.

Osler, W. (1910) "Angina Pectoris", *Lancet*, I: 839.

Osteras, H. and Hammer, S. (2006) "The Effectiveness of a Pragmatic Workplace Physical Activity Program On Maximal Oxygen Consumption and the Physical Activity Level in Healthy People", *Journal of Bodywork and Movement Therapies*, 10: 51–7.

Ostroff, C. (1992) "The Relationship between Satisfaction, Attitudes and Performance: An Organizational Level Analysis", *Journal of Applied Psychology*, 77: 963–74.

Parker, S.K., Wall, T.D. and Cordery, J.L. (2001) "Future Work Design Research and Practice: Towards an Elaborated Model of Work Design", *Journal of Occupational and Organizational Psychology*, 74: 413–40.

Parkes, K, R., Mendham, C.A. and von-Rabenau, C. (1994) "Social Support and the Demand Discretion Model of Job Stress: Tests of Additive and Interactive Effects in Two Samples", *Journal of Vocational Behaviour*, 44: 91–113.

Pearlin, L.I., Lieberman, M.A., Menaghan, E.G. and Mullan, J.T. (1981) "The Stress Response", *Journal of Health and Social Behaviour*, 22: 337–56.

Pennington, R.R., Kelton, A.S. and DeVries, D.D. (2006) "The Effects of Qualitative Overload on Technology Acceptance", *Journal of Information Systems*, 20 (2): 25. DOI: 10.2308/jis.2006.20.2.25

Perrewe, P.L. and Ganster, D.C. (1989) "The Impact of Job Demands and Behavioural Control on Experienced Job Stress", *Journal of Organizational Behavior*, 10: 213–29.

Personnel Today (2008) "Job Cuts Hit Older Workers as Unemployment Levels Reach 10-Year High", 22 September.

Peters, T.J. and Waterman, R.H. (1982) *In Search of Excellence: Lessons from America's Best Run Companies*. New York: Harper Row.

Petticrew, M., Fraser, J.M. and Regan, M.F. (1999) "Adverse Life Events and Risk of Breast Cancer: A Meta-Analysis", *British Journal of Health Psychology*, 4: 1–17.

Phelan, J., Schwartz, J.E., Bromet, E.J., Dew, M.A., Parkinson, D.K., Schulberg, H.C., Dunn, L.O., Blane, H. and Curtis, E.C. (1991) "Work Stress, Family Stress and Depression in Professional and Managerial Employees", *Psychological Medicine*, 21: 381–92.

Pierce, J.L., Newstrom, J.W., Dunham, R.B. and Barber, A.E. (1989) *Alternative Work Schedules*. Boston: Allyn & Bacon.

Pincherle, G. (1972) "Fitness for Work", Proceedings of the Royal Society of Medicine, 65 (4): 321–4.

Piotrkowski, C.S., Cohen, B.G. and Coray, K.E. (1992) "Working Conditions and Well-Being among Women Office Workers", special issue, *Occupational Stress in Human–Computer Interaction. International Journal of the Human–Computer Interaction*, 4 (3): 263–81.

Pitt, G. (2009) *Employment Law*, 7th edn. London: Thomson Reuters.

Porter, A.M.D., Howie, J.G.R. and Levinson, A. (1987) "Stress and the General Practitioner", in R. Payne and J. Firth-Cozens (eds), *Stress in Health Professionals*. Chichester: Wiley: 45–70.

Porter, A.M.D., Howie, J.G.R. and Levinson, A. (1985) "A Measurement of Stress as it Affects the Work of the General Practitioner", *Family Practice*, 2: 136–46.

Poulton, E.C. (1978) "Blue Collar Stress", in C.L. Cooper, and R. Payne (eds), *Stress at Work*. Chichester and New York: Wiley.

Powell, G.N. and Mainiero, L.A. (1999) "Alternative Work Arrangements", *Journal of Occupational and Organizational Psychology*, 72 (1): 41–56.

Proper, K., Hildebrandt, V., van der Beek, A. and Green, B.B. (2003) "A Patient-Centred, Work-Based Counselling Programme May Increase Workers' Physical Activity", *Evidence-Based Healthcare*, 7: 138–9.

Prossin, A. (1983) "The Ocean and Occupational Health", *Canadian Family Physician*, 3 (23): 1135–40.

Quick, J.C. (1979) "Dyadic Goal Setting and Role Stress in Field Study", *Academy of Management Journal*, 22: 241–52.

Quick, J.C. and Quick, J.D. (1984) *Organisational Stress and Preventive Management*. New York: McGraw-Hill.

Quinlan, M. (2007) "Organisational Restructuring/Downsizing, OHS Regulation and Worker Health and Well-Being", *International Journal of Law and Psychiatry*, 30 (4–5): 385–99.

Ramanthan, C.S. (1992) "EAP's Response to Personal Stress and Productivity: Implications for Occupational Social Work", *Social Work*, 37: 232–9.

Ramsey, J.D. (1983) "Heat and Cold", in Robert Hockey (ed.), *Stress and Fatigue in Human Performance*. Chichester and New York: Wiley.

Randall, R., Cox, T. and Griffiths, A. (2007) "Participants' Accounts of Intervention Processes and Context in Organization-Level Stress Management Interventions", *Human Relations*, 60 (8): 1181–209.

Randall, R., Griffiths, A. and Cox, T. (2005) "Evaluating Organizational Stress-Management Interventions using Adapted Study Designs", *European Journal of Work and Organizational Psychology*, 14: 23–41.

Reason, J. (1998) "Achieving a Safety Culture: Theory and Practice", *Work and Stress*, 12 (3): 293–306.

Reason, J. (1988) "Stress and Cognitive Failure", in S. Fisher and J. Reason (eds), *Handbook of Life Stress, Cognition and Health*. Chichester: Wiley.

Rees, D. and Cooper, C.L. (1991) "A Criterion-Oriented Validation of the OSI Outcome Measures on A Sample of Health Services Employees", *Stress Medicine*, 7: 125–7.

Rhoades, L. and Eisenberger, R. (2002) "Perceived Organizational Support: A Review of the Literature", *Journal of Applied Psychology*, 87: 698–714.

Richards, J.H. (1987) "Time Management – A Review", *Work and Stress*, 1 (1): 73–8.

Rico-Sanz, J., Rankinen, T., Rice, T., Leon, J.S., Skinner, J.S., Wilmore, J.H., Rao, D.C. and Bouchard, C. (2004) "Quantitative Trait Loci for Maximal Exercise Capacity Phenotypes and their Responses to Training in the HERITAGE Family Study", *Physiological Genomics*, 16(2): 256–60.

Rimmele, U., Seiler, R., Marti, B., Wirtz, P.H., Ehlert, U. and Heinrichs, M. (2009) "The Level of Physical Activity Affects Adrenal and Cardiovascular Reactivity to Psychosocial Stress", *Phsychoneuroendocrinology*, 34: 190–8.

Robertson, I., Warr, P.B., Butcher, V., Callinan, M. and Bardzil, P. (2003) "Older People's Experience of Paid Employment: Participation and Quality of Life". Sheffield: Growing Older Programme.

Robertson, I.T. and Cooper, C.L. (1990) "The Validity of the Occupational Stress Indicator", *Work and Stress*, 4: 29–39.

RobertsonCooper (2007) "Case Studies" Accessed on 26 February 2010 from www.robertsoncooper.com

Robinson, D., Perryman, S. and Hayday, S. (2004) "The Drivers of Employee Engagement", IES Report. Brighton: Institute for Employment Studies.

Roethlisberger, F. and Dickson, J.J. (1939) *Management and the Worker*. Cambridge, MA: Harvard University Press.

Rogers, S. (1998) "Reduce Stress to Work Happier", *Canadian Living*, November: 102.

Rook, K.S. (1995) "Support, Companionship and Control in Older Adults' Social Networks: Implications for Well-being". In J.F. Nussbaum and J. Coupland (eds), *Handbook of Communication and Aging Research*. Mahwah, NJ: Erlbaum: 437–63.

Rosa, R.R., Colligan, M.J. and Lewis, P. (1989) "Extended Workdays: Effects of 8-hours and 12-hour Rotating Shift Schedules on Performance, Subjective Sleep, Sleep Patterns, and Psychosocial Variables", *Work and Stress*, 3(1): 21–32.

Rosegger, R. and Rosegger, S. (1960) "Health Effects of Tractor Driving", *Journal of Agricultural Engineering Research*, 5: 241–75.

Rosenman, R.H. (1985) "Health Consequences of Anger and Implications for Treatment", in M.A. Chesney and R.H. Rosenman (eds), *Anger and Hostility in Cardiovascular and Behavioural Disorders*. Washington, DC: Taylor & Francis: 103–25.

Roskies, E. and Louis-Guerin, C. (1990) "Job Insecurity in Managers: Antecedents and Consequences", *Journal of Organizational Behavior*, 11: 345–59.

Rousseau, D.M. (2003) "Extending the Psychology of the Psychological Contract: A Reply to 'Putting Psychology Back into Psychological Contracts'", *Journal of Management Inquiry*, 12: 229.

Rousseau, V., Salek, S, Aubé, C. and Morin, E.M. (2009) "Distributive Justice, Procedural Justice, and Psychological Distress: The Moderating Effect of Co-Worker Support and Work Autonomy", *Journal of Occupational Health Psychology*, 14 (3): 305–17.

Royal College of Psychiatrists (1995) "'Defeating Depression' – Depression in the Workplace", Conference, April. London: Royal College of Psychiatrists.

Rubery, J., Smith, M. and Fagan, C. (1995) *Changing Patterns of Work and Working-Time in the European Union and the Impact on Gender Provisions*, April. European Commission.

Russek H.I. and Zohman, B.L. (1958) "Relative Significance of Heredity, Diet and Occupational Stress in CHD of Young Adults", *American Journal of Medical Sciences*, 235: 226–75.

Ruys, T. (1970) "Windowless Offices", MA Thesis, University of Washington, cited in D.J. Oborne, *Ergonomics at Work*, 2nd edn. Chichester: Wiley.

Sainfort, P.C. (1990) "Job Design Predictors of Stress in Automated Offices", *Behaviour and Information Technology*, 9: 3–16.

Sainsbury Centre for Mental Health (2007) "Mental Health at Work: Developing the Business Case", Policy Paper 8. London: Sainsbury Centre for Mental Health.

Sand, R.H. (1990) "OSHA Pre-Emption of State Criminal Prosecutions, Fetal Protection, and Workers' Compensation for Emotional Stress", *Employee Relations Law Journal*, 15: 441–7.

Sargent, L.D. and Terry, D.J. (1998) "The Effects of Work Control and Job Demands on Employee Adjustment and Work Performance", *Journal of Occupational and Organizational Psychology*, 71: 219–36.

Saurel-Cubizolles, M.J., Zeitlin, J., Lelong, N., Papiernik, E., Di Renzo, G.C. and Breart, G (2004) "Employment, Working Conditions, and Preterm Birth: Results from the Europop Case-Control Survey", *Journal of Epidemiology and Community Health*, 58: 395–401.

Scase, R. and Goffee, R. (1989) *Reluctant Managers, Their Work and Lifestyles*. London: Unwin.

Schabracq, M.A.J. and Cooper, C.L. (2000) "The Changing Nature of Work and Stress", *Journal of Managerial Psychology*, 15 (3): 227–41.

Schabracq, M.J. and Cooper, C.L. (1997) "Flexibility of Labour, Well-Being and Stress", *International Journal of Stress Management*, 4: 259–74.

Schaubroeck, J., Ganster, D.C., Sime, W.E. and Ditman, D. (1993) "A Field Experiment Testing Supervisory Role Clarification", *Personnel Psychology*, 46: 1–25.

Schein, V. and Davidson, M.J. (1993) "Think Manager – Think Male – Managerial Sex Typing Among Uk Business Students", *Management Development Review*, 6 (3): 24–8.

Schleifer, L.M., Galinsky, T.L. and Pan, C.S. (1996) "Mood Disturbances and Musculoskeletal Discomfort: Effects of Electronic Performance Monitoring under Different Levels of VDT Data-Entry Performance", *International Journal of Human–Computer Interaction*, 8 (4): 369–84.

Schuler, R.S. (1980) "Definition and Conceptualisation of Stress in Organisations", *Organisational Behaviour and Human Performance*, 25: 184–215.

Schweiger, D.M. and DeNisi, A.S. (1991) "Communication with Employees Following a Merger: A Longitudinal Field Experiment", *Academy of Management Journal*, 34: 110–35.

Schweiger, D.M. and Ivancevich, J.M. (1985) "Human Resources: The Forgotten Factor in Mergers and Acquisitions", *Personnel Administrator*, November: 47–61.

Schweiger, D.M., Ivancevich, J.M. and Power, F.R. (1987) "Executive Actions for Managing Human Resources Before and After Acquisitions", *Academy of Management Executive*, 2: 127–38.

Schweiger, D.M. and Lee, C. (1993) "Longitudinal Effects of Merger and Behavioral Intentions on Job Insecurity", in D.P. Moore (ed.), *Best Paper Proceedings*. Atlanta: Academy of Management.

Scott, A.J. (1994) "Chronobiological Consideration in Shiftworker Sleep and Performance and Shiftwork Scheduling", *Human Performance*, Special Issue, 7(3): 207–33.

Scott, H. (2002) "Nursing Profession is Finding it Harder to Retain Nurses", *British Journal of Nursing*, 11: 1052.

Scott-Ladd, B. and Chan, C.A. (2004) "Emotional Intelligence and Participation in Decision Making: Strategies for Promoting Organizational Learning and Change", *Strategic Change*, 13.

Selye, H. (1983) "The Stress Concept: Past, Present and Future", in C.L. Cooper (ed.), *Stress Research*. Chichester: Wiley.

Selye, H. (1976) *Stress in Health and Disease*. London: Butterworth.

Selye, H. (1974) *Stress without Distress*. Philadelphia: J.B. Lippincott.

Selye, H. (1956) *The Stress of Life*. New York: McGraw-Hill.

Seymour, L. and Grove, B. (2005) *Work Interventions for People with Common Mental Health Problems*. London: British Occupational Health Research Foundation.

Sherizen, S. (1986) "Work Monitoring: Productivity Gains at What Cost to Privacy", *Computer World*, 20 (27): 55.

Shigemi, J., Mino, Y., Ohtsu, T. and Tsuda, T. (2000) "Effects of Perceived Job Stress on Mental Health: A Longitudinal Survey in a Japanese Electronics Company", *European Journal of Epidemiology*, 16: 371–76.

Shostack, A.B. (1980) *Blue-Collar Stress*. Reading, MA: Addison-Wesley.

Siegrist, J. (1997) "Working Conditions and Cardiovascular Disease", *Safety and Health Practitioner*, I, November: 35–7.

Siegrist, J., Peter, R., Junge, A., Cremer, P. and Seidel, D. (1990) "Low Status Control, High Effort at Work and Ischaemic Heart Disease:

Prospective Evidence from Blue Collar Men", *Social Science and Medicine*, 31: 1127–34.

Siegrist, J., Siegrist, K. and Weber, I. (1986) "Biological and Psychological Factors in Cardiovascular Disease", *Social Science and Medicine*, 22 (247): 104–26.

Simpson, R. (1998) "Presenteeism, Power and Organisational Change: Long Hours as a Career Barrier and the Impact on the Working Lives of Women Managers", *British Journal of Management*, 9, special issue, September: S37–S50.

Sinetar, M. (1981) "Mergers, Morale and Productivity", *Personnel Journal*, 60: 863–67.

Singer, G. (1985) "New Approaches to Social Factors in Shiftwork", in M. Wallace (ed.), *Shiftwork and Health*. Bundoora, Australia: Brain, Behaviour and Research Institute.

Skipper, J.K., Jung, F.D. and Coffrey, L.C. (1990) "Nurses and Shiftwork: Effects on Physical Health and Mental Depression", *Journal of Advanced Nursing*, 15: 835–42.

Smith, L., Totterdell, P. and Folkard, S. (1995) "Shiftwork Effects in Nuclear Power Workers: A Field Study using Portable Computers", *Work and Stress*, 9, (2/3): 235–44.

Smith, M.J., Cohen, H.H., Cleveland, R. and Cohen, A. (1978) "Characteristics of Successful Safety Programs", *Journal of Safety Research*, 10: 5–15.

Smith, M.R., Fogg, L.F. and Eastman, C.I. (2009) "Practical Interventions to Promote Circadian Adaptation to Permanent Night Shift Work: Study 4", *Journal of Biological Rhythms*, 24: 161–72.

Snow, D.L., Swan, S.C., Raghavan, C., Connell, C.M. and Klein, I. (2003) "The Relationship of Work Stressors, Coping and Social Support to Psychological Symptoms among Female Secretarial Employees", *Work and Stress*, 17: 241–63.

Sparks, K., Cooper, C.L., Fried, Y. and Shirom, A. (1997) "The Effects of Hours of Work on Health: A Meta-Analytic Review", *Journal of Occupational and Organizational Psychology*, 70: 391–408.

Sparks, K., Faragher, B. and Cooper, C.L. (2001) "Well-Being and Occupational Health in the 21st Century Workplace", *Journal of Occupational and Organizational Psychology*, 74: 489–509.

Sprigg, C.A., Stride, C., Wall, T.D., Holman, D.J. and Smith, P. (2007) "Work Characteristics, Musculoskeletal Disorders and the Mediating Role of Psychological Strain: A Study of Call Center Employees". *Journal of Applied Psychology*, 92: 1456–66.

Spurgeon, A., Harrington, J. and Cooper, C.L. (1997) "Health and Safety Problems associated with Long Working Hours: Review of the Current Problem", *Occupational and Environmental Medicine*, 54 (6), June: 367–75.

Spurgeon, P., Mazelan, P., Barwell, F. and Flanagan, H. (2007) "New Directions in Managing Employee Absence: An Evidence-Based Approach". London: Chartered Institute of Personnel Development.

Standard, The (2005) "Asia Slowly Shifts to Shorter Working Week", 28 September.

Stansfeld, S., Fuhrer, R. and Shipley, M.J. (1998) "Types of Social Support as Predictors of Psychiatric Morbidity in a Cohort of British Civil Servants (Whitehall II Study)", *Psychological Medicine*, 28: 881–92.

Steer, R. and Rhodes, S. (1978) "Major Influences on Employee Attendance: A Process Model", *Journal of Applied Psychology*, 63 (4): 391–407.

Sterns, H. and Alexander, R. (1988) "Performance Appraisal of the Older Worker", in H. Dennis (ed.), *Fourteen Steps to Managing an Aging Workforce*. Lexington, MA: Lexington Books: 85–93.

Steward, W.F., Ricci, J.A., Chee, E., Hahn, S. and Morganstein, D. (2003) "Cost of Lost Productive Work Time among US Workers with Depression", *Journal of the American Medication Association*, 289: 3135–44.

Strazdins, L. (2002) "Emotional Work and Emotional Contagion", in N.M. Ashkanasy, W.J. Zerbe and C.E.J. Hartel, *Managing Emotions in the Workplace*. New York: Sharpe: 232–50.

Sturges, J., Conway, N., Guest, D. and Liefooghe, A. (2005) "Managing the Career Deal: The Psychological Contract as a Framework for Understanding Career Management, Organizational Commitment and Work Behavior", *Journal of Organizational Behavior*, 26 (7): 821–38.

Sunday Times (2009) "The Best Companies To Work For 2009". Accessed on 26 february 2010 from http//business.timesonline.co.uk/tol/business/career_and_jobs/article6850595.ece

Surry, J. (1968) *Industrial Accident Research: A Human Engineering Appraisal*. Canada: Ontario Department of Labour.

Susser, P.R. (1988) "Electronic Monitoring in the Private Sector. How Closely Should Employers Supervise Their Workers?", *Employee Relations Law Journal*, 13: 575–98.

Sutherland, V.J. (1990) "Managing Stress at the Worksite", in P. Bennett, J. Weinman and P. Spurgeon (eds), *Current Developments in Health Psychology*. London: Harwood Academic.

Sutherland, V.J. (1995) "Stress and the New Contract for General Practitioners", *Journal of Managerial Psychology*, 10 (3): 17–28.

Sutherland, V.J. and Cooper, C.L. (1992) "Job Stress, Satisfaction and Mental Health among General Practitioners Before and After the Introduction of the New Contract", *BMJ*, 304: 1545–8.

Sutherland, V.J. and Cooper, C.L. (1991a) "Stress Personality and Accidents in the Offshore Environment", *Journal of Personality and Individual Differences*, 12 (3): 195–204.

Sutherland, V.J. and Cooper, C.L. (1991b) *Stress and Accidents in the Offshore Oil and Gas Industry*. Houston, Texas: Gulf Publishing.

Sutherland, V. J. and Cooper, C. L. (1990) *Understanding Stress: A Psychological Perspective for Health Professionals*. London: Chapman & Hall.

Sutherland, V.J. and Cooper, C.L. (1986) *Man and Accidents Offshore: The Costs of Stress among Workers on Oil and Gas Rigs*. London: Lloyd's List/ Dietsmann.

Sutherland, V.J. and Davidson, M.J. (1996) "Managing Diversity: Using an Equal Opportunities Audit to Maximise Career Potential and Opportunities in UK bank", *European Journal of Work and Organizational Psychology*, 5 (4): 559–82.

Sutherland, V.J. and Davidson, M.J. (1993) "Using A Stress Audit: The Construction Site Manager Experience", *Work and Stress*, 7 (3): 273–86.

Sutherland, V.J. and Davidson, M.J. (1989) "Stress among Construction Site Managers: A Preliminary Study", *Stress Medicine*, 5: 221–35.

Szwergold, J. (1994) "How to Juggle Business Demands ... Literally", *Human Resources Focus*, 71 (6), June: 3.

Takao, S., Tsutsumi, A., Nishiuchi, K., Mineyama, S. and Kawakami, N. (2006) "Effects of The Job Stress Education for Supervisors on Psychological Distress and Job Performance among their Immediate Subordinates: A Supervisor-Based Randomized Controlled Trial", *Journal of Occupational Health*, 48: 494–503.

Talbot, R., Cooper, C.L. and Barrow S. (1992) "Creativity and Stress", *Creativity and Innovation Management*, 1 (4), December: 183–93.

Tarafdar, M., Tu, A., Ragu-Nathan, B. and Ragu-Nathan, T. (2007) "The Impact of Technostress on Role Stress and Productivity", *Journal of Management Information Systems*, 24 (1): 301–28.

Taylor, M.F., Brice, J., Buck, N. and Prentice-Lane, E. (2004) *British Household Panel Survey User Manual Volume A: Introduction, Technical Report and Appendices*. Colchester: University of Essex.

Terra, N. (1995) "The Prevention of Job Stress by Redesigning Jobs and Implementing Self-Regulating Teams", in L.R. Murphy, J.J. Hurrell Jr, S.L. Sauter and G.P. Keita (eds), *Job Stress Interventions*. Washington, DC: American Psychological Association: 265–82.

Theorell, T. (2001) "Employee Effects of an Educational Program for Managers at an Insurance Company 964", *Psychosomatic Medicine*, 63: 724–33.

Thomas, L. and Williams, M. (2006) "Promoting Physical Activity in the Workplace: Using Pedometers to Increase Daily Activity Levels", *Health Promotion Journal of Australia*, 17: 97–102.

Thomas, L.T. and Ganster, D.C. (1995) "Impact of Family-Supportive Work Variables on Work–Family Conflict and Strain: A Control Perspective", *Journal of Applied Psychology*, 80: 6–15.

Throne, L.C., Bartholomew, J.B., Craig, J. and Farrar, R.P. (2000)"Stress Reactivity in Fire-Fighters: An Exercise Intervention", *International Journal of Stress Management*, 7: 235–46.

Tidd, S.T. and Friedman, R.A. (2002) "Conflict Style and Coping with Role Conflict: An Extension of the Uncertainty Model of Work Stress", *International Journal of Conflict Management*, 13 (3): 236–57.

Times Online (2009) "Racism 'Alive and Vile' in Metropolitan Police says Boris Johnson", 26 February. Accessed on 28 January 2010 from http://www.timesonline.co.uk/tol/news/uk/crime/article5809800.ece

Toffler, A. (1970) *Future Shock*. London: Pan.

Totterdell, P, Wood, S. and Wall, T. (2006) "An Intra-Individual Test of the Demands–Control Model: A Weekly Diary Study of Psychological Strain in Portfolio Workers", *Journal of Occupational and Organizational Psychology*, 79: 63–84.

Touitou, Y. and Bogdan, A. (2007) "Promoting Adjustment of the Sleep–Wake Cycle by Chronobiotics", *Physiological Behavior*, 90: 294–300.

Towers Perrin/ISR (2006) *The ISR Employee Engagement Report*.

Trade Union of Congress (1994) *Part-time Working in Britain: Analysis of Trends in Part-Time Work and the Characteristics of Part-Time Workers in 1994.* London: TUC.

Travaglione, A. and Cross, B. (2006) "Diminishing the Social Network in Organizations: Does There Need to be Such a Phenomenon as 'Survivor Syndrome' after Downsizing?", *Strategic Change*, 15.

Turnley, W.H. and Feldman, D.C. (2000) "Re-Examining the Effects of Psychological Contract Violations: Unmet Expectations and Job Dissatisfaction as Mediators", *Journal of Organizational Behaviour*, 21: 1–25.

Tyers, C., Gifford, J., Gordon-Dseagu, V., Lucy, D., Usher, T. and Wilson, S. (2007) "Workplace Health Connect, Research Report", March. Accessed on 26 November 2009 from http://www.employment-studies.co.uk/pubs/summary.php?id=hse_

Tyers, C. and Lucy, D. (2008) Workplace Health Connect Progress Report, January. Accessed on 26 Novembeer 2009 from http://www.hse.gov.uk/workplacehealth/jan08.pdf

Uehata, Tetsunojo (1991) "Long Working Hours and Occupational Stress-Related Cardiovascular Attacks among Middle-Aged Workers in Japan", *Journal of Human Ergology*, 20 (2): 147–53.

Ulleberg, P. and Rundmo, T. (1997) "Job Stress, Social Support and Absenteeism among Offshore Personnel", *Work and Stress*, 11 (3): 215–28.

Unger, H. (1986) "The People Trauma of Major Mergers", *Journal of Industrial Management*, 10: 3–17.

US Congress, Office of Technology Assessment (1987) *The Electronic Supervisor: New Technology, New Tensions*, OTA-CIT-333. Washington, DC: US Government Printing Office.

US Department of Health and Human Services (1996) Accessed on 26 February 2010 from http://www.nhlbi.nih.gov/health/public/heart/obesity/phy_act.htm

Vahtera, J., Kivimaki, M. and Pentti, J. (1997) "Effect of Organizational Downsizing on Health of Employees", *The Lancet*, 350: 1124–8.

Vakola, M. and Nikolaou, I. (2005) "Attitudes towards Organizational Change: What is the Role of Employees' Stress and Commitment?", *Employee Relations*, 27 (2):160–74.

Van Dongen, H.P.A. (2006) "Shift Work and Inter-Individual Differences in Sleep and Sleepiness", *Chronobiology International*, 23: 1139–47.

Van Doornen, L.P. and de Geus, E.J.C. (1993) "Stress, Physical Activity and Heart Disease", *Work Stress*, 7 (2): 121–39.

Van Mierlo, H., Rutte, C.G., Seinen, B. and Kompier, M. (2001) "Autonomous Working and Psychological Well-Being", *European Journal of Work and Organizational Psychology*, 10 (3): 291–301.

Van Vegchel, N., de Jonge, J., Bosma, H. and Schaufeli, W. (2005) "Reviewing the Effort–Reward Imbalance Model: Drawing Up the Balance of 45 Empirical Studies", *Social Science and Medicine*, 60 (5):1117–31.

Vartia, M. and Hyyti, J. (2002) "Gender Differences in Workplace Bullying Among Prison Officers", *European Journal of Work and Organizational Psychology*, 11: 113–27.

Verrier, J.R. (1989) "Mechanisms of Behaviourally Induced Arrhythmias", *Circulation*, 76 (supplement 1): 48–56.

Voit, S. (2001) "Work-Site Health and Fitness Programs: Impact on the Employee and Employer", *Work*, 16: 273–86.

Waddell, G. and Burton, A.K. (2006) *Is Work Good for Your Health and Well-Being?* Norwich: Stationery Office.

Wajcman, J. (1996) "Women and Men Managers: Careers and Equal Opportunities", in R. Crompton, D. Gallie and K. Purcell (eds), *Changing Forms of Employment*. London: Routledge: 259–77.

Waldman, D. and Avolio, B. (1986) "A Meta-Analysis of Age Differences in Job Performance", *Journal of Applied Psychology*, 71: 33–8.

Waldron, V.R. (2000) "Relational Experiences and Emotion at Work", in S. Fineman (ed.), *Emotion in Organizations*, 2nd edn. London: Sage.

Wall, T.D. and Clegg, C.W. (1981) "A Longitudinal Study of Group Work Redesign", *Journal of Occupational Behaviour*, 2: 31–49.

Wall, T.D., Jackson, P.R., Mullarkey, S. and Parker, S.K. (1996) "The Demands–Control Model of Job Strain: A More Specific Test", *Journal of Occupational and Organizational Psychology*, 69: 153–66.

Walsh, J.P. (1988) "Top Management Turnover following Mergers and Acquisitions", *Strategic Management Journal*, 9: 173–83.

Wardwell, W.I., Hyman, M. and Bahnson, C.B. (1964) "Stress and Coronary Disease in Three Field Studies", *Journal of Chronic Diseases*, 17: 73–84.

Waring, J.J. (2004) "A Qualitative Study of The Intra-Hospital Variations in Incident Reporting", *International Journal of Quality Health Care*, 16 (5): 347–52.

Warr, P. (2007) *Work, Happiness and Unhappiness*. Mahwah, NJ: Erlbaum.

Warr, P. (1999) "Well-being in the workplace", in D.Kahneman, E.Diener and N.Schwartz (eds), *Well-being: The Foundations of Hedonic Psychology*. New York: Russell Sage.

Warr, P. (1996) "Job-Related Well-Being Scale", in S. Mullarkey, T.D. Wall, P.B. Warr, C.W. Clegg and C.B. Stride (eds), (1999) *Measures of Job Satisfaction, Mental Health and Job-Related Well-Being: A Bench-Marking Manual*. Sheffield University: Institute of Work Psychology.

Warr, P. (1995) "Age and Job Performance", in J. Snell and R. Cremer (eds), *Work and Aging. A European Perspective*. Basingstoke: Taylor & Francis: 309–22.

Warr, P. (1989) *Work, Unemployment and Mental Health*. Oxford: Clarendon.

Warr, P., Cook J. and Wall, T. (1979) "Scales for the Measurement of Some Work Attitudes and Aspects of Psychological Wellbeing", *Journal of Occupational Psychology*, 52: 129–48.

Warr, P. and Wall, T. (1985) *Work and Well Being*. Harmondsworth: Penguin.

Warshaw, L.J. (1979) *Managing Stress*. Reading, MA: Addison-Wesley.

Watzlawick, P., Beavin, J.H. and Jackson, D.D. (1968) *Pragmatics of Human Communication*. London: Faber & Faber.

Weinberg, A. (2009a) "Counselling Service Evaluation Report", November, University of Salford.

Weinberg, A. (2009b) "The Relationship between the Psychological Contract and Emotional Labour at Work and the Implications for Psychological Well-Being and Organizational Functioning", in A.-S.G. Antoniou, C.L. Cooper,

G.P. Chrousos, C.D. Spielberger and M.W.Eysenck, *Handbook of Managerial Behaviour and Occupational Health*. Cheltenham: Edward Elgar: 397–412.

Weinberg, A. (2008) "Management Coaching Initiative Final Report", July, University of Salford.

Weinberg, A. (2005) "The Seeds of Stress in the Organizations of Tomorrow: The Impact of New Technology and Working Methods", in A.-S.G. Antoniou and C.L. Cooper (eds), *Research Companion to Organizational Health Psychology*. Cheltenham: Edward Elgar: 151–9.

Weinberg, A. (2002) "Findings of a Staff Stress Audit", summer, University of Salford.

Weinberg, A. and Cooper, C.L. (2007) *Surviving the Workplace: A Guide to Emotional Well-Being at Work*. London: Thomson Learning.

Weinberg, A. and Cooper, C.L. (2003) "Stress among National Politicians Elected to Parliament for the First Time", *Stress and Health*, 19: 111–17.

Weinberg, A. and Creed, F. (2000) "Stress and Psychiatric Disorder in Healthcare Professionals and Hospital Staff", *The Lancet*, 355: 533–7.

Welch, B.L. (1979) "Extra-Auditory Health Effects of Industrial Noise: Survey of Foreign Literature", Aerospace Medical Research Laboratory, Aerospace Medical Division, Air Force Systems Command, June, Wright Patterson.

Wells, D.L., Moorman, R.H. and Werner, J.M. (2007) "The Impact of Perceived Purpose of Electronic Performance Monitoring on an Array of Variables", *Human Resource Development Quarterly*, 18 (1): 121–38.

Wen, L.M., Orr, N., Bindon. J. and Rissel, C. (2005) "Promoting Active Transport in a Workplace Setting: Evaluation of A Pilot Study in Australia", *Health Promotion International*, 20: 123–33.

Westerlund, H., Alexanderson, K., Akerstedt, T., Hanson, L.M., Theorell, T. and Kivimaki, M. (2008) "Work-Related Sleep Disturbances and Sickness Absence in the Swedish Working Population, 1993–1999", *Sleep*, 31 (8): 1169–77.

Whatmore, L., Cartwright and Cooper, C.L. (1999) "Evaluation of a Stress Management Programme in the Public Sector", in M. Kompier and C. Cooper, (eds), *Preventing Stress, Improving Productivity: European Case Studies in the Workplace*. London: Routledge: 149–74.

Wheatley, M. (1992) *The Future of Middle Management*. Corby: Institute of Management.

Whitfield, A. (1997) "Many Mental Health Nurses Stressed Out", *Health and Safety Bulletin*, 262, October.

WHO (World Health Organization) (2010) "Mental Health". Accessed on 8 February 2010 from http://www.who.int/topics/mental_health/en/

WHO (World Health Organization) (1984) *Psychosocial Factors and Health: Monitoring the Psychosocial Work Environment and Workers' Health*. Geneva: WHO.

Wilkinson, R. (1969) "Some Factors Influencing the Effect of Environmental Stressors upon Performance", *Psychological Bulletin*, 72: 260–72.

Williams, C. (1997) "Implications For Employer's Liability Insurance – What Premiums Will You Have to Pay?", in "An Employer's Guide to Stress at Work Litigation", IBC UK Conferences, May, London.

Williams, J.E., Paton, C.C., Siegler, I.C., Eigenbrodt, M.L., Nieto, J. and Tyroler, H.A. (2000) "Anger proneness Predicts Coronary Heart Disease Risk:

Prospective Analysis from the Atherosclerosis Risk in Communities (ARIC) Study", *Circulation*, 101: 2034–9.

Williams, S., Dale, J., Glucksman, E. and Wellesley, A. (1997) "Senior House Officers' Work Related Stressors, Psychological Distress, and Confidence in Performing Clinical Tasks in Accident Emergency: A Questionnaire Study", *BMJ*, 314: 713–18.

Wing, R.R., Blair, E.H., Epstein, L.H. and McDermott, M.D. (1990) "Psychological Stress and Glucose Metabolism in Obese and Normal-Weight Subjects: A Possible Mechanism for Differences in Stress-Induced Eating", *Health Psychology*, 9 (6): 693–700.

Wirral, L. and Cooper, C.L (1997) "IM-UMIST, Quality of Working Life Survey". London: Institute of Management.

Wolf, S. and Wolff, H.G. (1943) *Gastric Function: An Experimental Study of a Man and His Stomach*. New York: Oxford University Press.

Wolf, S.G. (1960) cited in H. Lewis, H. Griswold, and H. Underwood (eds), *Stress and Heart Disease: Modern Concepts of Cardiovascular Disease*. New York: American Heart Association, 29: 559–603.

Wood, S. (2008) "Job Characteristics, Employee Voice and Well-Being in Britain", *Industrial Relations Journal*, 39 (2): 153–68.

Wood, S. (1989) *The Transformation of Work*. London: Unwin Hyman.

Worrall, L. and Cooper, C.L. (2001) "The Long Working Hours Culture", *European Business Forum*, 6: 48–53.

Wright, M., Marsden, S. and Antonelli, A. (2004) "Building an Evidence Base for the HSC Strategy to 2010 and Beyond: A Literature Review of Interventions to Improve Health and Safety Compliance", Research Report 196. Norwich: HMSO.

Wright, P.K. and Bourne, D.A. (1988) *Manufacturing Intelligence*. Reading, MA: Addison-Wesley.

Wright, T.A. and Staw, B.M. (1999) "Affect and Favourable Work Outcomes: Two Longitudinal Tests of the Happy-Productive Worker Thesis", *Journal of Organizational Behaviour*, 20: 1–23.

Wynne, R. and Clarkin, N. (1992) *Under Construction: Building for Health in the EC Workplace*. Dublin: European Foundation for the Improvement of Living and Working Conditions.

Wynne, R., Clarkin, N., Cox, T. and Griffiths, A. (1995) *Guidance on the Prevention of Violence at Work*. European Commission.

Yu, S., Yarnell, J.W.G., Sweetnam, P.M. and Murray, L. (2003) "What Level of Physical Activity Protects against Premature Cardiovascular Death? The Caerphilly Study", *Heart*, 89: 502–6.

Zemke, R. (1993) "Rethinking the Rush to Team Up", *Training*, November: 55-61.

Zheng, H., Ehrlich, F. and Amin, J. (2009) "Economic Evaluation of the Direct Healthcare Cost Savings resulting from the use of Walking Interventions to Prevent Coronary Heart Disease in Australia", *International Journal of Health Care Finance and Economics*, DOI: 10.1007/s10754-009-9074-2.

Zohar, D. (1980) "Safety Climate in Industrial Organizations: Theoretical and Applied Implications", *Journal of Applied Psychology*, 65: 96–102.

Cited cases

Barber v. *Somerset County Council* HL [2004] UKHL13.

Connor v. *Surrey County Council* [2009] (Unreported)

Dickins v. *O2 plc* [2008] EWCA Civ 1144.

Gogay v. *Hertfordshire County Council* [2000] IRLR 703

Green v. *Deutsche Bank Group Services Ltd.* [2008] EWHC 1898 (QB)

Hatton v. *Sutherland* [2002] 2 All ER 1

Industrial Cases Reports (1993) *Petch* v. *Customs and Excise Commission*, ICR 789.

Industrial Relations Law Reports (1991) *Johnstone* v. *Bloomsbury Health Area Authority*, London, IRLR 118.

Industrial Relations Law Reports (1997) *Waltons & Morse* v. *Dorrington*, IRLR 448.

Industrial Relations Law Reports (1993) *Mughal* v. *Reuters Limited*, IRLR 571.

Intel Corporation Ltd v. *Tracy Ann Daw* [2007] EWCA Civ 70.

LSM v. *Royal Navy*, Case No. 55542/95.

Multiple Claimants v. *MOD* [2003] EWHC 1134 (QB)

Walker v. *Northumberland County Council* [1995] 1 All ER 737

Walton and Morse v. *Dorrington* [1997] IRLR 488

INDEX